Laura Engelstein
52 Cedar Lane
Princeton, NJ 08540

Chernyshevsky and the Age of Realism

Chernyshevsky
and the Age of Realism

A Study in the Semiotics of Behavior

 IRINA PAPERNO

Stanford University Press, Stanford, California   1988

Stanford University Press
Stanford, California
© 1988 by the Board of Trustees of the
Leland Stanford Junior University
Printed in the United States of America
CIP data appear at the end of the book

Published with the assistance of a special grant
from the Stanford University Faculty
Publication Fund to help support nonfaculty work
originating at Stanford.

SOURCES OF ILLUSTRATIONS

1, 10. N. G. *Chernyshevsky v vospominaniiakh sovremennikov* (Saratov, 1958), vol. 1. *2, 3.* N. G. Chernyshevsky, *Polnoe sobranie sochinenii* (Moscow, 1939), vol. 1. *4.* N. M. Chernyshevskaia, *Sem'ia N. G. Chernyshevskogo* (Saratov, 1980). *5.* V. Zhdanov, *Dobroliubov* (Moscow, 1961). *6.* N. V. Shelgunov, L. P. Shelgunova, and M. L. Mikhailov, *Vospominaniia* (Moscow, 1967), vol. 2. *7, 8.* T. A. Bogdanovich, *Liubov' liudei shestidesiatykh godov* (Leningrad, 1929). *9.* I. M. Sechenov, *Avtobiograficheskie zapiski* (Moscow, 1945).

Acknowledgments

I wish to acknowledge a debt of intellectual gratitude to Lidia Yakovlevna Ginzburg and Iurii Mikhailovich Lotman. I am indebted to the scholarly generosity and help of William Mills Todd III. I would also like to thank the following friends and colleagues who read the drafts of this book and offered valuable advice: Edward J. Brown, Michael Flier, Joseph Frank, Gregory Freidin, Monika Frenkel, Boris Gasparov, Hugh McLean, Michael Heim, Olga Raevsky Hughes, Robert Hughes, Emily Klenin, Olga Matich, and Dean Worth. I gratefully acknowledge generous financial support from the University of California, Los Angeles, including Academic Senate grants, College Institute Grant, Career Development Award, and resources of the Center for Russian and East European Studies. Andrew Wachtel edited the manuscript, and the book benefited greatly from his stylistic improvements. I would like to thank him and Slava Paperno for their translations of the Russian material quoted in the text. I also thank Robbie Nester for helping with the picture captions. I am extremely grateful to Stanford University Press and to the superb editorial help of Helen Tartar, Barbara Mnookin, and John Ziemer. Finally, I want to record my unbounded appreciation for the support I have received over many years from my teachers, colleagues, students, and friends at Tartu University, Stanford University, and the University of California, Los Angeles.

Unless otherwise indicated, all quotes from Chernyshevsky's works were specially translated by Slava Paperno. Translations from other works, unless otherwise indicated, were done by Andrew Wachtel.

I have used the Library of Congress system of transliteration, adopting the traditional *-sky* and *-oy* as personal name endings.

I.P.

Contents

Eight pages of photographs appear following page 94

Chernyshevsky and the Age of Realism

This mutual interaction of people and books is a strange thing. A book takes its whole shape from society that spawns it, then generalizes the material, renders it clearer and sharper, and then is outstripped by reality. The originals make caricatures of their own sharply drawn portraits and real people take on the character of their literary shadows. At the end of the last century all German men were a little like Werther, all German women like Charlotte; at the beginning of this century the university Werthers began to turn into "Robbers" à la Schiller, not real ones. Young Russians were almost all out of *What Is to Be Done?* after 1862, with the addition of a few of Bazarov's traits.

—Alexander Herzen

Introduction: The Individual and Literature

A work of literature is an intrinsic structure, created out of a particular life experience, individual and historical; in turn, it exercises a formative influence on the life of the individual and society. But is it possible to trace the transformation of personal experience into the structure of a literary text representative of a historical epoch and the text's reverse influence on the experience of others? This task is closely connected to the traditional aesthetic problem of the relationship between art and life, or reality. The goal of this book is to explore this problem from the perspective of the semiotics of culture.

According to Ernst Cassirer's philosophy of symbolic forms, the principal aim of all forms of culture is to create and organize reality—our human world, human behavior, and human experience. The chaos of immediate sensory perceptions, emotions, desires, intuitions, and thoughts assumes shape and order and is endowed with definite meaning only when it is permeated with the connectedness, form, and expression of a symbolic system. The function of language, myth, religion, historical and scientific thought, art, and literature is not merely reproductive but productive. These systems do not reflect or imitate an empirically given, ready-made reality; rather, they form and construct what we call the real or objective world.

Whereas Cassirer spoke of the "creatability" of the real world, contemporary semiotics talks about the "creatability" of psychic structures. It views human personality as a product of organization—the selection, correlation, and symbolic interpretation of the elements of mental and life experience: that is, as a structure created by a method analogous to that used in language and other forms of culture. The principle of creative organization inherent in human language reaches its ultimate realization in works of art (especially in literature as the verbal art). Literary models possess a high degree of deliberate internal organization; projected onto the flow and flux of human life, they reveal distinct and meaningful structure in it. From this it follows that literature plays a special role in shaping, ordering, and defining the life of the individual and of society.[1]

From these general ideas, contemporary semiotics has developed a unified approach to the study of the relation of the literary text (an artistic world with its own organization) to the real world that stands beyond the text. This approach can be called the *semiotics of behavior*. The everyday behavior of people who belong to historically distinct cultural groups (such as, for example, the Russian nobility in the second half of the eighteenth century, or the Decembrists, or the members of the philosophical circles of the 1830s and 1840s) is "read" and explicated as the realization of cultural codes that were directly influenced by the literature (and art) of the period. Many events and situations in the lives of participants in cultural life are elucidated by uncovering literary texts and categories (such as literary characters, plot movements, or rhetorical conventions) that encoded this behavior. It is from these studies, specifically those of Lidia Ginzburg and Iurii Lotman, that my work takes its departure.[2]

The project that I pursue here is an extension of the semiotic study of culture. First, my focus is essentially different. So far semiotics has been concerned primarily with one side of the interaction between the individual and culture—the influence of literature on individual behavior. I propose to examine as well the role of the individual and the individual psychological process in the formation of literary models and patterns. Semioticians have acknowledged that the individual is not merely a passive recipient of culture and that a cultural code is not a self-enclosed and self-determined whole. Culture is the result of human activity. Personality is an important factor in literary development and literary structure. Historical laws "work through the mechanisms of human psychology which become in turn important mechanisms of history," writes Lotman.[3] "We must remember," urged Jan Mukařovský, one of the pioneers of the semiotics of culture, "that all external influences enter the work [of literature] through the mediation of personality and that even in the study of historical periods the problems of personality as a developmental factor do not lose their urgency."[4]

The relationship between the creative personality and culture is dynamic. In the course of development, a person encounters a variety of cultural material circulating in the surrounding society. He absorbs those cultural elements, which resonate with what can tentatively be called his psychological predispositions, his psychic needs and inclinations. Having been selected by an individual, the elements of the existing cultural codes are juxtaposed in new and idiosyncratic combinations and thus reinterpreted and given new meaning. As part of the same process, the cultural material that is adopted encourages the retention of those elements of mental and life experience that can be correlated with current cultural concerns and shapes this psychological material in accordance with the conceptual system and rhetoric of contemporary culture. Thus, a person's psychological potentialities are realized in terms of existing cultural codes, and at the same time, existing cultural codes are rearranged in accordance with his predispositions.

In the end, a more or less coherent structure emerges. Individual predispositions and psychological potentialities are converted into the structure of personality that is intimately related to a certain society and culture. Viewed in this way, the individual psychological process appears as an integral part of culture. It can thus become a legitimate object of semiotic research. In fact, it is as difficult to understand the literary text isolated from its author and its real-life context as it is to understand the life of the individual and of society in isolation from the literary models that organize this life.

My project further extends the semiotic study of culture by expanding the chronological limits of the semiotic analysis of Russian cultural history. To date, we have a more or less systematic description of the period from the mid-eighteenth century to the 1840s (with occasional excursuses into medieval and seventeenth-century culture). The limitation of the object of study to such highly ritualized periods as the Middle Ages and the eras of classicism and romanticism is not accidental. A deliberate and programmatic expansion of literary categories into real life was typical of these periods: ordinary life, patterned on the norms and rules governing artistic texts, was meant to be experienced as an aesthetic form. Realism in the second half of the nineteenth century, on the contrary, affirmed the separateness of art and reality and the primacy of life over art. This caused art forms to be experienced as essentially de-aestheticized ("real"). Because realistic literature imitates a lack of literariness and aesthetic organization, some argue that the influence of realistic literary models on real-life phenomena is less accessible to semiotic analysis.[5]

This book attempts to deal with the central period of realism in Russian culture—the 1860s. In keeping with the task of focusing on the individual's role in the development of culture, I examine the life and works of a concrete individual—Nikolai Gavrilovich Chernyshevsky (1828–89), the most influential cultural figure and prototypical personality of his time. A theoretician of the aesthetic relationship of art to reality, Chernyshevsky is the author of the novel that has had the greatest impact on human lives in the history of Russian literature—*What Is to Be Done?* (*Chto delat'?*; 1863).

The New Man

The 1860s were a turning point in Russian cultural history, a time when new cultural principles and new principles of behavior came into being. What historians call the "sixties" began in 1855 with the death of Nicholas I and the accession of Alexander II, who reduced the political repressions introduced after the

European revolutions of 1848–49 and undertook major political and social reforms. These events marked the transition between two cultural generations, known in Russian intellectual history as the "men of the forties" and the "men of the sixties," or between the romantics, immersed in the philosophical tradition of idealism, and the realists, with their adherence to positivism. The general sentiment of the sixties was that of "a new age," an era of "liberation" and "spiritual renewal." The liberation of the serfs and other social reforms undertaken during these years were seen as symbolic events of global significance that opened the way for what, in the language of the day, was called a "transfiguration of all life" (*preobrazhenie vsei zhizni*), from the organization of state and society, to metaphysical, ethical, and aesthetic conceptions, to the arrangement of human relations and customs of domestic life. Ultimately, this would result in the "transfiguration" of the human being and the rise of the "new man." In the words of a contemporary, "Everything that had existed traditionally and had formerly been accepted without criticism came up for rearrangement. Everything—beginning with theoretical peaks, religious views, the basis of the state, and the organization of society, all the way to quotidian customs, to clothing, and to hair styles."[6]

An era of rapid development of literary institutions, the sixties witnessed a proliferation of universities and the rise of journalism, which claimed the role of consolidator of public opinion. A large number of "thick" journals (combining belles-lettres, literary criticism, politics, and science) were published in Petersburg and Moscow during these years, ranging from the liberal *Russian Messenger* (*Russkii vestnik*) to the radical *Contemporary* (*Sovremennik*) and *Russian Word* (*Russkoe slovo*).

These journals actively debated the need for reform and renewal in all spheres of life, addressing such problems as the means of emancipating the serfs and reforming landownership (the "peasant question"); freedom of the press and open legal proceedings (*glasnost'*); women's liberation from social inequality and family tyranny (the "woman question"); the introduction of modern bourgeois institutions, such as railroads and credit (the "Europeanization of Russia"); and the metaphysical and ethical implications of the contemporary expansion of science.

The Emancipation Edict of February 19, 1861, was followed by reforms in the legal system, local government, the army, finances, education, and the press. But the reforms failed to satisfy a need for reconstruction; they were followed by an outbreak of peasant riots, which had to be repressed by military force. In the same year, some proclamations appearing in St. Petersburg (such as "To the Young Generation" ["K molodomu pokoleniiu"], written and distributed by the radical journalists Nikolai Shelgunov and Mikhail Mikhailov) contained an ultimatum to the government issued by "public opinion." Student disturbances and general disorder troubled Petersburg, culminating in an outbreak of fires in May 1862. The common people of Petersburg blamed rebellious students for these fires (most probably, accidental); they were seen as the possible beginning of a bloody revolution. The government responded by arresting radical journalists and temporarily closing the *Contemporary*, the *Russian Word*, and Petersburg University. The sixties ended in 1866 when all activities associated with liberation came to an abrupt halt with Dmitry Karakozov's attempt on the life of Alexander II and the new wave of repressive measures that followed it. But the cultural processes started during these years, especially those associated with the radical intellectual movement of the 1860s (*shestidesiatnichestvo*), left a powerful imprint on Russian culture.

The intellectual emancipation of the 1860s was connected with a major social change—the appearance of the non-noble intelligentsia (*raznochinnaia intelligentsiia*). This group of university-educated, professional intellectuals of varied origins (mostly clerical and petit bourgeois) were bound together by a shared sense of alienation from their social roots and an all-encompassing spirit of opposition to the existing order. In the 1860s, the *raznochinnaia* intelligentsia (or *raznochintsy*, "people of various ranks," a term that emphasizes their motley roots) attained a position of power and significance in society, which had previously been dominated by the educated nobility.[7]

The radical ideology and style of behavior of the new intelligentsia exercised a preponderant influence on the intellectual life of society as a whole. Nikolai Nekrasov's *Contemporary*, a journal that established itself as a militant partisan of materialism and socialism and an active proponent of "civic aesthetics" (the affirmation of the social purpose of literature), was by far the most popular periodical of the day. The opposition's intellectual hegemony can be sensed in the testimony of a young contemporary, Elena Shtakenshneider (Stackenschneider), the daughter of a court architect whose mother kept a famous literary salon. In 1857, the young girl complained in her private diary:

I once worked up the courage to tell my friends that I don't like Nekrasov. That I don't like Herzen—I wouldn't have the courage. . . . We now have two censorships and, as it were, two governments, and it's hard to say which one is more severe. The Gogolian officials, clean-shaven and wearing medals around their necks, are fading into the background, while new ones are coming on stage. They wear sideburns and haven't got medals around their necks, and they, simultaneously, are the guardians of order and the guardians of disorder.[8]

In the intellectual realm, the "new age" construed itself negatively, as a radical rejection of the "old world" and its beliefs and traditions (hence the term nihilism). In reaction against romanticism and idealism in philosophy, in politics, and in everyday life, the intellectual movement of the mid-nineteenth century espoused realism, denying everything not based on pure and positive reason, on sensory data and practical considerations. But although a man of the sixties saw himself as a new man who had shaken off the "old Adam," one can justifiably speak of continuity and succession between the two eras and the two generations. It was in the intellectual atmosphere of the philosophical and literary circles of the 1840s, centered around Mikhail Bakunin, Nikolai Stankevich, Timofei Granovsky, Alexander Herzen, Nikolai Ogarev, and Vissarion Belinsky, that the men of the sixties were reared. It is not surprising, therefore, that romantic consciousness was a tangible (though at times vehemently denied) presence, a substratum of the consciousness of the realist.

Realism as a Weltanschauung rejected philosophical idealism for positivism, theology for Feuerbachian anthropology, traditional Christian ethics for English utilitarianism, constitutional liberalism for socialism and radicalism, and romantic aesthetics for the aesthetics of realism. The basic notion of "reality" implied a conception of the world as "the orderly world of nineteenth-century science, a world of cause and effect, a world without miracle, without transcendence even if the individual may have preserved a personal religious faith,"[9] and the conception of man as a corporeal being living (and acting) in society, an object of natural and social science. A true realist had to forsake miracles, personal immortality, and "ideality" (*ideal'nost'*) in approaching feelings, human relations, and everyday life, in favor of rationalism, practicality, energetic activity (including political action), and an unshakable belief in science and education as guarantees of moral, social, and economic progress.

It was universally believed that the avant-garde of realism was literature: Russian realism as an intellectual movement began in the realm of letters through the efforts of the literary critic Vissarion Belinsky. The groundwork of literary realism was laid in the 1840s, and the trend continued to develop throughout the 1850s and 1860s. The question What is realism? became one of the central issues of the day, vigorously discussed in journals of different persuasions.

A keystone of the aesthetics of realism is the issue of the relations between literature and reality and, in the long run, the function of literature in real life. In its attitude toward these issues, realism saw itself as a reaction against romanticism. Romanticism insisted on the deliberate linkage of life and art and, ultimately, on the complete aesthetization of life. This view was based on the idea of the inherent primacy of art—as pertaining to the realm of the ideal—over "base" empirical reality. In contrast, realism subordinated art to reality. Realistic aesthetics saw the involvement of literature with life as essentially twofold. On the one hand, the intention of realism (as proclaimed by radical critics) was the direct and precise representation of social reality, as close to the empirical object, or as true to life, as possible. (Truth, *istinnost'*, or authenticity of representation, became the central aesthetic category, more important than Beauty.) On the other hand, realism clearly had a didactic intent and wished to have a direct impact on reality. Thus, literary characters and literary situations were claimed to have been derived from "life itself" and thereafter, "returned to reality" and offered to society as examples worthy of imitation in real life.

Of course, in terms of modern literary theory, a realistic work, like any other work of art, is not a mere reproduction but a complex model of reality constructed in accordance with a set of artistic conventions. It is, however, a model that essentially involves the imitation of a lack of modeling, conventionality, or literariness.[10] The contradiction between the programmatic principle of natural, unmediated mimesis and the awareness that literature is a product of construction was resolved with the help of the concept of *type*. In realistic aesthetics, the concept of type was a hybrid of the sociological category referring to a representative member of a class ("social type") and the Hegelian notion of ideal. For Belinsky and his followers among the radical critics, type is an individual fact of reality (a social fact) that, having "passed through the imagination of a poet," acquires a universal significance of mythic proportions. As we might say today, a literary type is a result of the aesthetic organization and generalization of reality, and deals with material that has already undergone social organization.[11] This literary model possesses a remarkable power to organize the actual life of a reader who, through familiar configurations of a social role that lies behind the text, recognizes himself in the world of a literary text. This principle was formulated in Dostoevsky's novel *The Idiot*: "Writers mostly attempt in their stories and novels to take social types and represent them imaginatively and artistically; these types are extremely rarely met with in actual life in their entirety, but they are nevertheless almost more real than real life itself."[12]

As a corollary of these principles of realistic aesthetics, literature was seen as a major force in the development of society (this attitude toward literature is usually regarded as a specifically Russian phenomenon).[13] Taking its material from life, refashioning it, and then returning to life for imitation and actualization, literature regenerates and extends contemporary life into the future and recasts man as he is into a new man. This principle was formulated by M. E. Saltykov-Shchedrin:

Literature predicts the laws of the future, produces the image of the man of the future. . . . The types created by literature always go on ahead of those circulating on the market, and that is why they in particular make their mark even on a society that seems to be entirely under the yoke of empirical cares and fears. Under the influence of these new types, modern man, without realizing it himself, acquires new habits, assimilates new views, and receives a new point of view. In a word, he gradually makes a new man of himself.[14]

A necessary part of this process is the literary critic, who mediates between the literary work and its actualization in reality. The radical school of aesthetics, the "real criticism" (*real'naia kritika*), advanced the idea that an author can reveal things in reality (such as future types) that are independent or even contrary to his intentions. On this view, the critic is a full co-author of the text (even though his presence is frequently uninvited and unwelcome).*

A special nuance was added by the orientation of realistic literature in the mid-nineteenth century toward science (a part of the general orientation toward objectivity). Literature readily incorporated and absorbed elements of contemporary scientific and social thought, even neurophysiology, political economy, and statistics. The resulting literary model appeared to be a product of the scientific analysis of data, hence its special trustworthiness and effectiveness. Ideally, according to Nikolai Dobroliubov and Dmitry Pisarev, science and fiction should merge. But since this goal had not yet been achieved, the literary critic had to play the role of the scientist in literature and "complete" the artistic analysis of reality, making it a truly objective and thus openly prescriptive scientific analysis. It is notable that most radical literary critics actively engaged in popularizing the

---

*A typical example is the story concerning Turgenev's novel *On the Eve* (*Nakanune*). Dobroliubov discovered a "type," the active revolutionary who is about to appear on the Russian scene, in the main character, Insarov ("Kogda zhe pridet nastoiashchii den'?" [When will the real day come?]; 1860). Turgenev considered this a major distortion of his novel and insisted that the *Contemporary* force Dobroliubov to make changes in his critical article. This conflict, which was viewed by its participants as a conflict between two cultural generations, resulted in Turgenev's withdrawal from the journal, an event that signified the victory of the "sons."

achievements of contemporary science and wrote numerous articles devoted to scientific topics.

Thus, in the 1860s literature was almost universally regarded as an all-encompassing "guide to life" (Chernyshevsky's term) and a driving force of social and historical progress; and literary criticism was viewed as an essential part of literature. This view of a work of literature as a means to the global organization of life and a prophecy of the future was accompanied by a special attitude toward authorship; the author was seen as the acting head of society and, moreover, as a figure surrounded by a special aura of sanctity. As Nikolai Shelgunov wrote in his memoirs:

Never, neither earlier nor later, did writers occupy such an honored place here in Russia. When a writer who enjoyed the favor of the public appeared on stage for a reading (they had just begun at the time), there was a groan of ecstatic shouts, applause, and the banging of chairs and heels. It wasn't mere enthusiasm, but some kind of raving [*besnovanie*] that accurately expressed the fervor that the writer called forth from the public.[15]

Chernyshevsky, in his early diaries, called the major Russian writers (such as Lermontov and Gogol) "our saviors"; Chernyshevsky himself was called a "prophet of the young generation." It is noteworthy that the prophet of the sixties was not the poet (as in the age of romanticism), but the leading journalist (or "publicist"), a role that combined the occupation and expertise of literary critic, popularizer of science, and public activist. As early as 1842, Belinsky proclaimed, in his prophetic "Speech on Criticism" ("Rech o kritike"), that in the age of realism "a clever and energetic critic," and not "a great poet," stands "at the head of society." Twenty years later, in an article devoted to Chernyshevsky's *What Is to Be Done?*, Shelgunov pointed out that in that epoch "creative writers formed the rearguard of the movement; the avant-guard of the advancing literary hordes consisted of publicists."[16]

Another outgrowth of the basic principles of realism was a far-reaching confusion between the realms of literature and real life. Since literature was regarded as a maximally precise and direct representation of reality, the literary world was easily and eagerly equated with the real world. Not only the "real critics" but even their ideological opponents engaged in the practice of discussing fictional characters as living people and literary situations as real-life situations. The "real critics" canonized this practice, claiming that a work of realistic art (provided that it is trustworthy, a definition with distinct moral overtones) can be treated as a phenomenon of actual life.[17]

At the same time, the reverse side of the confusion—the application of aesthetic norms to life—seems quite consistent with the declared principles of realistic aesthetics. The contradiction is inherent, I believe, in the main thesis of Chernyshevsky's tract "The Aesthetic Relations of Art to Reality" ("Esteticheskie otnosheniia iskusstva k deistvitel'nosti"; 1855) in which he advanced his notorious doctrine of the superiority of reality to art. Since it is not possible for the mind to conceive of anything that cannot be perceived by the senses, argued Chernyshevsky, nothing can be more beautiful than what actually exists in reality; therefore, "Beauty is life" (*Prekrasnoe est' zhizn'*). (This thesis became a slogan of the radical school of realistic aesthetics.) But if reality is viewed as a realm of the beautiful, it follows that aesthetic categories can be applied to phenomena of real life. It is, perhaps, the greatest paradox of realism that radical realistic aesthetics, in spite of its affirmation of the separateness of art and reality, inspired a wide expansion of literature into life, quite comparable to that in the ages of romanticism and symbolism with their conscious intention of merging art and life.

The principles of realistic aesthetics regarding the relationship of art to reality and their concrete realization are best illustrated by the events surrounding the appearance of the literary model of the new man. These events started with the polemic surrounding the publication of Turgenev's *Fathers and Sons* (in the February 1862 issue of the *Russian Messenger* [*Russkii vestnik*], at that time the main opponent of the *Contemporary*).[18] *Fathers and Sons* was universally regarded as a novel that addressed the burning issue of contemporary life: the emergence of a new type in Russian life (Turgenev gave it the name "nihilist") and the change of generations on the cultural scene. The polemic concerned the interpretation of the main character, Bazarov; it focused on establishing the authenticity of the image (that is, on whether it was an accurate statement about actual life) and on its moral evaluation.

For the younger generation, Bazarov was a model against which they were invited to judge themselves. Their reactions differed. The critics of the *Contemporary* refused to recognize themselves in Bazarov; in a notorious article "An Asmodeus of Our Time" ("Asmodei nashego vremeni"; 1862), M. A. Antonovich declared the image of Bazarov a lampoon of the younger generation and a deliberate distortion of reality. The resulting judgment was twofold: the novel failed to be true to reality and was thus both an aesthetic failure and an ethical transgression. (A contributing factor was the widespread feeling that Bazarov was a deliberate and spiteful caricature of Dobroliubov, whose quarrel with Turgenev had resulted in Turgenev's withdrawal from the *Contemporary*.)

In his memoirs, the radical activist G. Z. Eliseev called *Fathers and Sons* "an atrocious action by Turgenev" (*bezobraznyi postupok Turgeneva*), an action that caused the younger generation to lose credibility. Eliseev saw the ascribing of the fires of the summer of 1862 to students, the shutdown of the *Contemporary*, and the arrest of its leading author, Chernyshevsky, as direct effects of *Fathers and Sons*: "It turned out that a horrible suspicion, if not a direct accusation, could arise in our society because of such a trivial thing as a well-written little novel by an unthinking man. And with what weight did it fall on a blameless journal and on its blameless staff and, even more so, on blameless students and, finally, on the equally blameless liberal party." [19]

M. N. Katkov, the editor of the *Russian Messenger*, maintained in opposition to Antonovich that the novel was a great aesthetic achievement and, therefore, an authentic picture of Russian life. Katkov then proceeded to analyze and condemn what he called "the Bazarovs of Russian reality" and "Russian nihilism." But in criticizing Bazarov for various human faults, Katkov stepped beyond the boundaries of Turgenev's image and discussed Bazarov's possible behavior in a variety of situations that had not been described in *Fathers and Sons*. He pronounced Bazarov "immoral in intention and action." Katkov admitted that Bazarov's essential immorality did not manifest itself within the novel; he explained this by pointing out that the plot of the novel did not call for a "significantly immoral action."

And yet, Pisarev, another leader of the young generation and the main critic of the *Russian Word*, joined Katkov in defining the novel as a mirror image of reality, eagerly recognizing himself and his cohorts in the image of Bazarov. Pisarev blamed Antonovich for paying too much attention to Turgenev and his novel ("although the public did not care a whit about Turgenev or his novel") and thus overlooking both the "truth" and the rich human potential of Bazarov as such. In his article "Bazarov" (1862), Pisarev recast Turgenev's character. He eagerly supplied additional ("missing") details of Bazarov's life and provided ingenious psychological motivations for those of his actions described in the novel. He explained, for example, that Bazarov had naturally been led to his radical persuasions by his experiences as a poor plebeian at the university; and behind Bazarov's cruelty to his parents was his painful realization of the inevitable alienation from them. All of these deductions, claimed Pisarev, were based on a "correct" understanding of the "astonishingly accurate" factual material presented in Turgenev's novel.[20] Herzen, in the article "Bazarov Once Again" ("Eshche raz Bazarov"; 1868), said of Pisarev's Bazarov: "I don't care whether or not Pisarev understood Turgenev's Bazarov. What is important is that he recognized himself and his fellows [*svoikh*] in Bazarov and added what the book lacked."[21]

Thus reshaped, the image of Bazarov appeared to contemporary readers as a model of human personality acceptable for and worthy of imitation in real life. Various elements of real-life material, differentiated and particularized, found their place within the overall structure (which was based on the opposition of "sons" and "fathers"): adherence to natural science as opposed to the humanitarian inclinations of the previous generation, the radicalism of the men of the sixties contrasted with the political liberalism of the men of the forties, a rejection by the "sons" of the traditional rules of social propriety accepted by the "fathers." Minor details of the portrait of a nihilist (those that Pisarev found to be "astonishingly accurate" and that were instantly recognizable to contemporaries), such as Bazarov's routine of dissecting frogs, his chapped red hands and unkempt hair, and his smock with fringes (*balakhon s kistiami*), acquired symbolic value and meaning when treated as the components of a unified artistic image. In the course of Bazarov's second life as a standard for the young generation, even those negative characteristics of Turgenev's character that had offended the staff of the *Contemporary*—his rudeness and insolence, cruelty and disdain for emotions, rejection of art, and lack of aesthetic feeling—were reevaluated positively as the meaningful signs of a new social position.[22]

Shortly after the publication of *Fathers and Sons*, in the midst of vigorous discussions of Bazarov and nihilism, Chernyshevsky started work on a novel entitled *What Is to Be Done? From the Tales About the New People* that was intended as a direct response to Turgenev by a member of the younger generation.[23] What the novel offered was not a negatively defined image, but a coherent and all-encompassing positive program of behavior, from important social actions to minor details of domestic arrangement; with it came another name—the "new men," a positive alternative to nihilists.* Chernyshevsky deliberately designed the new men of his novel as models for reproduction in real life:

All the prominent traits by which they [the new men in the novel] are marked are traits, not of individuals, but of a type. . . . These general traits are so prominent that they eclipse all individual peculiarities. . . . This type has recently appeared in our midst. . . . It has been multiplying rapidly. It is born of an epoch, it is a sign of the times, and—must I say it?—it will disappear with the fast-flying epoch that produced it. . . . And then it will reappear in a greater number of individuals

*Many authors commented on the importance of the name nihilism in creating a reputation for the new intellectual movement. Characteristically, the term itself appeared before *Fathers and Sons*, but it was only after the novel was published that the term acquired general significance and symbolic connotations. Turgenev later remarked that he regretted equipping the "reactionaries" with "the word," "the name," that was used as "a stigma, almost a mark of disgrace" (Turgenev, *Polnoe sobranie sochinenii*, 11: 93). However, though initially used in a contemptuous sense, the label was later accepted by those against whom it was employed. By giving a name to the movement, Turgenev helped to bring it to the level of social awareness.

under better forms. . . . There will no longer be any special type, for all men will be of this type.[24]

Several years later, in a footnote to "Bazarov Once Again," Herzen testified to the effectiveness of Chernyshevsky's creative efforts and, in addition, attempted to explain the dual interrelation between human reality and literature:

This mutual interaction of people and books is a strange thing. A book takes its whole shape from the society that spawns it, then generalizes the material, renders it clearer and sharper, and then is outstripped by reality. The originals make caricatures of their own sharply drawn portraits and real people take on the character of their literary shadows. At the end of the last century all German men were a little like Werther, all German women like Charlotte; at the beginning of this century the university Werthers began to turn into "Robbers" à la Schiller, not real ones. Young Russians were almost all out of *What Is to Be Done?* after 1862, with the addition of a few of Bazarov's traits.[25]

The words of Katkov, in 1879, attest that the literary model of the new man had received real-life embodiment, bringing significant changes to Russian society:

What Is to Be Done? was a prophet of sorts. Much that seemed a dream to him [Chernyshevsky] was fulfilled in life: the new men spread into the cities and hamlets trying to put the lessons of their teacher into practice, going far beyond his hopes, which had a slight tinge of sentimentality. And now, as before, the problem is that Kirsanovs can be professors, Mertsalovs can be archpriests, their friends can be justices of the peace [*mirovye sud'i*], members of law courts, colonels of the general headquarters, privy councilors [*tainye sovetniki*].*

Thus, an integral model of behavior based on a new conception of personality appeared in Russian culture crystalizing around literary images and their critical interpretations (and around the names given to it in literature). As defined by a con-

Moskovskie vedomosti, 1879; cited in *Literaturnoe nasledstvo*, 25–26 (1936): 544. Curiously enough, a social distinction soon appeared within the nihilists' camp between plebeian nihilists, nicknamed "browns" (*burye*), and the "gentry," or "salon nihilists." There was even a nihilist salon, at the home of Countess L. N. Tolstaia. See Zhukovskaia, *Zapiski*, p. 208; and Kovalevskaia, *Vospominaniia*, pp. 231, 491. On the salon, see Stites, *Women's Liberation Movement*, p. 119.

temporary, the configurations of this new personality type rested on the "three hypostases of the 'trinity' prescribed by *What Is to Be Done?*": "freethinking," "an enlightened woman as a life-companion," and "rational labor."[26] The new man was a rationalist and a positivist who held an unquestioning belief in science (to quote Pisarev's colorful formula, "the salvation and the renewal of the Russian people" lay in the "spread frog" *rasplastannoi liagushke*).[27] In the realm of feelings and relations with women, the new man was motivated by a concern for promoting the "freedom of the heart" and "rehabilitation of the flesh" (doctrines that included a permissive attitude toward sexual behavior) as well as women's free access to higher education and the professions in affirmation of total equality (in this sense, Bazarov was not a complete new man). Finally, the new man was a man of action, a "worker in the laboratory of nature" (in the words of Turgenev's Bazarov) or a "proletarian of the intellect" (Pisarev's words).

But through literature (and most important, through *What Is to Be Done?*), nihilism received not only these commandments of moral conduct, but also, as one of the new men, A. M. Skabichevsky, put it, "obligatory manifestations in day-to-day quotidian life, including diet, clothing, living arrangements, and so on."[28] Skabichevsky gave a comprehensive description of the external signs that marked a person who belonged to the new type:

The desire to look different from the despised philistines extended to the very external appearance of the new men, and thus appeared the notorious costumes in which the youth of the 1860s and 1870s showed themselves off. Plaids and gnarled walking sticks, short hair [for women] and hair to the shoulders [for men], dark glasses, Fra Diavolo hats and Polish caps [*konfederatki*]—my God, all of that was bathed in such a poetic aureole then, and how it made the young hearts beat.[29]

A perceptive (though disapproving) portrait of a female nihilist in daily life appeared in the newspaper *Newsword* (*Vest'*) in 1864:

Most *nigilistki* are usually very plain and exceedingly ungracious, so that they have no need to cultivate curt, awkward manners; they dress with no taste, and in impossibly filthy fashion, rarely wash their hands, never clean their nails, often wear glasses, always cut their hair, and sometimes even shave it off. . . . They read Feuerbach and Büchner almost exclusively, despise art, use *ty* [informal address] with several young men, light their cigarettes not from a candle, but from men who smoke, are uninhibited in their choice of expressions, live either alone or in phalansteries, and talk most of all about the exploitation of labor, about the silliness of marriage and family, and about anatomy.[30]

The most penetrating remark in this depiction concerns the cultivation of curt and awkward manners. The awkwardness and lack of social skills characteristic of the original *raznochintsy*, who came from lower social strata and had not received instruction in manners (an important part of the upbringing of the gentry), were deliberately cultivated, both by those who were naturally ungracious and by those trained in the social graces. Rudeness and curt manners, negligent styles of dress and even untidiness became meaningful, ideologically weighted signs, which immediately distinguished the nihilists both from the members of the opposing camp (the traditionalists, the reactionaries) and from ordinary people. (Many contemporaries mentioned dirty, chewed fingernails, a sign that apparently carried special significance, since it was opposed to Onegin's famous manicured fingernails, canonized in a work of literature of the preceding period as the mark of an aristocratic dandy.)

It appears that these signs were identified as nihilist and so interpreted by wide circles of contemporaries. An interesting example is given in the memoirs of another nihilist, V. K. Debogory-Mokrievich. After returning from the university to his hometown, he paraded in his new attire under the windows of his old schoolteacher. The "elder," writes Debogory-Mokrievich, "looked at my long hair, spectacles, and thick walking stick, and said: 'I can see you've drunk the whole fill of nihilist wisdom.'"[31]

The young people of the new persuasion apparently felt themselves to be a closely knit clan alienated from the rest of society (a feeling akin to the sense of clanship uniting the aristocracy). Both obvious and more subtle signs helped those who "belonged to the tribe" to recognize each other and to communicate. Sofia Kovalevskaia remembered: "No sooner would two or three young people meet at a party of elders, where they had no right to make themselves heard, than they understood one another immediately by a look, a sigh, an intonation of the voice." [32]

The area of social relations most affected by the revolution in manners was behavior toward women. Deliberate disregard of traditional forms of gallantry was interpreted as affirming equality between the sexes; by contrast, special courtesy in social intercourse with women was regarded as offensive. The anarchist Petr Kropotkin wrote:

> He [the nihilist] absolutely refused to join in those petty tokens of politeness with which men surround those whom they like so much to consider as "the weaker sex." When a lady entered a room a nihilist did not jump from his seat to offer it to her, unless he saw that she looked tired and there was no other seat in the room. He behaved towards her as he would have behaved towards a comrade of his own sex; but if a lady—who might have been a total stranger to him—manifested the desire to learn something which he knew and she did not, he would walk every night to the far end of a large city to help her. [33]

A parody of these attitudes appears in Dostoevsky's *Crime and Punishment*, in the scene in which Lebeziatnikov (a lampoon of the new man) is educating Sonia about kissing hands ("it is an insult to a woman for a man to kiss her hand, because it is a sign of inequality"), about workmen's associations, and about "the question of free entry into rooms" (whether a member of the commune has a right to enter another's room without permission). The last detail is a direct reference to *What Is to Be Done?*, which offered couples of the new persuasion special rules for entering each other's rooms, based on considerations of equality.

The overt motivations behind these attitudes were ideological: anti-aristocratism in daily conduct was directly associated with anti-aristocratism in social life. Shelgunov wrote: "Aristocratism, with its external comeliness, elegance, and shine, was the highest form of our culture then. But that beautiful flower had grown in the soil of the serfdom that had completely confused all concepts." [34]

But at the same time, nihilism as a unified style of behavior arose from the extension of the principle of liberation from the political arena and the realm of religious beliefs and philosophical convictions into the spheres of human relations and the customary habits of daily life. Conventions of polite behavior accepted by the polished "fathers" were viewed as a manifestation of the lies and hypocrisy of the old world. Kropotkin pointed out that nihilism "declared war upon what may be described as the conventional lies of civilized mankind."[35] In this sense, nihilism, or realism, in behavior paralleled realism in literature: both disparaged conventionality and proclaimed an ideal of direct reference to reality, a mode of expression that was candid and natural. Viewed in this light, nihilism in daily life appears an integral part of the realist movement.

Nikolai Chernyshevsky

According to Nestor Kotliarevsky, the historian of the intellectual movement of the 1860s,

There are names that encompass the spiritual work of a whole generation, the activity of a gigantic number of people, people who are otherwise independent and strong. The name of a single man becomes the expression of a mass movement—the movement, not of an uneducated mass, but of a whole group of *intelligenty*. For the young generation of the sixties, in radical groups of various shades, the name Chernyshevsky was such a conventional name.[36]

Indeed, the symbolic value of Chernyshevsky's name is a historical fact amply supported. His political influence was remarkable, as attested by contemporaries of not only his own camp but that of ideological opponents. Though frequently of an anecdotal nature, involving highly improbable situations, such evidence points to the strength of his public image. The revolutionary movement in ideology and politics was sometimes, in all earnestness, ascribed to Chernyshevsky's influence alone. Thus, the historian Boris Chicherin, a distinguished liberal activist of the 1860s, told the equally distinguished scientist Ivan Sechenov: "There was a time when Russia stood on a healthy path that promised much. Those were the first years of the reign of Alexander II. But then the revolutionary ferment began and everything got messed up, and so it goes to this very day. It's all Chernyshevsky's fault: it was he who injected the revolutionary poison into our life."[37]

Vsevolod Kostomarov, the agent provocateur who played a crucial role in Chernyshevsky's arrest and conviction on false evidence, was of similar opinion.[38] Dostoevsky was also convinced that Chernyshevsky controlled the rebellious forces: when fires broke out in Petersburg in May 1862, Dostoevsky, seeing in them an omen of impending calamity, appeared at Chernyshevsky's door (although the two writers hardly knew each other) and begged him to put a stop to them.[39] This belief was apparently shared by the governor of St. Petersburg, Prince A. A. Suvorov who, according to Shelgunov, boasted that in his time (that is, before Karakozov's assassination attempt) he had easily managed to control the city: "Informers tell me that a disturbance is being prepared. I send for Chernyshevsky and say to him: 'Please, arrange things so that it won't take place.' He gives me his word, and I go to the sovereign and report that everything will be calm."[40] An oral legend of peasant origin credited Chernyshevsky with being Alexander II's right-hand man in the emancipation of the serfs.[41] On the other hand, a loyal landowner, in an anonymous letter of June 1862 to the chancellor of the Third Section (Russia's secret police), begged the government to save society from imminent bloodshed by removing Chernyshevsky, "the scourge of revolt."[42]

On the eve of the "sixties," in April 1856, the secret police opened and copied a letter written by a student at Kazan University to a friend in the province of Mogilev (the letter was included in a police report prepared for the emperor). The student described rowdy parties with political flavor:

It's time for toasts—first of all for N. G. Chernyshevsky, then we sing the praises of liberty and freedom. Then we curse everything and everyone mercilessly, beginning with N. P. [Nikolai Pavlovich, i.e., Nicholas I]—well, you, I think, can guess with whom we start . . . because it's impossible that the words of our enlightener Nikolai Gavrilovich are not branded in your soul.[43]

A police agent underlined the last sentence in red, and in the margin the Manager of the Third Section, L. V. Dubelt, noted that Nikolai Gavrilovich was "unknown" (by that time Cherny-shevsky was an active participant in the *Contemporary*).

In July 1862, Chernyshevsky was arrested and then convicted of subversion, despite an obvious lack of evidence of any subversive activities; he was sentenced to seven years of penal servitude, followed by exile in Siberia for life. Chernyshevsky was believed to be an object of Alexander II's personal hatred. He was permitted to return to the European part of Russia (still as an exile) in 1882 at the demand of the terrorist organization the People's Will (Narodnaia volia); his release, a result of secret negotiations between the government and the terrorists, was offered in exchange for a guarantee of peace during the coronation of Alexander III, who ascended the throne after Alexander II was assassinated by terrorists on March 1, 1881.

What was the precise scope of Chernyshevsky's political activities that they provoked such horror in the government and its loyal subjects and such enthusiasm in several generations of radicals? Although some historians, like the government of Alexander II, consider Chernyshevsky the creator of an influential underground party, there is absolutely no documentary evidence to support this view. There is not even any proof that Chernyshevsky wrote the proclamation "To the Landlord's Peasants" ("K barskim krest'ianam"; 1861), which figured as the main charge against him at his trial.[44]

Though uninvolved in any outright illegal and violent actions or an underground organization, Chernyshevsky was an influential journalist and writer, the main contributor to, and a member of the editorial board of, the most widely read journal of the day, the *Contemporary*. In his numerous articles, book reviews, translations, and compilations of Western treatises on politics and science, Chernyshevsky was an ardent propagandist of materialism in epistemology and aesthetics, utilitarian ethics, and the politics of anti-liberalism. He devoted special effort to establishing literature as a force for social development and to proselytizing political economy as a tool of social organization and change, and he promoted communal forms of labor and communal land tenure (*obshchina*) and women's emancipation—all that was called socialism or communism in that day—and he did it with a distinct style of arrogant and militant self-righteousness.[45]

The influence of his writings on society and its ways of thinking is difficult to overestimate: it is this influence that was mistaken by contemporary readers and governmental officials alike for political influence achieved through organized underground political activities. His influence was acknowledged both by police agents[46] and by enthusiastic readers. N. Ia. Nikoladze, a Georgian student in Petersburg and later a prominent member of the radical movement, left one of the many records of this type: "At home I studied old issues of the *Contemporary* and digested from the first to the last line each new number, whose publication I awaited as manna from heaven."[47] M. Iu. Aschenbrenner, a cadet at a military school in Petersburg who became a member of the People's Will in the 1880s, remembered that "Chernyshevsky had a strong and direct impact on us [cadets]. We knew him by heart, we swore by his name as a believing Moslem swears by the name of Mohammed, the prophet of Allah."[48] An activist in the *zemstvo*, M. Krasnoperov, maintained that in the late 1850s and early 1860s Chernyshevsky's articles in the *Contemporary* were meticulously studied, for entire nights, by seminarians in the theological seminary in Viatka, under the supervision of a teacher.[49] Shelgunov testified that he "had opportunities to see seventy-year-old men for whom the *Contemporary* was a 'guidebook to life' and a mentor in correct understanding of contemporary issues."[50] Another contemporary, the liberal activist A. V. Evald, an opponent of Chernyshevsky's, wrote that even those young women who read the *Contemporary* without understanding anything at all "regarded themselves as sorts of Joans of Arc, called to recreate mankind; naturally, in the company of their admirers."[51]

But it was Chernyshevsky's novel *What Is to Be Done?*, written in prison after his public activities had been halted (and published in the *Contemporary* in the spring of 1863 through an egregious oversight of the censors[52]), that expanded his influence even further: from the arena of ideological struggle, from the realm of political programs and philosophical creeds, into the everyday private life of readers.

What Is to Be Done? is a social as well as an emotional utopia; the plot rests on what is essentially a complicated love story with a feminist flavor. The heroine, Vera Pavlovna Rosalskaia, is an ordinary Petersburg girl of petit-bourgeois origin who suffers from family despotism in the house of her greedy and unscrupulous mother, Maria Alekseevna. Maria Alekseevna is trying to force her daughter into a marriage of convenience with a wealthy gentry libertine (Storeshnikov). The intrigue almost ends in Vera's dishonor, and she is saved only through the intervention of a French courtesan, Julie. In the meantime, a young man of the new type, a medical student of non-noble origin, Dmitry Lopukhov (he tutors Vera's brother) takes an active interest in the girl's fate. First, Lopukhov devotes his efforts to raising the level of her social consciousness by reading such books as Victor Considérant's *Destinée sociale* and Ludwig Feuerbach's *Das Wesen des Christentums* with her. He then tries to rescue her, and when finding her a job proves impossible, he offers her his hand in fictitious marriage—an arrangement that allows her to leave her parents' home. In order to support her, Lopukhov gives up his medical career and takes a managerial position at a factory.

After "marrying," the young people arrange their lives in accordance with the ideas of equality and independence in marital relations; of course, since Lopukhov married Vera in order to liberate her, he does not exercise his conjugal rights. Vera organizes a cooperative workshop and a residential commune of seamstresses, enterprises that not only ensure her own financial independence, but also help other (unmarried) young girls become self-sufficient. All the arrangements (both economic and quotidian) in the Lopukhovs' home and in the commune are described with exactitude and precision. Throughout their business career, Lopukhov and Vera are unfailingly successful because of the rational organization of their enterprises, which have been planned with the objectivity and precision of scientific methods. The perfect equilibrium of the rational world of the new people is upset, however, when Vera begins to feel a powerful need for strong emotions and for the excitements of society that her union with Lopukhov, an even-tempered and reserved man, is unable to satisfy.

In the meantime, the couple has been joined by Lopukhov's best friend from his student years, Alexander Kirsanov, a distinguished physiologist of materialistic bent, who becomes an ardent participant in the merry amusements of the Lopukhovs' household. Without realizing it, Vera falls in love with Kirsanov, and her feeling is returned. It is at this point that the marriage of Vera and Lopukhov is sexually consummated—at the initiative of Vera Pavlovna. Kirsanov discreetly withdraws; he is distracted by an affair with a prostitute (Nastia Kriukova), whom he reforms and restores to a decent life. Nastia soon dies of consumption, and Kirsanov and Vera are confronted with their love for each other. Lopukhov becomes aware of the situation; he first suggests that all three "remain close to each other" in a ménage à trois, but when this proves to be unacceptable to Vera (who is somewhat affected by public opinion), Lopukhov decides—on the basis of rational calculations—to remove himself physically. He fakes a suicide, escapes to America, and allows Vera and Kirsanov to unite in marriage; a child is later born to them, and most important, with Kirsanov's help Vera Pavlovna undertakes the study of medicine. After Lopukhov's disappearance, his plan is disclosed by his friend Rakhmetov, whose appearance introduces an image of the ideal human being into the novel.

A rationalist and, as the reader is allowed to guess, a dedicated professional revolutionary, Rakhmetov renounces common pleasures, personal feelings, and the love of women in order to prepare himself for the struggle for social equality in the name of the common people. A wealthy aristocrat by birth, he has given away his fortune to revolutionary causes and refashioned his behavior and physique by joining a crew of *burlaks* (laborers towing boats) on the Volga; he eats only those foods accessible to common people (with a few carefully explained exceptions) and even attempts sleeping on a bed of nails. Toward the end of the novel, Rakhmetov mysteriously disappears from Petersburg; his return is associated with the impending revolution.

After a period of time, Lopukhov returns to Russia disguised as an American businessman, Charles Beaumont. He marries Katia Polozova, a girl from a rich and well-connected family who happens to have been saved by Doctor Kirsanov from dying of grief over frustrated love. The two couples eventually settle together in the perfect harmony of a joint household.

In the epilogue, a mysterious lady in black appears, surrounded by a noisy crowd of admirers who are apparently young men of the new persuasion. The author hints that her husband is in confinement in Siberia. She then reappears (dressed in jubilant pink) with her husband at her side. There is a masked suggestion that this is the author of the novel himself, liberated by a successful revolution. Elaborate calculations place the event in the spring of 1865.

But the highlights of the novel are Vera's four dreams—allegories that illustrate the main points of Chernyshevsky's philosophical, ethical, and social doctrine. The culminating point is the fourth dream, a utopian vision of the society of the future. A grandiose palace of iron and glass equipped with technological wonders is the communal domicile of morally and physically perfect human beings who live under conditions of rationally (communally) organized labor. Their working day ends with a magnificent ball (superior diet and physical exercises allow for tireless dancing and singing), with special arrangements for free sexual fulfillment (all the arrangements are described in precise technical detail).

Most critics agree that *What Is to Be Done?* is badly written (a contemporary critic called it "the most atrocious work of Russian literature"). The novel abounds in banal situations and plot movements; above all, it is clumsy and awkward in style (Turgenev commented that Chernyshevsky's style aroused physical revulsion in him). Nevertheless, its profound influence on the lives of contemporary readers was unprecedented in the history of Russian literature.

For contemporaries, the novel was a bombshell and created a tremendous public uproar. Official circles considered it a serious threat to the stability of the existing social order. Although the central issue of the novel was the reorganization of relations between the sexes, it was projected, both by the author and by readers, onto the reorganization of all social relations. The censor who, after the appearance of the novel, was asked to evaluate its potential implications wrote that "such a perversion of the idea of marriage also destroys the idea of the family, which is the foundation of society. The ideals [expounded in the novel] stand in direct opposition to the basic principles of religion, morality, and civil order." He concluded that "the book . . . is in the highest degree pernicious and dangerous."[53]

The reaction of the reading public varied with the reader's ideological convictions. The poet Afanasy Fet wrote: "Katkov and I were beside ourselves with amazement, and the only thing we didn't know was what surprised us most: the cynical silliness of the whole novel or the obvious collusion of the censorship."[54] According to Skabichevsky, there were rumors (which originated in the circle of aesthetes around the critic Apollon Maikov) that the censors had permitted the novel's publication in the hope that such a highly inept work of art would ruin Chernyshevsky's reputation. In a critical analysis of *What Is to Be Done?*, D. K. Shedo-Ferroti, a journalist and a government agent, assessed the novel as an inadvertent self-parody, a novel so amoral and so absurd as to be not only harmless, but even useful and desirable as an antidote to nihilism for youth inclined to political and philosophical fantasies.[55]

But contrary to expectations, nothing of the sort happened. Russian youth, wrote Skabichevsky, did not seek aesthetic merits in the novel, but a program of action (a "guide to life"): "It would not be an exaggeration to say that we read the novel practically on bended knee, with the kind of piety that does not permit the slightest smile on the lips, the kind with which sacred books are read. The novel had a colossal effect on our society."[56] Eliseev wrote: "Manna from heaven never brought so much joy to the starving as this novel brought to the young people who had previously been wandering aimlessly around Petersburg. It was just like a vision sent from on high. In real life they began to do exactly what they were supposed to do according to the sense of the novel."[57] Another contemporary remembered: "We made the novel into a kind of Koran in which we looked for and found not only a general guide to a correct life, but also exact instructions on how to act in specific situations."[58]

Petr Kropotkin wrote that "for the Russian youth of the time it was a revelation and it became a program." In his view, "no novel of Turgenev and no writings of Tolstoy or any other writer [had] ever had such a wide and deep influence upon Russian society as this novel had."[59] His appraisal was echoed by the Marxist philosopher and literary critic Georgy Plekhanov; conceding that "of aesthetic merits the novel has very few," he added: "From the time that printing presses appeared in Russia up to our times, no single printed work has been as successful in Russia as *What Is to Be Done?*" [60] Plekhanov, who notably enough expressed doubts concerning Chernyshevsky's revolutionary activities, offered an ingenious explanation for the novel's power: it met the demand for a 'scientific' formula of universal applicability. [61]

A similar judgment, though with different emotions, was made by members of the opposite ideological camp. A professor at Odessa University, P. P. Tsitovich, wrote in his 1879 anti-Chernyshevsky pamphlet:

What Is to Be Done? is not only an encyclopedia, a reference book, but a codex for the practical application of the new word. . . . In the guise of a novel (an awkward novel, an extremely coarse one), a complete guide to the remaking of social relations is offered: most important, to the remaking of relations between men and women. . . . In my sixteen years at the university I never did meet a student who had not read the famous novel while he was still in school. A fifth- or sixth-grade girl was considered a fool if she was unacquainted with the adventures of Vera Pavlovna. In this respect, the works, for example, of Turgenev or Goncharov—not to mention Gogol or Pushkin—are far behind the novel *What Is to Be Done?* [62]

Almost immediately after its publication, the novel was banned (the ban was lifted only after the Revolution of 1905); its numerous readers had to use either the original magazine version (which became a bibliographic rarity) or one of the émigré editions (1867, 1876, and 1902), which were smuggled into Russia. The price of a copy of *What Is to Be Done?* ranged from 25 rubles in the 1860s to 60 rubles at the end of the century—a tremendous sum at the time. One memoirist remembers that some people sold their most valuable possessions to acquire a copy of the novel, another that in certain circles it was a precious graduation or wedding gift. There is evidence that the whole novel was often copied by hand, and dozens of such copies were in circulation (one person claimed to have produced four copies in his lifetime). [63]

There is also ample evidence of young people attempting to turn the fictional situations into real life. Skabichevsky wrote:

Producers' and consumers' associations, sewing, shoemaking and bookbinding workshops, laundries, residential communes, and family apartments with neutral rooms began to be founded everywhere. Fictitious marriages in order to liberate the daughters of generals and merchants from familial despotism in imitation of Lopukhov and Vera Pavlovna became normal phenomena. It was, in addition, quite rare if a woman liberated in this way did not open a sewing workshop and did not relate vatic dreams in order to resemble the novel's heroine exactly.[64]

One of the most famous residential communes modeled on *What Is to Be Done?* was established by a popular writer, Vasily Sleptsov, in 1863 and lasted for about a year.[65] A public activist, Ekaterina Vodovozova, describes a cooperative business enterprise with female labor (one of many) that was planned, to the last detail, by a group of young people gathered around an open copy of *What Is to Be Done?* When one of them pointed out the story of the successful rehabilitation of a prostitute in the novel, the others agreed to introduce prostitutes into their workshop.[66] A similar attempt was undertaken in a laundry cooperative organized in the spring of 1864 by a certain Mme Garshina. Both ended in total disaster.[67]

Literary reverberations of these events appeared in many contemporary novels. In the drafts of *The Idiot*, Dostoevsky had Prince Myshkin think about organizing a women's cooperative and a residential commune.[68] Nikolai Levin in Tolstoy's *Anna Karenina* contemplates a project for a cooperative workshop (it is notable that both Myshkin and Levin are also involved in the salvation of "fallen women").

The communes mentioned above were organized by people of the new persuasion who were uninvolved in the revolutionary underground. But the novel also had an impact on the revolutionary movement; the professional revolutionary, a social type that emerged after the 1860s, was without doubt directly influenced by the image of Rakhmetov—the model of an unbending and austere leader, coldly rational and calculating, who shows strict self-discipline and even cruelty to himself and to others in the name of the cause. Two members of the first revolutionary organization to appear in the mid-1860s, Dmitry Karakozov and Nikolai Ishutin (according to their comrade P. F. Nikolaev), consciously mimicked Rakhmetov.[69] Another revolutionary, M. P. Sazhin, remembered: "I grew up on Chernyshevsky, and one of the heroes of his novel *What Is to Be Done?*, Rakhmetov, was my ideal. Of course, I couldn't bring myself to sleep on a bed of nails, but I did sleep on bare boards for a year. Not only that, I tried to eat as little as possible and chose the simplest possible foods."[70] One Osipanov, a member of the terrorist organization the Group of March 1 (*pervomartovtsy*), so-called because of their March 1, 1887, assassination attempt on the life of Alexander III, did sleep on nails.[71]

It is a remarkable fact that Dmitry Karakozov set the date April 4, 1866—exactly three years after the completion of *What Is to Be Done?*—for his fateful attempt on the life of Alexander II (an act that, by causing a radical change in the political climate, marked the end of the "sixties"). He was undoubtedly inspired by Chernyshevsky's calculations of the date of the future revolution (two years after the first scene of the epilogue, though the calculations of the date of Rakhmetov's return involve the number three). M. N. Murav'ev, the official in charge of investigating the attempt, took this as evidence of art depicting life, rather than life imitating art: he was convinced that the date on which the text of the novel concludes (April 4, 1863) revealed that Chernyshevsky knew well in advance of the upcoming assassination attempt and of its exact timing.[72]

What Is to Be Done? was the favorite book of another member of the Group of March 1, Alexander Ul'ianov. His younger brother, Vladimir Ul'ianov (Lenin), claimed that Chernyshevsky, whom he read in 1887 following his brother's execution, played a crucial role in making him a revolutionary. He read and reread every line of Chernyshevsky's articles in the *Contemporary*, published more than twenty years earlier, but it was *What Is to Be Done?* that overturned (in Lenin's words "plowed over") his whole life. Characteristically, Lenin saw the novel's power to influence the lives of its readers as proof of its literary merit (according to memoirists, he became extremely annoyed with people who pointed out the book's aesthetic flaws). Chernyshevsky's greatest service, claimed Lenin, was that his novel showed the particular type of man that a revolutionary should be, and specified the methods and means of attaining this ideal. Lenin even accepted the novel's program for resolving marital conflicts: separate rooms for complete privacy and the rational handling of love triangles. I believe that Lenin's simultaneous relations with Inessa Armand (who later became a Bolshevik theoretician of love) and his wife Nadezhda Krupskaia in 1915 were ideologically motivated and directly influenced by *What Is to Be Done?*[73]

Apart from becoming a catechism of the Russian revolutionary, *What Is to Be Done?* provided a pattern for several generations of Russians to organize their emotional lives and personal relations. This aspect of the novel's influence was compared with that of Rousseau's *La Nouvelle Héloïse* and *Emile* on the emotional life of the people of the eighteenth century.[74] Even concerned censors were well aware of this side of the novel's effect. In 1865, P. Kapnist reviewed for the Ministry of Internal Affairs the impact of *What Is to Be Done?* on Russian society and noted: "There were cases of daughters running away from their fathers and mothers, wives from husbands; some even went to all the extremes that resulted from this."[75]

Judging from various memoirs, this is an accurate assessment. All over Russia, young women began leaving their parents' homes, and fictitious marriages became a regular way to elude parental restrictions, if not the normal way for the free-spirited young women to marry. In the words of one such woman, Anna Evreinova (who became the first woman doctor of law in Russia), "we were seeking people like ourselves, warmly devoted to a cause and whose principles were identical to ours, who would not so much marry us as liberate us."[76] The peculiar code of honor of the new people commanded a young man to be prepared to offer his hand in pro forma marriage to a domestically oppressed young lady whose beliefs and aspirations he shared. After the wedding the couple would usually separate; another variant involved living together under pretense of real marriage but with the understanding that the husband would not exercise his conjugal rights.[77]

A typical marriage of this type, which took place in the early 1870s, is described in detail in the memoirs of Sergei Sinegub. This young man from St. Petersburg, a member of the populist Chaikovtsy circle, went to a remote village near Viatka and offered his hand in marriage to the daughter of the local priest because he had heard that she was sufficiently enlightened to desire to arrange her life by the new beliefs. In the course of the common work "among the people" that followed their "marriage," the young man fell in love with his fictitious wife but in accordance with the new morality did not dare to declare his love ("It would have been a crime, an infringement of her freedom, since I was her legal husband"). However, the girl, who secretly shared his feelings, initiated the consummation of their marriage ("The conversation began with various moral and social themes, shifted by association to the question of love, and ended with a declaration"). Another member of the same circle, Dmitry Rogachev, offered himself as a fictitious husband to a girl named Vera Pavlovna Karpova, the sister of the playwright Evtikhy Karpov. The girl's name, no doubt, served as a source of inspiration for both of them: it was "read" as a sign directing them to "what is to be done."[78]

At the same time, a husband's failure to provide a meaningful common life dedicated to the cause (a goal that often served as a primary motivation for marrying) became, in the morality of the new people, an acceptable reason for his wife to leave him (and sometimes the children). One notable case was Ekaterina Maikova, wife of the well-known literary figure Vladimir Maikov (according to some sources, she served as a prototype for Olga in Ivan Goncharov's *Oblomov*), who left her husband in the early 1860s, after having re-examined her marriage (apparently a stable one) in the light of *What Is to Be Done?*[79] Finally, some love triangles were resolved, or rather maintained, in the manner suggested by Lopukhov (but rejected by Vera Pavlovna). Such cases became quite common (a literary reverberation of this practice can be found in a novel by S. Stepniak-Kravchinsky, written in English, *The Career of a Nihilist*; 1889).

But the best-known real-life experiment in human relations prompted by Chernyshevsky's novel was undertaken many years later by Vladimir Mayakovsky, Lilia Brik, and Osip Brik when, after the victory of the long-expected revolution, Chernyshevsky's influence surged. Early in their lives, Mayakovsky and the Briks formed a close and affectionate friendship based on a remarkable affinity "in art, in politics, and in everything" (the words of Lilia Brik). Mayakovsky's love for Lilia, so openly and ardently expressed in his poetry, did not seem to mar his friendship or his artistic and ideological alliance with Osip. When, in 1918, Mayakovsky and Lilia became lovers, the three of them made a decision "never to part." At one time during the 1920s they even shared an apartment; the arrangement of its private and neutral rooms is described in detail in Lilia Brik's memoirs. *What Is to Be Done?* apparently served as their model and inspiration. Notably, Mayakovsky was reading the book shortly before his suicide in 1930. "The life described in it," wrote Lilia Brik, "resonated in our life." [80]

A remarkable example of a whole life shaped in the spirit of the new men and under the direct influence of *What Is to Be Done?* is that of Sofia Kovalevskaia (1850–91), the first woman to make a significant contribution to mathematics. The story deserves to be related in detail, especially since Kovalevskaia's biographers have paid little attention to the special impact of Chernyshevsky's novel. [81]

Sofia and her elder sister Anna, daughters of a wealthy landowner, General V. Korvin-Krukovsky, were among those children of aristocratic families affected by the "epidemic of nihilism." They were introduced to the new faith by the son of the parish priest in their ancestral village of Palibino; a seminarian who became a student at Petersburg University, he claimed to have seen "the great Chernyshevsky, Dobroliubov, and Sleptsov." Anna was an aspiring author who, to her family's great dismay, published a short novel in Dostoevsky's journal *The Epoch* (*Epokha*). (Dostoevsky later fell in love with Anna and proposed to her in 1865; she declined.) Sofia had an active interest in, and a gift for, mathematics, but she was not allowed to pursue serious studies.

The sisters decided to escape from parental tyranny through fictitious marriages and, joined by a like-minded friend, initiated a search for suitable candidates (the code word was "brother" or "doctor"). They approached a science student at Petersburg University, Vladimir Kovalevsky, who eagerly accepted the challenge. He chose to marry the younger one, Sofia, whom he considered to be a promising scientist and therefore a more appropriate object for deliverance than her elder sister. The marriage took place in 1868 despite strong parental opposition. A husband for Anna, however, could not be found; Ivan Sechenov was approached, but being involved in a similar undertaking already, he could not "doctor" Anna Krukovskaia. In a letter to her sister, Sofia expressed regret that "brother" (that is, Kovalevsky) was not a Moslem and could not marry them both.[82]

The young couple soon left for Germany, where both became engrossed in studies. Anna was then allowed to settle with her married sister, and a little later, several other liberated young girls joined what turned into a small commune. Sofia and Vladimir became close friends and collaborators. For the most part, they lived and traveled together (and even engaged in a dramatic exchange of mutual demands and accusations), while faithfully continuing to maintain the initial arrangement and to live in the chastity of a fictitious marriage. Sofia's parents eventually learned of the true nature of their relationship and vainly tried to persuade her to become Kovalevsky's real wife. In contrast, Anna and the other members of the commune disapproved of Sofia's closeness to Kovalevsky and accused him of "an emotional violation" of the new code: they insisted that, since the marriage was fictitious, Kovalevsky ought not give too intimate a character to his relations with Sofia.[83]

Like Vera Pavlovna in *What Is to Be Done?*, Sofia was soon consumed by what a friend called "a craving for great emotions."[84] Her marriage with Kovalevsky was finally consummated; they were brought together, it seems, by the death of Sofia's authoritarian yet beloved father in 1875.[85] A little later, a daughter was born to the Kovalevskys. In full accord with the canon established by Chernyshevsky's novel, Sofia had peculiar dreams, which she habitually described to friends; she took them for prophetic visions, and indeed, according to one of these friends, they frequently came true.[86]

After their return to Russia in 1875, the Kovalevskys started a series of business enterprises (to which many of their friends contributed money). Sofia believed that, with her command of mathematics, she could arrange these enterprises on a totally rational, scientific basis that would guarantee their financial success. It is an error, I believe, to treat these enterprises (which included low-cost apartments and public baths in a working-class neighborhood) as a purely financial undertaking inspired by the bourgeois spirit of the time, as some biographers do. Many details attest that they were inspired by the ideas of the rational organization of labor, which found their clearest expression in *What Is to Be Done?* The profits, for example, were not intended solely for individual benefit: when Kovalevsky announced (mistakenly) that they had made a fortune, Sofia immediately "laid plans for founding a phalanstery." [87]

The Kovalevskys were notorious for their indifference to the material side of life and for their devastating impracticality, and it is no surprise that, unlike Vera Pavlovna and Lopukhov, they were not successful. In the midst of the difficulties caused by their business failure, the couple separated. Sofia took up a professorship at Stockholm University (unprecedented for a woman); Vladimir lived through a major financial disaster and committed suicide in 1883.

Toward the end of her life, Sofia, by then an internationally acclaimed mathematician, began to write. A drama, *Struggle for Happiness*, written collectively with A. C. Leffler, grew out of her reflections on her husband's tragic end. Centering around the theme of marriage, the drama's two parts relate the story of a marriage. One part describes things as they are in reality, the other as they might have been if the couple had been able to arrange their marriage in full accord with their youthful aspirations. The drama culminates in a vision of a small, ideally arranged family commune, with the heroine dreaming of the People's Palace, a domicile of the workmen's association. With her characteristically unshakable belief in science, Sofia's foreword states what she believed to be the scientific foundation for her view of love, proving the omnipotence of love "with mathematical stringency" (in the words of a contemporary reader). [88]

Sophia intended the drama to bring ultimate happiness to all mankind. Her other literary project, an unfinished novel entitled *The Nihilist*, was based on Chernyshevsky's life.

The literary response to *What Is to Be Done?*, and to the personality and behavior model it promoted, was also significant. In the years following its publication, a special genre of anti-nihilist literature appeared, distinguished by a set of specific conventions and devices for the parodistic treatment of the new people. This was seen as a necessary antidote to the evil effects of *What Is to Be Done?* Among the works in this genre are Lev Tolstoy's play *The Infected Family* (*Zarazhennoe semeistvo*, 1863–64); Alexander Pisemsky's *Troubled Sea* (*Vzbalomuchennoe more*, 1863), a novel devoted to the effects of "free love" in a circle of nihilists; and Nikolai Leskov's novels *Nowhere to Go* (*Nekuda*, 1864), a lampoon of Sleptsov's commune, and *The Bypassed* (*Oboidennye*, 1864), which offered an alternative to cooperative workshops. In the 1860s and 1870s, works in this genre practically flooded the literary market.[89] Chernyshevsky appeared as a fictional character in many works of Russian literature, from contemporary works, such as D. V. Grigorovich's play *The School of Hospitality* (*Shkola gostepriimstva;* 1855), to a major twentieth-century Russian novel, *The Gift* (*Dar;* 1937) by Vladimir Nabokov.

Indeed, Chernyshevsky became such an inseparable part of Russian culture in the second half of the nineteenth century that his presence is felt in most writings of his contemporaries, including the major achievements of Russian prose. Traces of *What Is to Be Done?* can be found in Dostoevsky's *Notes from Underground, Crime and Punishment, The Idiot, The Devils,* and *The Brothers Karamazov* and in Tolstoy's *Anna Karenina.* But most important, Dostoevsky and Tolstoy, as well as many other contemporaries, were involved throughout their life and work in a constant and intense dialogue with the view of man and his destiny on earth espoused by Chernyshevsky.

For more than a century, Chernyshevsky has remained a center of popular and scholarly controversy. He has been described as an active revolutionary who controlled revolutionary forces and as a person who merely appeared to do so. He has been considered an independent thinker and a mere popularizer of intellectual innovations for magazine readers. Almost universally regarded as an inept writer, he is nevertheless credited with the development of such innovative literary techniques as "polyphony" (Mikhail Bakhtin) and "stream of consciousness" (Gleb Struve).[90]

Chernyshevsky's personality has attracted almost as much attention as his writings. Attention has focused on his "existential dilemma":[91] the profound idealism of this devoted materialist, the Christian asceticism and sacrificial zeal of this "rational egoist," the Orthodox sentiments of this accomplished atheist, the *a priori* thinking of this sociologist and economist committed to science, the aesthetic helplessness of this successful novelist and theoretician of art, the deep feeling of social inferiority in this militant revolutionary, and the tormenting doubts that this propagandist for the complete objectivity of sensory perception experienced in relation to his own senses. But regardless of how we assess the merits of Chernyshevsky's activities and works, or his personal worth, his enormous impact on the lives of many significant people and the works of major Russian writers cannot be overestimated. "By the sheer weight of his influence," he established himself as one of the leading figures in the Russian culture of the 1860s.[92]

But Chernyshevsky's impact on Russian culture cannot be fully explained by his political activity, his participation in ideological and literary polemics, or his journalism and artistic writings. His most significant act was the creation of a unified model of behavior for the age of realism, the conception of a new type of personality, with a different orientation to the world and different patterns of behavior, that contemporaries eagerly adopted.[93]

For Chernyshevsky, a prototypical personality was to be formed not only in works of literature but also in private life. The task involved subjecting one's personal life to the demands of a public role (hence Chernyshevsky's famous self-discipline and self-denial and his desire to set a worthy example of conduct in his own behavior); but it also entailed a deliberate psychological self-organization in which one's private personality, one's psychic life itself, was shaped to conform to a historical mold. For Chernyshevsky, this was an essential, if not the most important, part of the vocation of the writer, who (in his words) "stood at the head of social development." It is in this spirit that, shortly after his arrest, working on *What Is to Be Done?* in prison confinement, Chernyshevsky wrote to his wife: "My life and yours belong to history."[94] "Thrust forward," in Hegelian terms, at a turning point in Russian history, Chernyshevsky succeeded in promoting cultural mechanisms for ordering human reality and organizing individual behavior in an era of ultimate disarray, when "everything came up for rearrangement."

Why Nikolai Gavrilovich Chernyshevsky was a particularly appropriate person for this creative task and how exactly it was achieved will, I hope, become clear in the course of this book. What follows is a detailed description of the development of Chernyshevsky's model, focusing on the interrelation between the personal and the cultural. This process is studied in three different phases; each of the three parts of the book is devoted to a particular phase. In the first part, I discuss the general problems that young Chernyshevsky confronted on the eve of the sixties and show how they correlated with important social and cultural issues. In the second part, I focus on Chernyshevsky's marriage and on the marriage design that he developed in the course of this experience; in this design, psychological and cultural elements converged into a coherent pattern ready to be offered to contemporaries as a cultural model. In the third part, I examine the structure of Chernyshevsky's writings, in which his model was embodied. In *What Is to Be Done?*, the model became all-encompassing. Not only was it realized in plot, characterization, and ideology, but it also penetrated the texture of the narrative and was manifested through the artistic principles behind the organization of the text: psychological structure merged with literary structure. I conclude with an analysis of the novel from this perspective.

ONE

Exposition

In June 1846, the eighteen-year-old Chernyshevsky arrived in St. Petersburg to become a student at Petersburg University. Born and raised in the provincial town of Saratov on the Volga, he was the only son in the family of an archpriest (*protoierei*). At first he was educated at home under the guidance of his father (a learned man by contemporary standards), and then in an Orthodox seminary, an institution that prepared students for careers in the clergy.[1] In the seminary he earned a reputation as a student of truly outstanding abilities, whose academic achievements far surpassed the generally accepted standards. Great things were expected of him. His family decided to give Nikolai a university education, and he was sent to St. Petersburg. There this voracious reader (in his own words, a "bibliophagus"[2]) decided to enroll in the faculty of philology.

The confrontation with the real world of independent life in the capital proved to be a cruel and painful experience. In Saratov the Chernyshevskys enjoyed the general respect of their fellow countrymen and a comfortable living. A beautiful, bright, and gentle child and adolescent, Nikolai was the object of attention and admiration in his family and at school, as well as in the circles of local society his family frequented.[3] From the socially sheltered environment of his Saratov home, Chernyshevsky entered a world in which he and his family were nobodies and about which they knew almost nothing.* From the point of view of Petersburg society, the status of the provincial parish clergy, even at his father's relatively high rank, was far from privileged. In Petersburg, Chernyshevsky's financial circumstances were reduced almost to the level of poverty. His education was quite solid and thorough, but as a seminary graduate, he was unprepared for a university course and for social interaction in the educated circles of the capital. The entrance examinations immediately revealed gaps. Most notably, Chernyshevsky received a low grade in French (the first low grade in his life). By that time, the beautiful child had turned into an awkward and ungainly-looking youth, nearsighted and painfully shy.

During his university years, Chernyshevsky apparently experienced a serious crisis. His diaries, begun in May 1848, reveal the inner life of a youth gripped at once by a deep sense of inadequacy and a desire for glory. Tormented by his unsociability and emotional inhibitions, young Chernyshevsky engaged in constructing plans, projects, and theoretical systems for destroying and rebuilding society. He worked on a *perpetuum mobile* that was supposed to liberate humanity from material need and open the way to moral reformation. The invention was to make Chernyshevsky a "second Savior" (1: 281), as well as to enable him to have an audience with the emperor, an opportunity for aiding his father's advancement in rank (1: 158).† He was also contemplating becoming a thinker of genius such as Plato or Hegel or a great writer who would move humanity, or at least the Slavic world, "in a somewhat new direction" (1: 127).

In spite of his grand plans, he saw the difficulties in the way of

*Randall, *N. G. Chernyshevskii*, p. 24. Chernyshevsky's cousin Alexander Pypin wrote: "In our immediate circle there was nobody who knew anything about Petersburg. It was an inconceivable, remote land, a dwelling place of all the authorities, a place with its own special ways and great hardships of living" (cited in Oksman, *N. G. Chernyshevsky*, 1: 64).

†The in-text citations are to Chernyshevsky, *Polnoe sobranie sochinenii*. His father's career suffered because of an incident that happened a short while before young Chernyshevsky's graduation from the seminary. A mistake in birth records cost Father Gavriil his post as a member of the consistory. The family was deeply shaken by what they saw as an injustice, and the incident influenced the decision to give Nikolai a secular education (Oksman, *N. G. Chernyshevsky*, 1: 48–49).

self-fulfillment as almost insurmountable. Chernyshevsky's self-doubt focused on conflicts and situations that revealed a lack or weakness of emotional response to events and impressions of the real world around him. "I feel not a thing, absolutely nothing," he records in sorrow and bewilderment (1: 113). "Insensitivity," or "coldness," becomes the dominant theme of the diaries, a characteristic that encompasses a whole range of problems: doubts about seemingly obvious matters of life; reticence and timidity in approaching others, especially women; a disparity between rational thinking and spontaneous feeling; a gulf between pure love (or rather lack of love) and tormenting carnal desires; and weakness of will, inertia, and inactivity ("lifelessness").

In his intense search for solutions to these problems, young Chernyshevsky drew on the resources of culture. In the words of a contemporary, "Starting with Hegel and Feuerbach and ending with French pulp novels, Chernyshevsky read everything."[4] He absorbed whole theoretical systems and fragments of knowledge and ideas, metaphysical and scientific concepts, and rhetorical devices. Chernyshevsky's attention focused on those materials that were in tune with his private concerns, a complex of issues connected with the idea of reality. This chaotic experimentation with his own psychic life, defined and organized in the language of contemporary culture, could be called a phase of *cultural* language acquisition.

The Diaries: Attention to Pennies

Between 1848 and 1853, Chernyshevsky kept detailed and candid diaries. They were intended primarily as a means of self-definition and self-improvement, but because he was preparing for a career as a writer, he could not help seeing the exercise as a literary undertaking. Later he used these diaries as source materials for his literary works: whole scenes and many details were transferred to his fiction. In addition, since young Chernyshevsky was assiduously preparing for glory, the diaries were meant to be useful for an autobiography or for the researchs of future biographers (1: 193).[5]

In their emphasis on psychological self-examination and in

their confessional character, Chernyshevsky's diaries are by no means unusual for the period. A year earlier, Lev Tolstoy (who was also born in 1828) had started a diary aimed at the scrupulous investigation of his own character. This diary became a psychological testing ground for his later novels. A similar diary was begun in 1852 by Nikolai Dobroliubov (born in 1836); a section of it was entitled "Psychotorium"—a laboratory of mental processes. Thus, the concern with psychological introspection and the intense interest in personality that prompted Chernyshevsky to scrutinize his mental life in a diary were part of a general cultural wave in mid-nineteenth-century Russia. Symptomatic of this concern was the intense interest in Rousseau, especially in his *Confessions*, shown by Chernyshevsky's generation, including Tolstoy and Dostoevsky,[6] and the growing interest in memoiristic and documentary literature (Russian translations of Chateaubriand's *Mémoirs d'outre-tombe*, Lamartine's *Confidences*, the letters of Benjamin Constant, and Goethe's *Dichtung und Wahrheit* appeared during these years).

An immediate source of the new psychological self-analysis was the cult of the "inner man" among members of the philosophical circles of the 1830s and 1840s. Such "private" works of literature of the 1840s as Herzen's diaries, Ogarev's letters (and his later *Confession*), the letters of Stankevich and Bakunin, and the early letters of Belinsky contained astounding self-revelations and thoughtful generalizations based on private experience. But since the form assumed by documentary accounts of private life is always related to the literary currents of the epoch, there is a marked difference between human documents written in the age of romanticism and those from the age of realism.

For the men of the 1830s and 1840s, the road to the inner workings of the soul lay through philosophy. They viewed the individual human being, human emotions, and even the routine situations of daily life in terms of metaphysical categories. Looking back at this time, Herzen described the psychological practices of his youth: "Everything in reality direct, every simple feeling was lifted into abstract categories and came back from them without a drop of living blood, a pale algebraic shadow. . . . The very tear glistening on the eyelash was strictly referred to its proper classification, to *Gemüt*, or to the 'tragic in the heart.'"[7]

As a result, the letters and diaries of this generation are almost entirely devoid of concrete psychological material as well as of concrete details of everyday existence.[8]

A new approach to the analysis and apprehension of human life was introduced by Belinsky, a major theoretician of Russian realistic aesthetics and a forerunner of the men of the sixties, in his private correspondence. As early as 1837, in his letters to Mikhail Bakunin (who was especially famous for "engaging in the practice of mystical and semi-philosophical interpretations of life phenomena"[9]), Belinsky raised the issue that he saw both as a defect of psychological analysis and as a moral problem: "disharmony between the external life and the inner life." He saw its cause in a "disdain for pennies." By that he meant the romantic taboo on the facts of "low reality," that is, those concerned with the material circumstances of being—money, living conditions, and the human body. As a result, Belinsky implies, the romantic saw no relationship between external conditions and the inner life and intellectual activity.[10]

Belinsky's passionate appeal to Bakunin, a nobleman by birth and upbringing, urging him to be aware of pennies and to be scrupulous about them had a special poignancy, a special nuance; it was made by the only plebeian in Bakunin's circle, a man who by virtue of his lowly status was enmeshed in "low reality." In a letter to Bakunin of November 1, 1837, Belinsky described in vivid detail the material side of his life, which by the cultural canon of the time should have remained outside the writings (if not outside the consciousness) of a literary-minded person:

I sit down to work, to translate from the German or to do something else. . . . And what happens? I shake from the cold, my hands are incapable of holding a pen, my animal side comes to the fore. . . . Or another time, just as I want to do something, to take advantage of a moment of inner harmony, suddenly I get a letter reminding me that I owe 30 paper rubles this month on the 500 that I borrowed. I reply asking whether they can pay those 30 rubles for me plus give me about 800 more at the same rate.[11]

But Belinsky's appeal to Bakunin, made in full awareness of the difference in their social positions and, therefore, in their behavior (Bakunin, with the characteristic carelessness of a noble-man, ignored his large debts), contained much more than purely moral and social implications. The famous "dispute over pennies" was a confrontation between romanticism and nascent realism. Realism as a style of literature claimed to be all-inclusive in subject matter (and thus objective in method); the trivial and low became legitimate subjects of art.[12] Realism as a style of life meant an awareness of the details of concrete, material existence, even the petty, ugly, or revolting ones, for they were inseparable from the "life of the spirit." The inner life was perceived as inter-locking with external circumstances. In the mature stages of real-ism, previously unmentionable and "contraband" details of exis-tence, including, in Belinsky's terms, "pennies," "groceries," and "the animal side of human nature" (bodily needs), became legitimate facts of culture. They became meaningful elements of literary discourse and meaningful and noticeable elements of be-havior. In daily life they became a requirement of "everyday positivism," which replaced "everyday Byronism."

The new principles for apprehending the inner life—prin-ciples that proved decisive for the methods of nineteenth-century Russian psychological prose—were originally introduced and developed in the personal writings of cultural figures, in inti-mate letters and diaries. The private personalities of the authors of these documents, or rather the correlation between the indi-vidual characteristics of writers and the historical quality of their activity, became an important factor in the cultural develop-ments of the age of realism.

Chernyshevsky played an extremely important role in these developments, and his early diaries are an interesting example of private experiments with realism understood in a direct sense. The strategy adopted in his diary was fairly simple and remark-ably straightforward: he strove to make as complete, specific, and precise an account of each day as possible. The record of his day unfolded gradually, going from descriptions of routine ac-tions (for example, his daily morning walk to the university) and observations on the weather to justifications of his actions in rela-tion to external conditions (what he was wearing and why). The extensive discussions of his readings and conversations at times grew into reflections on global problems of human existence:

2 [December 1848], 11 [o'clock].—It was not so cold as it was yesterday, and I was able, especially when I was walking to the university, to wrap myself up so well that my ears did not freeze at all. For the second time this winter, I walked without galoshes, among other things, for reasons of economy. Will this pair of boots and my old galoshes last until summer? Of course not, but even so. Got to the university at 10:30. Did not go to Grefe's class as I had wanted, but went to the library where I read Limayrac's critical articles in the *Revue de deux mondes*. Vulgarity, just as his remarks about the lack of spirituality, inconsistency, and general lack of principles in the work of Benj. Constant. The clowns—they think that if a man says in indignation, "I don't believe, people are base and stupid," it is because he has a soul that desires to believe, that loves mankind less than theirs do and not because, on the contrary, he harbors a force that searches for satisfaction more eagerly and the disparity between the real and the rational is all the more bitter for him. (1: 185)

The orientation toward all-inclusiveness and precision resulted in juxtaposition of materials of different orders. Commonplace details of external life and generalizations of global significance expressed in metaphysical terms appeared as links in the uninterrupted chain of human existence in which "boots and old galoshes" are intertwined with "the disparity between the real and the rational." As if echoing Belinsky's passionate epistolary monologues on the significance of pennies, Chernyshevsky filled his diaries with budget calculations and shopping lists (which later found their way into *What Is to Be Done?*). In contrast, the diary of the young aristocrat Lev Tolstoy for the same year is almost devoid of concrete details of everyday life.[13]

But even when viewed against the background of common cultural developments of the age of realism, in which non-gentry intellectuals like Chernyshevsky played a special role, his diaries are unique in their extreme degree of precision and in the scope of the material included. Chernyshevsky meant to account for "everything, absolutely everything" (1: 471); he recorded serious thoughts, reflections, and feelings; fleeting associations and sensations; conversations; habitual actions; movements around the city; dinner menus; budget calculations; and even bodily functions (including the minutest details of excretory and sexual functions). Still more striking is the precision of these accounts, for Chernyshevsky tried to define every component of his experience by specifying, whenever possible, the location of events in time and space and their quantity, and by revealing causal connections between them.

Plans of houses he had visited and even diagrams of his movements around a room are frequently included. For his description of a dance party (the first in his life) that he attended with a friend, Chernyshevsky drew a diagram in which the position of each participant is marked with a letter of the alphabet: "At first I stood by the door to their room, next to the piano, and then later by the entrance, and in all that time only six— four to be exact—couples danced. . . . At first (i.e., during the first dance), she stood on *l* while Iv. Vas. and I stood at the door, on *b*, and I was watching her and almost never took my eyes off her" (1: 210).

If he moved around the city visiting friends and business acquaintances, Chernyshevsky recorded not only his routes but also the time taken:

The time I spent walking was 100 minutes going from Maksimovich to Bulychev's and back, then 16 minutes going to Al. Fed.'s, then back home another 16 minutes, then to Bulychev's 50 or at least 48 minutes, which totals 180 minutes, i.e., 3 hours, and then I walked from there to the cottage, arriving at a quarter to 9, and since I was at Bulychev's at 6, this makes another 2 and ½ hours at least. So, totaling all the above, 5 and ¼ hours and 32 miles. (1: 278)

A whole day is thus translated into a chain of calculations.

But the closest attention by far is given to emotions and sensations, especially those relating to women. By defining the smallest events of his emotional life with particular precision, Chernyshevsky was able to investigate the connections between the inner life and external circumstances. Thus, he made careful observations of where and when he experienced a sensation or impression: "As we walked (around the corner, turning into the Second Lane from the Prospect, past the barracks), I was struck by the impression that the way she walks isn't attractive" (1: 71). The woman in question was an object of Chernyshevsky's affection, although that affection was accompanied by agonizing doubts about the reality of these feelings.

After a series of such observations and experiments, Chernyshevsky concluded that "feelings are determined by the time rather than by the location" (1: 99). But on further reflection, he admitted that he had not established definite ties between the internal and external. Bewildered that the emotion he felt for a friend whom he supposedly dearly loved was no stronger in its concrete manifestations than the emotions evoked by the routine events of university life, he pondered that "perhaps the quickening of the heart is not caused by events, but rather it comes about without any reason whatsoever" (1: 99). Thus arose the disturbing supposition that perhaps "sensations come from within rather than from without" (1: 99).

When Chernyshevsky could establish no tangible connection between a sensation and the time, location, or external circumstances, he tried to pinpoint the emotion by measuring its external physical manifestations (for example, by tracing sadness through the tears it evoked, which could then be defined numerically). "Three to four tears trickled out" is how Chernyshevsky related his reaction to the death of a childhood friend (1: 53). Whereas for young romantics, described with such irony in Herzen's *My Past and Thoughts* (*Byloe i dumy*; 1852–68), "the tear glistening on the eyelash" referred to the abstract categories of German idealism, the young realist defined emotions with the positive, scientific precision of mathematics.

These operations—recording both mental and physical experience in its totality, locating it in time and space and defining it numerically—indicate a condition that Chernyshevsky referred to as his "insensitivity": a lack of direct emotional response to external events, which leads to the loss of a sense of conviction about the world.[14] But Chernyshevsky correlated what was a matter of psychological necessity (hence the extreme intensity with which he followed these procedures) with the concerns and strategies of culture. He interpreted his strong urge to attach the self securely to the outside world (an operation that he as an individual apparently could not achieve through immediate sensory perception) in terms of the current cultural code as "a striving for reality," in contrast to the "idealization" and emotional barrenness of the idealists of the 1830s and 1840s. This urge found expression in a series of concrete psychological strategies that captured the actuality of real-life events and emotional states, and were prompted by such central cultural principles as Belinsky's attention to pennies and to bodily needs, the positivistic concern with determinism (ties and links in a chain of psychic states and events), and the general principle of scientific precision.

On the one hand, Chernyshevsky's behavioral idiosyncrasies turned out to be particularly appropriate for the period's expectations of personal behavior. On the other hand, the emerging cultural and literary principles particularly suited his personal needs. In his acceptance of these principles for the goals of self-definition in his diary, the individual and the cultural converged.

Living Merged with Writing

Diary accounts of the events of each day are regularly interrupted by detailed inventories of the diary itself. Thus, Chernyshevsky transferred his attention from the event to the process of its recording. Apparently, the writing process and the physical presence of the text represented tangible evidence of the reality of his existence.

Oh Lord, such abundance of detail! Everything is described, absolutely everything, with the precision of a stenographer's report! . . . Well, of course—it fills 44 single pages plus 10 double pages! . . . 64 pages full of writing, neither more nor less! If one should take the trouble to calculate it all, it will come to 64 times 27 lines, then multiply that by 80 characters in a line, and you get 138,200 characters! This equals 140 pages of regular print! This, after all, is a short novel, really. My, what a productive writer! (1: 471)

Shortly after this inventory was made, in the spring of 1853, Chernyshevsky abandoned the diary, but he did not abandon the feverish pace of his writing, which he kept up, in one form or another, as long as he lived. Writing became an essential part of the life process.

As a professional writer, Chernyshevsky was in fact extremely productive. During the years of his active participation in the *Contemporary* (1855–62), he filled, almost single-handedly, issue after issue, taking care of the sections on criticism, bibliography, and (from 1859) politics, as well as supplying translations of studies in history and political economy. The external motivations for this frenzied activity were not just the demands of his editorship, but also his desire to ensure a steady and ample income (mainly for his wife's sake, for Chernyshevsky himself was a man of ascetic inclinations). Friends and relatives remembered him as a person who wrote almost unceasingly—through conversations with visitors, hasty meals, and even the noisy parties given by his wife.* He continued to write throughout the 22 months he spent in the Peter-and-Paul Fortress (1862–64). By one estimate, Chernyshevsky produced the equivalent of approximately 215 printed pages a month during this period.[15]

In Siberia, throughout almost 20 years of penal servitude and exile, he wrote constantly, both to pass the time and in the hope that his writings could be published to help support his family. During some periods of his exile, Chernyshevsky wrote for at least fifteen hours every day, and sometimes through the night. He wrote thousands of pages of fiction, and promised his cousin and executor, Alexander Pypin, that he would send him "masses" of his writings (14: 619) and "flood" Russian literature with his compositions (14: 496) as soon as the censors allowed him to resume publishing (which never happened): "I keep writing novels. I have written dozens of them. I write them and then tear them up. One needn't keep old manuscripts because everything that has been written down remains in one's memory. And as soon as you tell me that I can start publishing, I will start sending about 400 pages a month" (15: 87).

His memory, indeed, was extraordinary, and once written, the texts were permanently fixed in his mind; on his return from Siberia, Chernyshevsky could recite whole chapters of the novels he had written there. Seeing that none of his manuscripts could be published (those sent by mail never reached the addressee), Chernyshevsky burned masses of manuscripts and then resumed writing again.[16] He was driven by an irresistible urge to write, and those of his Siberian manuscripts that were

---

*A friend remembered: "Sometimes he would wake up at night, jump out of bed, and begin to write" (Lebedev, "N. G. Chernyshevsky," p. 303).

preserved (and published posthumously) testify, both in quantity and in quality, to his graphomania.

In penal servitude in Aleksandrovsky zavod (1864–70), surrounded by fellow prisoners, Chernyshevsky improvised endless stories, with complicated plots and psychological analyses, sometimes looking into an empty notebook on the pretense that he was reading a previously written text.[17] Actually, he found this form of composition preferable to writing, and in later years, in Astrakhan' and Saratov (1883–89), Chernyshevsky dictated everything to a stenographer. This way he could work even faster; for example, four days before he died, already gravely ill, Chernyshevsky translated eighteen pages of Georg Weber's *Universal History* in this fashion. Curiously enough his words in his final delirium were also recorded by the secretary in shorthand (the record was later published by his son).[18]

Chernyshevsky was much intrigued by the possibilities of stenography and mentioned it frequently in his writings. The perfect example of the motif is found in a novel he dictated in Astrakhan', *Evenings at Princess Starobelskaia's* (*Vechera u kniagini Starobel'skoi*; 1888). Its hero, Viazovsky, is an autobiographical character, an old scholar and writer; he is invited to speak to a group of aristocrats who have gathered to listen to his improvisations. The stories are recorded by a whole team of stenographers, whose arrangement in the room is described in meticulous spatial detail:

Two tables were placed between the stage and the first semicircle of chairs, one table a little to the left of the stage and one a little to the right, and six stenographers sat at the one that was to the left (i.e., to the left if you are facing the stage), those six were all young men, whereas the five stenographers at the other table were all women. With them was a man, about 35 years of age or perhaps a little older. Apparently he was the head of this group of male and female stenographers. (13: 788)

This episode was of such importance to Chernyshevsky that he continued working on this scene even after he had submitted the manuscript for publication to the magazine *Russian Thought* (*Russkaia mysl'*). Erroneously assuming that the novel was being printed, he sent insertions specifying the position of the stenographers.[19]

As one of Chernyshevsky's fellow prisoners who listened to the Siberian improvisations commented in his memoirs, "for him to write meant to live."[20] But Chernyshevsky's preference for stenography—the instantaneous recording of a verbalization—over other methods of composition reveals an important aspect of the psychological function that writing had for him. The principle that unites the recording of improvised discourse and diary writing was a "coincidence between verbalization and perception or experience."[21] Beginning in the diaries, Chernyshevsky equated a living person with a verbalizing person, whose existence was further confirmed by the material product of that verbalization. Only in the verbal flow of instantaneous description of sensations did experience acquire reality, continuity, and permanence. The early diaries and the Siberian fiction, which belong to the two major periods of mental stress, exemplify this phenomenon of living merged with writing.

It was only after he discontinued his diaries that Chernyshevsky found, and immediately identified, the literary model that fulfilled his need to use literature as "equipment for living": Tolstoy's technique of the literary presentation of consciousness. The discovery was made in 1856, in a review of Lev Tolstoy's early prose, including the autobiographical *Childhood* and *Boyhood* (*Detstvo* and *Otrochestvo*). It is, incidentally, one of Chernyshevsky's best articles as well as one of the most insightful analyses of Tolstoy's narrative.

Chernyshevsky claimed that the essence of Tolstoy's innovative artistic method, and his main merit, was his concentration on the inner life, on the psychological process (or "psychic movements") per se. Chernyshevsky named this process the "dialectics of the soul" (*dialektika dushi*). In Chernyshevsky's words, Tolstoy's literary craftsmanship opened the way to "capturing the dramatic transition of one emotion into another, one thought into another," to penetrating into "the mysterious process through which a thought or a feeling is developed." Whereas most writers "give us only the two extreme links of the chain, the starting point and the finish of a psychic process," Tolstoy analyzes the "process itself." Thus he succeeds in capturing and fixing the "elusive manifestations of inner life, which succeed one another with extraordinary rapidity and inexhaustible variety" (3: 425–26).[22]

For Chernyshevsky, Tolstoy's technique of fixing the flux of human consciousness was an important addition to two principles of realism developed in earlier literature: all-inclusiveness and precision of detail. In his experiments with narrative, Tolstoy went far beyond the task of early realism with which Chernyshevsky had struggled in his diaries—the presentation and analysis of the connections between the internal and the external. In the narrative mode developed in Tolstoy's early works, Chernyshevsky saw a tool for capturing the "elusive manifestations of inner life itself," of sensations that, in Chernyshevsky's words, "came from within" and thus remained entirely out of reach and control—as good as nonexistent. These new narrative techniques allowed mental processes to be securely fixed on paper, and thus, human life in its totality received ultimate reality through writing.

In his review, Chernyshevsky, who knew nothing of Tolstoy's diary, made an ingenious guess about the source of Tolstoy's technique, maintaining that only the practice of careful self-examination could allow an author to penetrate into the working of the human consciousness. Thus, at the time Chernyshevsky was struggling with the "mysterious movements of the psychic life" in his early diaries, general interest in the problem of narrative modes of presentation of consciousness had become a major trend in contemporary literature. Even before the publication of *Childhood* (1852), *Boyhood* (1854), and *Sevastopol' Tales* (*Sevastopol'skie rasskazy*; 1855–56), Tolstoy had attempted to combine the technique of stream of consciousness with the task of depicting the events, thoughts, and impressions of a single day in someone's life, presented through his own consciousness in a first-person narrative. This is the unfinished story "The History of the Previous Day" ("Istoriia vcherashnego dnia"; 1851), which is partially based on material from Tolstoy's own diary.

In similar attempts, Dostoevsky experimented with confessional discourse (adopting Rousseau or entering into polemics against him) and the technique of the "inner monologue" in *The Double* (*Dvoinik*; 1846), a book that made a tremendous impression on Chernyshevsky; in *Notes from Underground* (*Zapiski iz podpol'ia*, 1864); and in such other works as *A Gentle Creature* (*Krotkaia*; 1876).[23]

Both in the diaries and at the more mature stages of his writing, Chernyshevsky worked on developing new techniques to record consciousness. He was, however, more successful in theory than in practice. A stenographic novel of the Siberian period, *Gleams of Radiance* (*Otbleski siianiia*), written some time between 1879 and 1882, represents a failed attempt to depict a whole day in the life of its hero. Indeed, Chernyshevsky did not start with the idea of limiting his novel (which, like Tolstoy's story, remained unfinished) to a single day; instead, he saw that episode as part of a large, complicated work. He abandoned the novel, however, when, after writing the equivalent of 150 pages of small print, he still had not completed the account of one morning.

Thus, in his own diary writing, in his critical analysis of Tolstoy's experiments with narrative form, and in his later fiction, Chernyshevsky identified and formulated those principles and techniques of literary presentations of reality that had a potential to be adapted to the needs of daily life (to his struggle with his "insensitivity"). Innovative narrative techniques served as defense systems of an idiosyncratic nature; at the same time, these defense systems proved to be innovative literary principles and narrative techniques. Culture did not merely prescribe certain types and norms of behavior; it also offered structural mechanisms and principles of organization that could be applied to the organization and structuring of a personality. And, on the reverse side, the principles and techniques of personality organization became part of the cultural inheritance, not only as behavior patterns, but also as literary principles and narrative techniques.

The Intermediary: Lobodovsky

Chernyshevsky's diary opens with a detailed account of a marriage—the marriage of his closest friend at the time, Vasily Petrovich Lobodovsky. The first entry recounts, in epic tones: "In late April 1848, Vasily Petrovich announced to me that he was getting married" (1: 29). The diary also ends with a detailed account of a marriage—Chernyshevsky's own marriage to Olga Sokratovna Vasil'eva in 1853 (he too was wed in late April, around Easter time). Lobodovsky's marriage obviously served as a prototype for Chernyshevsky's own marriage. Moreover, his friend's experience, and Chernyshevsky's participation in it, influenced *What Is to Be Done?*

Vasily Petrovich Lobodovsky was a fellow student at Petersburg University and, like Chernyshevsky, was the seminary-educated son of a provincial priest. In the full romantic tradition of tender friendship, young Chernyshevsky formed a passionate attachment to Lobodovsky. "I love you, Vas. Petr., I love you!," he confided to his diary (1: 68). Idealizing his more mature and experienced friend ("A great man!" 1: 95), Chernyshevsky relied on, and was easily influenced by, Lobodovsky's opinions and tastes, and eagerly shared in his friend's emotions. Chernyshevsky's identification with Lobodovsky was based on an awareness of their similarities: the predicament of their origins and their shared aspirations for glory and sacrifice on the path to social reformation. The expectation of future shared glory was reflected in endless conversations between the two young men: "At last we began to talk about the social upheavals that are due in this country. He [Lobodovsky] thinks that he will be their perpetrator, their hero" (1: 363); "He was telling me that I should be a second Savior, which he had hinted at before" (1: 281).

Chernyshevsky's awareness of many similarities was complemented by his projection of desired qualities onto his close friend. Thus, Lobodovsky was endowed with a strong will and feelings. "Greatness of heart" (a gap in Chernyshevsky's own character) was combined with "greatness of mind," a quality that Chernyshevsky saw as a strength common to both: "V. P. is truly a great man. The greatness of his heart is perhaps even stronger than the greatness of his mind" (1: 115). By identifying with Lobodovsky, Chernyshevsky could participate vicariously in certain experiences not otherwise open to him and thus experience "mediated emotions." Lobodovsky eagerly admitted Chernyshevsky into his confidence and his intimate life, and made Chernyshevsky a party to his marriage.

According to Chernyshevsky, Lobodovsky married without love; he hardly even knew his bride, whom he met through a matchmaker. He had no means to support a family, and his bride, the daughter of a stationmaster, brought him no money. Lobodovsky married beneath himself socially, and ashamed to introduce this simple girl to his family, he kept his marriage a secret. A dropout from Kharkov University, Lobodovsky had moved to Petersburg hoping to complete a degree, find a position, and participate in the intellectual and social life of the capital. In a conversation with Chernyshevsky, recorded in the diary in the first person, Lobodovsky explained his reasons for marrying: "The main reason for marriage is this. It will be my duty to make this human being happy, and this will be a catalyst for activity, which is so necessary for me" (1: 29). Marriage was regarded as a stimulus for activity: for professional activity, for an active participation in social life, and for the spiritual activity of the mind. Several days after the wedding, Lobodovsky declared to Chernyshevsky: "I am becoming an active person" (1: 33).

Initially, Lobodovsky was convinced that he would not be able to love such a simple and unsophisticated girl; he reported that during the ceremony his heart remained cold, and "only the physical side was awakened" (1: 30). But on the day after the wedding, he told Chernyshevsky there had been a "significant moral change": the physical side turned out to be less strong than he had expected, and he discovered hopes for love in a project to develop his wife's mind (*razvitie*, a catchword of the day, tied to the "woman question"; 1: 33). These revelations pleased Chernyshevsky, not only for the sake of his friend, but also for his own: "This may initiate a change in my nature: I think I am positively beginning to feel something close to an understanding of the sweetness of love—meaning love for one's true love. In contrast I never thought about this seriously in the past, I never had any need to love, all I had were sensuous fantasies" (1: 37).

For many months Chernyshevsky's thoughts remained concentrated on the Lobodovskys and their relationship. He took an active part in their family life, practically becoming a family member. Lobodovsky shared with him the most intimate details of the couple's experience. They discussed the delay in consummating the marriage, for example, and, deeply sympathetic, Chernyshevsky tried to reconstruct the details; on hearing that on the third or fourth day after the wedding Lobodovsky "did not feel well," he speculated: "Before carrying out the ultimate act" (1: 36). Chernyshevsky visited the couple almost daily; he even strolled past their window unnoticed, glancing inside at scenes of family life, which deeply moved him (1: 81, 85). In addition, Chernyshevsky supported the Lobodovskys financially, secretly giving his friend considerable sums of money that he had received from his father for his own needs. The sacrifice was quite significant, reducing him to poverty. Apart from the financial sacrifice, there were moral inconveniences: Chernyshevsky did not reveal the reason for his expenditures to his family and was forced into elaborate lies.

The intense involvement in his friend's marriage became an experience of the utmost importance in young Chernyshevsky's life and had a formative influence on him. Love for his friend and participation in the marriage promised a possible resolution to his emotional problems. The relationship with Lobodovsky convinced him that he had the ability to form an emotional attachment to another person: "When I did not love Vas. Petr., I thought that there was no love in me at all" (1: 59). Lobodovsky's marriage produced another change in Chernyshevsky's emotional life: he developed an attachment for his friend's wife, Nadezhda Egorovna, a feeling that, with a remarkable degree of insight, he attributed to the mediation of his friend and double. It seemed to him that because he loved Lobodovsky so much, he thought about her through him and was perhaps beginning to feel "affectionate regard" for her, a "brotherly feeling," "love, or just sublime respect" (1: 80, 112). He speculated on the nature of this feeling, both wanting and not wanting to call it "love."

From the very beginning of this mediated relationship, Chernyshevsky hoped to achieve a direct emotional feeling for the woman: "I suppose in the future I will be fond of her for her own sake, not just because of Vas. Petrovich" (1: 35). At the same time, the presence of his friend protected him from physical temptation and "nuptial duties." His feeling for the wife of his friend was, by definition, a pure, "brotherly" attachment. Yet brotherly feeling was "conditioned by sex," and it was thus of both a spiritual and a material nature (1: 35). His feeling for Lobodovskaia was not devoid, therefore, of sexual feeling: he looks at her half-bared breast (euphemistically referred to as "a certain part beneath the neck") with a "certain pleasure, quite chaste," and a "truly brotherly feeling" (1: 148). He looks not only with brotherly feeling, but also for the sake of another—for her husband: "I looked—actually I looked because I desired to convince myself that Vas. Petr. would definitely be enchanted with it, especially when she is educated" (1: 148).

As the relationship developed, Chernyshevsky started to contemplate substituting himself for his friend. Lobodovsky was thinking of taking a position in Stuttgart. Excited by the prospect, Chernyshevsky thought of taking care of Nadezhda Egorovna in his friend's absence (she would always be happy to see him, he persuaded himself, because he was her husband's friend and would always talk to her about him), and of then accompanying her to Stuttgart to join Vasily Petrovich, if of course "mummy and daddy" (*papen'ka i mamen'ka*) or the government imposed no obstacles (1: 200). His fantasies went so far that he started contemplating Lobodovsky's possible death (say, from consumption). He would then be obligated to marry his friend's widow because the life of a widow was truly unbearable under present social conditions. He was both attracted and alarmed by the prospect of this future obligation and thought of this potential marriage as a sacrifice necessitated by his personal loyalty to his "dead" friend and by his general sympathy for woman's inferior and dependent position (another reference to the woman question). He imagined this marriage as a purely platonic relationship ("I have to marry her, etc., in the most chaste sense"); that is, it would be a fictitious marriage (1: 157–58).

Chernyshevsky saw the relationship as essentially a threesome, for not only did he require the mediation of Lobodovsky in order to establish contact with Nadezhda Egorovna, but he also regarded himself as an intermediary between the couple. He made every effort to encourage Lobodovsky's love for Nadezhda Egorovna. That love, he believed, depended on his intervention; at one point, he even planned to write an anonymous letter informing Lobodovsky that a certain Chernyshevsky was in love with his wife, in the hope that through jealousy he might stimulate love. The realization that he, Chernyshevsky, could play a decisive role in bringing two spouses together allowed him to view his participation in the marriage as a duty. To justify his affection for Nadezhda Egorovna and to dispel doubts, Chernyshevsky launched into long and complicated deliberations, trying to disentangle the chain of emotions and motivations that kept him involved in his friend's marriage:

I can strengthen his love for her—and therefore, though I am not aware of it, my sense of duty and my desire that she be happy (her happiness is a function of his love for her), i.e., my desire that he be happy because being what he is he will collapse if he doesn't make her happy—make me think of her incessantly (1: 36).

But for all Chernyshevsky's hopes and plans, marriage had quickly turned into a bitter disappointment for Lobodovsky. Indifferent to his wife, discouraged in his attempts to educate her (much to the regret of both young men, Nadezhda Egorovna did not want to study French and German or to read Gogol and Lermontov), and annoyed by the intervention of her vulgar family, Lobodovsky soon came to regret his decision to marry. About two months after the wedding, he declared to Chernyshevsky: "It was a mistake to marry, a miscalculation all around" (*oshibka vo vsekh raschetakh*; 1: 61). Lobodovsky was cold even to the physical side of the marriage: "I'll pass up the opportunity to be a husband, not because I am not able [*net sil*], but because I have no desire [*net okhoty*]" (1: 68). When, a week later, Chernyshevsky commented on Lobodovsky's mental alienation from his wife, he employed the same terms: "He is no longer able to understand this simple and charming creature that became legitimately his, i.e., he no longer has a desire to understand her" (*on uzhe ne v silakh, t.e. ne khochet*; 1: 83). In a later entry Chernyshevsky lamented Lobodovsky's failure to educate his wife, suggesting apathy as a reason: "The reason being of course his lack of desire because he has almost no desire for anything at all" (*okhoty v nem net pochti ni k chemu*; 1: 286).

Lobodovsky's gravest miscalculation was his hope that marriage would stimulate him to activity. Burdened by the obligations of family life, disappointed, desperate, he sank into ever deeper apathy and inactivity; he did practically nothing and grew to depend on Chernyshevsky's efforts to find him a position and on his friend's financial and moral support. One day, walking through their neighborhood (Chernyshevsky of course specified the location), Lobodovsky revealed a plan that he had conceived in a moment of despair: "We were walking across the cobbled space between the Vvedenskaia Church and the bridge when he [Lobodovsky] looked around and said, 'Truly, if I have a really bad moment, I will find a person with a thousand rubles in silver in his pocket, steal it, give half to Nadia, send the other half home, and go to Siberia.'" Chernyshevsky replied: "This is the material aspect, and there is also the moral aspect, the heart" (1: 99). The two students, who carried out this conversation in the summer of 1848 in the part of Petersburg where Dostoevsky later set his novel, shared more than a neighborhood with the characters of *Crime and Punishment* (1866).

Lobodovsky's disappointment in Nadezhda Egorovna caused Chernyshevsky to doubt his impressions concerning her beauty and grace. His ultimate disenchantment grew out of the conviction that she was an ordinary woman, unable to make Vasily Petrovich happy. Disappointment in the wife and marriage of his friend was followed by disappointment in Lobodovsky himself. As their relationship collapsed, Chernyshevsky's descriptions of Lobodovsky began to focus on the absence of the very qualities that he once thought Lobodovsky possessed in a superior degree: strong emotions and strong will. Chernyshevsky recorded Lobodovsky's declarations of his own coldness and insensitivity, inability to love (1: 246), and lack of willpower (1: 226). Cherny-shevsky proceeded to draw universal conclusions from his personal disappointment: marriage should be destroyed (1: 265), and will is nonexistent ("What an absurd thing is this, 'a man with a strong will'"; 1: 226).

Thus, Chernyshevsky's first contact with a woman and his first emotional experience of affection for a woman were achieved through the mediation of a third party. Sharing his friend's emotion and his marriage, Chernyshevsky experienced a "feeling by proxy" and participated in a "secondary marriage" that did not allow for sexual closeness (thus liberating him both from sinful carnal sensations and from dreaded sexual obligations), a marriage that was required by the call of duty inspired by contemporary ideas on the woman question.

Resources of Culture: Love and Reality

The men of the 1830s and 1840s attached extraordinary importance to matters of the heart, infusing love and relationships with women with metaphysical, religious, and social significance of global proportions. The cultural sources of these attitudes include not only German romanticism (Schiller and Goethe in literature, Schelling, Fichte, and Hegel in philosophy), but also French Christian socialism (expressed in the works of such thinkers as Saint-Simon, Fourier, and Pierre Leroux) and the novels of the social romantics (Balzac, Hugo, Eugene Sue, and, of special importance, George Sand).[24]

As intellectual historians have noted, Schiller's ideal of the *schöne Seele*—the self-fulfillment of the individual and the achievement of inner freedom through the cultivation of sublime love for a woman of ideal beauty and aesthetic feeling—had tremendous appeal for the post-Decembrist generation. The cult of tender feelings was further catalyzed by Fichte's metaphysical concept of love as the main source and driving force of life and by Schelling's treatment of love as a realization of the Absolute.

These ideas and their vague reverberations were known both to those who read German philosophers and to those who did not; they were part of intellectual conversation in the circles of the two capitals and part of the intimate exchange between lovers and close friends. Metaphysical notions became the idioms of everyday speech, part of the common language. As a result, abstract philosophical categories were, in complete earnestness and with striking naïveté, applied to daily life. A famous example is Mikhail Bakunin's intervention into the marital difficulties of his sister Varvara. He urged her to seek divorce in the name of the Absolute:

Do you want to enjoy a life of absolute love with him? This is also interesting. You have discovered that your husband lives in the Absolute. But what, tell me, is his connection with this Absolute? The potatoes that he eats or the stupid statements that he makes? No, Varenka, he does not live in the Absolute. He and the Absolute are the two extremes that are incompatible.[25]

One consequence of this expansion of German philosophical romanticism into daily life was the attaching of cosmic significance to the emotions and events of private experience.

In the Russian interpretation, Schiller's quest for inner freedom was understood in connection with Rousseau and the Enlightenment and directly associated with social freedom. In Russia, German romanticism coexisted with French Christian socialism, a social theory in which the issue of love and marriage became a touchstone of the whole system. The ultimate triumph of love involved two steps: love for humanity was to be infused with the emotional energy of love for a woman, which would rescue a society that had lapsed into emotional sterility and would stimulate love for a woman. The rearrangement of the relations between the sexes would lead to the rearrangement of the social order and propagate freedom.[26]

The blending of the idealistic sanctification of love and woman with the doctrines of Saint-Simon, the prophet of the New Christianity, plus a bit of romantic messianism, permeated such phenomena as the young Herzen's and Ogarev's attitudes toward love. It was in this spirit that Ogarev wrote to his bride, at four o'clock in the morning on April 23, 1836, three days before their wedding: "Our love, Maria, contains the germ of the liberation of humanity. The tale of our love will be told from age to age, and future generations will preserve our memory as holy."[27] The name of his bride, Maria (and the name of Herzen's bride, Natalie), and the date of the wedding (both friends were married soon after Easter) played important roles in the development of these sentiments. Herzen and Natalie originally meant their marriage to be a chaste union and planned to live as brother and sister, in the manner of the early Christians; this intention, however, was not fulfilled.[28]

Rousseau's revolt against the constraints of civilization in the name of the liberation of the human personality and the Christian socialists' "rehabilitation of the heart" for the sake of the harmonious rearrangement of the social order were synthesized in the novels of George Sand. The idea of freedom of love formulated in her novels, which virtually flooded Russia in the 1840s, was based on the injection of the romantic cult of love and woman into the social question of woman's subjection to man through the institution of bourgeois marriage.[29] The Christian connection was made through Christian socialism (Pierre Leroux directly influenced George Sand). In Russia, George Sand was proclaimed a "female Christ," "the second Savior."[30]

In Russia in the 1840s, the socialists grouped around Mikhail Petrashevsky, using the ideas of the French Christian socialists as a starting point, focused not so much on the political organization of society as on those "everyday, household, as it were, quotidian relations of people . . . that might seem trivial to careless observers, but that in fact play the most important role in the question of human happiness."[31] In their eyes, the rearrangement of interpersonal relations, especially of marital relations, would eventually bring "emotional harmony." That, in turn, would naturally result in social harmony. Accordingly, the main task of the struggle for social improvement was understanding those elusive laws and principles that rule human emotions. Literature, in its ability both to analyze and to organize human emotions, was a revolutionary force of crucial importance.

These ideas were universally known in educated Russian society in the mid-nineteenth century and had considerable power over beginning writers. Young Dostoevsky, who belonged to Petrashevsky's circle, was enthralled by them. Chernyshevsky, as we know from his diaries, was involved in intense discussions of them with his close friend Alexander Khanykov, a member of Petrashevsky's circle. Even Lev Tolstoy, who had no direct contact with the socialists, revealed an intense interest in these ideas in his early diaries. In short, they were an integral part of the "self-consciousness of the epoch."[32]

It has been pointed out that the prominence of the woman question in Russian radical thought is "somewhat difficult to explain," especially given the many other, more basic issues that "offered themselves to the energy of reformers," such as absolutism, serfdom, the restriction of civil liberties, poverty, and illiteracy.[33] Against the background of the developments discussed above, however, the importance of the woman question is not surprising. "Woman's liberation" grew to mean liberty, and liberation in personal relationships (emotional release and the dissolution of traditional marriages) almost became identified with the social and metaphysical liberation of mankind.

In a context in which love had metaphysical and social significance, insensitivity and coldness grew to mean more than a mere personal deficiency: they became symbolic of a global spiritual failure and a failure of civic duty. The gulf between the ethical ideal of all-encompassing love and the disappointing failure to realize this ideal was a measuring rod for several generations of literary Russians. In their letters, Stankevich and Belinsky discuss apathy, coldness, lack of love, and insensitivity as their "sins"—offenses or faults committed against the demands of the Spirit or the Absolute.[34]

At the end of the 1830s, the time of the disintegration of romanticism in Europe, most of the "idealists of the thirties" experienced a deep emotional and spiritual crisis, which they interpreted in metaphysical and ethical terms. The inner coldness and apathy that seized them, arresting attempts at emotional, spiritual, or social self-realization, provoked a sense of impotence of cosmic proportions. They blamed their "lifelessness" on their devotion to pure cerebration, limited to the conceptual level of phenomena; on the tragic hiatus between the ideal life of the spirit and the reality of the human body; and on the alienation of the realm of the ideal from the reality of living and acting human beings. They rejected the accursed *Schönseeligkeit* of

Schiller and Schelling in favor of newly appraised reality. These developments were associated with Hegel, who at about that time rose to extraordinary prominence in Russian thinking.[35]

In 1837, Nikolai Stankevich declared to Belinsky: "I have never loved. For me, love has always been a whim of the imagination, a game of the idle mind. . . . A true human being and a strong personality lives in reality, whereas a weak soul resides in *Jenseits* [the Beyond]."[36]

In a confessional letter to Stankevich written in 1839, during the period of "reconciliation with reality," Belinsky described the liberating effect of Hegelian philosophy (and the "words" that it brought) in terms of spiritual rebirth and renewal. The beginning of the Gospel of St. John shaped his account: "A new epoch has begun. . . . A new world has been discovered for us. . . . I can't describe the feeling with which I heard those words—it was liberation. . . . For me the word 'reality' became equivalent to the word 'God.'"[37]

Belinsky became the most ardent propagator of reality, proclaiming it, in his 1842 "Speech on Criticism" ("Rech o kritike"), the "slogan of the age": "Reality—that is the slogan and the last word of the modern world. Reality in facts, in knowledge, in the convictions of feeling, in the conclusions of the mind—in everything and everywhere reality is the first and the last word of our age."[38]

With the turn to reality, the concept of woman acquired additional overtones: the association between love for woman and liberation was combined with the association between woman and life, or reality. In his new "guidelines" for life (the "real life") addressed to his friends, Belinsky wrote: "Rush into life while you can. Be lovers of art, readers of books, but be prepared to throw it all overboard for the sake of life (i.e., for the sake of a woman)."[39]

Salvation from cerebration and alienation was found in Hegel's concept of activity and in the Left-Hegelian "philosophy of the deed" (in Belinsky's words, "in the living and rational *Tat*"[40]). The essential literary underpinning for the idea was Goethe's Faustian pronouncement, "In the beginning was the deed [*Tat*]." In the philosophical circles of the 1840s, as Herzen remarked in *My Past and Thoughts*, "A knowledge of Goethe, especially of the second part of *Faust*, was as obligatory as the wearing of clothes."[41] Goethe's *Faust* reinforced the love connection: the idea of salvation through *Tat* was inextricably interwoven with the idea of redemption through love and woman.

The next stage in the quest for reality involved the social interpretation of metaphysical concepts in the spirit of Left-Hegelianism. Belinsky, in his socialist period, reinterpreted "reality" as "sociality" (*sotsial'nost'*): "Sociality, sociality—or death!"[42] There were, in his eyes, but these two alternatives. The notion of "activity" (*deiatel'nost'*) was transformed into "social action" (*obshchestvennoe deianie*), a concept vaguely related to Feuerbach's "activity for others." For Herzen, "activity" meant "revolutionary activity."

Throughout all the stages of the disintegration of the romantic consciousness, the lofty ideal of woman and love for woman, the association of woman with reality, and the social connections of the issue of love were all retained. These connections were reinforced with the advent of positivism and materialism, which supplied additional corroboration. In the late 1840s, educated Russians became familiar with the ideas of Auguste Comte, who attached the greatest value to the experience of the senses, or, more loosely, sensibility. It was through sensibility that a human being became connected with others in a unity of humankind (in this lies the essence of Comte's "positive religion"). From this follows, once again, a special role for woman, who stands for the realm of the heart in human society. But positivism was not nearly so decisive an influence on Russian thought as the naturalist materialism of Ludwig Feuerbach. In the 1850s and 1860s, Feuerbach became an object of "a poetic cult with an overtone of religious worship."[43] Chernyshevsky, in his later work, played a crucial role in propagating this influence; during the period described in the diaries, immersed in his private struggle with insensitivity, he was already concerned with these ideas.

In Feuerbach, Chernyshevsky found a formula for the reconciliation of the romantic oppositions of ideal and real, soul and body (the hiatus between them being responsible for emotional

barrenness). The solution lay in the idea of the essential inseparability of spirit and matter. The principle of inseparability rested
on the cult of sense experience. "Everything," wrote Feuerbach,
"is sensibly apprehensible; if not immediately, at least medi-
ately; if not with the vulgar, untrained senses, at least with the
cultivated senses."[44] What proved of special importance for Russian thinkers of Chernyshevsky's generation was Feuerbach's
identification of sensibility with reality and, like the German
idealists before him, the tremendous importance he attached to
love. Love was the ontological proof of the existence of an external object, the only true criterion of reality and actuality. This
made it possible in common usage to equate "sense experience"
and "love." Finally, Feuerbach joined with the French Christian
socialists in appealing for the "rehabilitation of the flesh" (in
Feuerbach's terms, *jus corporis*), which was to accompany the
"rehabilitation of the heart." He proclaimed that the body was
the basis, the subject of personality; only by the body is a real
personality distinguished from the imaginary personality of a
specter. For Feuerbach, the ultimate reality in human life was
corporeal.[45]

The subsequent development of positivism, in the writings of
the German materialists Friedrich Büchner, Jacob Moleschott,
and Karl Vogt and in the works of the physiologists Claude Bernard, Rudolf Virchow, and others, introduced a biological approach to man and his feelings. In Russia in the 1860s, their
names became signs of adherence to radical ideology and symbols of the time (Bazarov, in *Fathers and Sons*, recommends
Büchner's *Kraft und Stoff* for the reeducation of the elder Kirsanov;
Doctor Kirsanov, a hero of *What Is to Be Done?*, enjoys the personal patronage of Claude Bernard). In Russia, Ivan Sechenov's
The Reflexes of the Brain (*Refleksy golovnogo mozga*; 1863) was also
of tremendous importance. The phrase "reflexes of the brain"
became, in the vocabulary of the nihilists, a regular replacement
for the outdated concept of "soul."* The view of man merely

---

*An amusing illustration of this appears in the memoirs of the radical activist
Leonid Panteleev: "In Eniseisk a merchant's wife loved to repeat: 'Our learned
professor Sechenov says that there is no soul but there are reflexes'" (Panteleev,
Iz vospominanii proshlogo, p. 573).

as a complex of physiological functions had important implications for the realistic reinterpretation of the romantic conception of love.

It was Chernyshevsky who in his famous article "The Anthropological Principle in Philosophy" ("Antropologicheskii printsip v filosofii"; 1860) first elaborated for a Russian audience the broad cultural and ethical implications of Feuerbach's teaching and of the nineteenth-century expansion of science.[46] In this work he justified the practice of applying the methods and concepts of recent advances in the physical sciences to the study of human nature and behavior.

This complex of ideas provided a vocabulary of self-definition and expression for the members of the new generation. All these ideas and notions had a long history, had been reinterpreted many times over by different metaphysical and artistic systems, and had absorbed and accumulated a variety of meanings. Some of them were so overused that they had become cultural clichés (mere words), such as "brotherly feeling," love as striving for "ideal beauty," and the opposition between "head and heart." But in the constant movement of culture, even such clichés can become the material from which new ideas are formed. New concepts or new meanings for old ones are arrived at by purely rhetorical means. At times, this process involves combining logically incompatible ideas, associating and identifying disparate notions, violating the epistemological coherence of philosophical systems, and resorting to figurative uses of philosophical and scientific concepts. This intellectual work, based on rhetorical principles, serves as a dynamic of cultural history.

In his diaries, Chernyshevsky defines the psychologically concrete theme of love and the incapacity for love in terms of the language described above. Thus, he closely associates the private experience of love for, and contact with, a woman with establishing relations with reality and with social service for the cause of liberation. He endows love with metaphysical and religious significance. In the diaries, Chernyshevsky makes his first approaches to the contemporary concern with "positive reality" and "science," but these new developments are mixed with the resources of his earlier upbringing and education, with naïve romanticism and intense Christian sentiments. In addition, in Chernyshevsky's usage, existing cultural notions and ideas received new overtones: he reinterpreted them in relation both to current cultural concerns and to his personal psychological needs.

Realization of Metaphor: Head and Heart

An interesting example of the process of adapting and reinterpreting an element of the cultural code is the treatment of the opposition between head and heart in Chernyshevsky's diary for 1848. By that time, this opposition had turned into a cultural cliché separated from its original literary and metaphysical contexts; it had become part of the common language.[47]

The opposition between reasoning and feeling, metaphorized as head and heart, originated in Plato's tripartite division of man (head, heart, and will). Rousseau evoked Plato's man to set reason apart from feeling on the ethical scale. In his system, which was directed against the Enlightenment and the Encyclopedists' cult of reason, tender feeling is a positive value, and reason a source of evil. Late romanticism emphasized the principle of opposition itself; the extremes of human consciousness were thought of as antinomies; antinomies served as the basis for the character of the demonic hero. During the disintegration of romantic thought in the 1840s in Russia, a reasoning person (one who loves with his head), as opposed to a truly sensitive man, was seen as the embodiment of the malaise of the age; reflection was a quality that blocked will and action (the tripartite division restored).

In the struggle against idealism for reality, the opposition between head and heart was correlated with another popular cliché: the opposition between spiritual and sensual love. Following Plato and Saint Augustine, Rousseau in his *Confessions* established the tradition of viewing pure love and physical passion as separate entities that can be experienced simultaneously and directed at different objects. Romanticism cultivated "ideal" or pure platonic love, which was opposed to "low" sensuality. Under the influence of positivism, the early Russian realists of

the 1840s reevaluated the traditional opposition: sensuality became associated with strength and energy as opposed to idealistic sterility and apathy. "Love is materialism," wrote Feuerbach. "Immaterial love is a chimera." [48]

Post-romantic thought regarded the principle of romantic dualism, or thinking in terms of oppositions, as evil. The disjunction of consciousness, not the negative pole of the opposition,
was regarded as intrinsically wrong and as a sign of weakness
of character. The problem gained social significance; the Saint-
Simonians established the goal of reeducating Plato's tripartite
man into a new, total man who would be simultaneously a rational being, a man of feeling, and an industrious activist.

The problem of the dualism of consciousness, focused on the
issue of love, became one of the central concerns in the diaries
once Chernyshevsky, a youth brought up on the romantic poetry of Schiller and Vasily Zhukovsky and an ardent reader of
Hugo, was confronted with the contemporary polemics over romantic dualism. In the diary for 1848, he seems almost obsessed
with the idea of the unity versus the disjunction of the human
personality. He concludes that a truly great man (such as Lobodovsky) is equally able to lead the life of the head and the life of
the heart. Nevertheless, he is painfully aware of the contradiction between his own intense intellectual life and remarkable
abilities and the poverty of emotional experience that make him
incapable of fulfilling the mission of love.

In almost daily recordings of the events of his emotional life,
which he defines through either the presence or the absence
of sensations, Chernyshevsky distinguishes between emotions
"felt with the head" and those "felt with the heart," dutifully
specifying what kinds of sensations he experienced in every
situation:

The day passed well. My sensations were all of the mind except when
I was with them [the Lobodovskys] I felt some pleasure in my heart.
(1: 51)

. . .

I was thinking about him and her, but it was purely intellectual thinking, no involvement of the heart. (1: 137)

. . .

When conversing [with Lobodovsky], I felt as if I were somewhere else and my heart was quite indifferent, while my mind was very much involved. . . . But the heart felt nothing, and still feels nothing now. This is strange, this is how it used to be with me before he was married. (1: 100)

In accordance with the new scale of values, the predominance of cerebral feelings becomes a matter of concern and bewilderment, and it is the sphere of the heart, of emotion, that receives special attention and is further elaborated in the diary.

In a search for solutions to a painful psychological problem (the pain being intensified by the awareness of the cultural inappropriateness of his emotional life), Chernyshevsky started to explore the psychological potential of positivistic and materialistic ideas. In his treatment of the theme of head and heart, Chernyshevsky goes beyond this common metaphor: in the accounts of his emotional life, the term "heart" is demetaphorized. He frequently treats "heart" (*serdtse*) not as a metaphoric representation of feeling, but literally—as an organ, a physiological agent of emotion. In reference to feeling, Chernyshevsky describes in graphic detail the evolution of the heart as an organ:

It is strange but my heart again beats fast when I think of Nad. Eg., as it used to do in the first days after their marriage. Again I experience a sensation of—of what? . . . And I enjoy this quickening of the heart; no, this is not the quickening of the heart, this is as if my heart somehow tightens and then expands, and indeed creates some sensation. (1: 80)

Chernyshevsky here equates physical sensation in the heart with emotion, and this connection is realized through the medium of language—through manipulation of the two modes of the meaning of feeling and to feel (*chuvstvovat'*, *chuvstvo*), metaphoric and literal. The starting point of the passage is a popular metaphor of emotion, *serdtse nespokoino* ("the heart is agitated"), which receives immediate explication, *est' chuvstvo* ("there is a feeling"). At the beginning of the train of reasoning, *chuvstvo* is used in its metaphoric meaning of emotion. There is a feeling— "what is a feeling?" (*chto èto takoe?*); there is a pleasant physical sensation in the heart, therefore, "you really feel something in the heart" (*i chto-to v samom dele chuvstvuesh v nem*). In the middle of the train of reasoning, "to feel" is used in its literal meaning of "to experience physical sensation"; in the conclusion the two meanings are blended.

Chernyshevsky performs a similar operation with another common figure of speech that refers to emotion: the metaphor *dvizhenie serdtsa* ("movement of the heart") or its popular contemporary variant *shevelenie serdtsa* ("stirring of the heart"): "The truth is that I am simply waiting for a signal, for an opportunity, and at the first opportunity, I will fall in love, and this began to stir my heart: indeed, I experience a painful or a pleasant sensation in my heart, in this physical part of my body, just as I feel various sensations in the external organs, for example, in the sexual organs, etc." (1: 270–71). The description of physical changes in the heart, as well as in other organs, such as the "outer parts of the body," serves to explicate the term "emotion."

Chernyshevsky also observed outward physical signs of emotion in other people. Comparing himself to Lobodovsky, supposedly a man of strong emotions, he comments: "Almost no sensations in my heart today, except when I was speaking to Vas. Petr., I felt something but not so much. But when he spoke, he was breathing so hard that he visibly trembled" (1: 96).

This attention to the sphere of the heart and the search for tangible evidence of its functioning were prompted by the contemporary positivist emphasis on sense experience and observable physical phenomena, which were part of the general striving for realism and concreteness. From this point of view, cerebral feeling, a phenomenon without physical manifestations, had no real existence and thus could not be accepted as true experience. In contrast, the reality of the spontaneous feelings of the heart, acclaimed by Rousseau and the sentimentalists and by the Russian realists of the 1840s, could be confirmed by observing palpable physical phenomena, including those of a sexual nature. But, in the end, the goal of explaining mental phenomena through the data of sense experience was achieved through linguistic operations—by the absolutization of discourse and the transformation of metaphor into physical reality.

The process may be viewed in the following way: Chernyshevsky moves both from discourse to physical sensation and from physical sensation to the emotion denoted by language. In other words, he adopts a metaphor for emotion in order to reveal the actual emotion present in his real-life experience. He finds the link between the two in the realization of the inner form of the metaphor, which in the case of metaphors of feeling refers to the plane of physical sensations. He takes the metaphors of feeling—heart (as opposed to head) and movements of heart—and, by absolutizing their inner form (physical sensation), arrives at the experience implicit in the metaphoric meaning.

But what is the direction of the process? Which comes first, physical sensation or metaphor? What are we dealing with, the sublimation of physiological phenomena or the materialization of cultural phenomena?[49] Apparently, for Chernyshevsky abstract constructs had more reality and substantiality than did sensual phenomena. In his case, the path went in the direction metaphor—physical sensation (inner form of the metaphor)—emotion (meaning of the metaphor). In his quest for emotion, Chernyshevsky retraced the steps of the process of metaphorization. In a literal sense, emotion was a product of the cultural code, which in this case was represented by a rhetorical expression. By reworking a romantic cliché through the positivist apparatus, Chernyshevsky transformed the symbolic material of culture into psychological reality.

The Ideal

Throughout his involvement in Lobodovsky's marriage, Chernyshevsky could not decide whether what he felt for Nadezhda Egorovna was truly love. Tormented by doubts, he sought external confirmation of the reality of his own feelings, equating subjective emotion for a woman with the objective qualities of that woman. Thus, his doubts about his own feelings and his reveries about Nadezhda Egorovna focused on probing her beauty and grace. To convince himself that what he felt was true love, Chernyshevsky had to assure himself of his beloved's *ideal* beauty.

Chernyshevsky developed a special technique to obtain proof of his beloved's beauty. The first step was to compare his chosen lady with other pretty young women. Chernyshevsky embarked

on special expeditions dedicated to observing women or portraits of them in public places: "I kept comparing the pretty
women with Nadezhda Egorovna and decided that they are all
inferior to her" (1: 49); "I walked along Nevsky Prospect on my
way home, and looked at the pictures and women. Nobody
looked better than Nad. Eg." (1: 111); "I must note that I constantly compare all women, both in life and in pictures, with
Nad. Eg." (1: 116). Through this process of comparison, Chernyshevsky concluded that his object was superior in beauty to
all other possible objects. He even described his fear that the
beauty of some other woman could, perhaps, match his beloved's beauty and a "sort of pride" that there was no such
woman (1: 138).

An important criterion was total perfection, faultless beauty.
He was tormented by doubts and suspicions that parts of his
lady's face and body were not perfect; either the "line between
the chin and the neck" or her nose, shoulders, or gait sometimes
seemed less than they should be in an ideal beauty.

I looked closely, trying to find something that is not as it should be in
her face, but I could find nothing wrong. I thought her face was very,
very pretty and quite charming, and I also thought (even though these
thoughts could not put an end to my doubts) that my doubts concerning her beauty, i.e., the true beauty, are quite wrong, and that there
is nothing coarse in her features—however, I still doubt and hesitate.
(1: 76)

Chernyshevsky, however, felt more inclined to doubt the reality
of his own impressions than the quality of the object: "The sides
of her nose seemed somewhat wrong. I suppose that I was mistaken" (1: 134).

The next step involved measuring his candidate against guaranteed, generally accepted examples of beauty—portraits of
popular beauties exhibited in fashionable galleries ("a portrait of
a woman . . . a celebrity or an ideal"; 1: 75):

I was walking along Nevsky Prospect, looking at the pictures. Junker
had many new beauties, and I spent a long time examining those two
that I thought were especially pretty. I was quite objective in my comparison, and I found that they looked inferior to Nad. Eg., quite inferior
because I can find no shortcomings in her face, whereas I found many

things wrong in their faces; particularly unsuccessful was the glabella as well as the parts lying near the nose, on both sides of the bridge. Yes, this is quite definitely so. (1: 83)

Such entries are frequent and typical.

Chernyshevsky accepted the popular belief that ideal and supreme beauty was to be found in aristocratic women—examples of a guaranteed quality. The impression that Lobodovskaia had "a common Russian, ordinary face" (1: 63) was alarming to him. As his admiration for Nadezhda Egorovna weakened and his evaluation of her beauty changed from "absolute" to "so-so," he began to fear that a day would come when it would become apparent to him that her face was definitely not aristocratic (1: 63). And, not surprisingly, that day came. When his ideal was dethroned, Chernyshevsky discovered crudities: "I noticed that the forehead was somehow excessively round, and there was something ignoble [*prostonarodnoe*] in her face" (1: 205).

At about the same time, Chernyshevsky espied a true ideal of beauty in a young noblewoman among the visitors at an exhibition that he attended specifically to observe and investigate feminine beauty: "Rather tall, at least much taller than Nadezhda Egorovna, thin, slender, rather pale face, wonderful eyes, quite perfect and intelligent features—she was beyond comparison with anyone who was there" (1: 290).

This episode, described in the diary with precise spatial details, was remembered 30 years later in Chernyshevsky's letters from Siberia. The whole scene became exaggerated: in the diary he mentioned that, enchanted by the girl's beauty, he followed her and her family, devouring her with his eyes from a distance for about five minutes; in the Siberian letter the period became "one or two hours." "Quite obviously," he added, "they were of noble birth indeed, which was obvious to everybody from their extraordinarily nice manners" (15: 177). Apparently, this young noblewoman, briefly glimpsed at an exhibition when Chernyshevsky was 21, remained a paragon of beauty in his eyes for the rest of his life. In the Siberian letter of 1879, the reminiscence is concluded with the following deduction: "That girl was beautiful, truly beautiful, for otherwise I would not have liked her" (15: 203).

The mental devices of orientation toward the ideal arose from Chernyshevsky's need to support his feeble apprehension of subjective experience and of the external world. His strategy for dealing with the problem was constructed from current cultural material: a metaphysical conceptual apparatus and social mythology. Behind the clichés he used to conceptualize his experience stood vague evocations of the "metaphysics of the ideal" that had had a tremendous influence on the thought and feeling of the previous generation. But Chernyshevsky merged the idea of "sublime love" for a woman of "ideal beauty" (a sure path, according to Schelling, to the "identity of the real and the ideal") with the contemporary positivist emphasis on "scientific facts," on the objective evaluation of perceptible external objects. He applied a special procedure for the evaluation of the object, a procedure that operated on the principles of objective method (this took the place of Schelling's "aesthetic intuition"), to the end of finding "positive" proof of the "ideal." This positively established ideal was to serve as a mediator between Chernyshevsky and potential love objects.

Shyness

The isolation of the individual from the external world (expressed in the concept of alienation) formed the metaphysical core of German idealism. For the idealists of the 1830s and 1840s, this idea had tremendous psychological implications. In the 1860s, with the emergence of the *raznochinnaia* intelligentsia, alienation was redefined within sociopolitical parameters. Social isolation and political powerlessness distinguished the new intelligentsia as a social group: they were déclassés who had "no place to go and nothing to do."[50] The intelligentsia were alienated both from the clerical/petit-bourgeois (*meshchanstvo*) strata of their origin and from the mainstream of the educated society to which they belonged by virtue of their education and cultural role. Because of their spiritual and political aspirations, they had little in common with the former; to the latter they remained unacceptable on social, ideological, and stylistic grounds. Separation from their roots and hostility toward society contributed to a spirit of loneliness and reticence in approaching others, and to an overwhelming feeling of social inferiority and embarrassed timidity.

In the 1860s, for the first time in Russian history, people of non-aristocratic origin entered polite society, not as gifted individuals admitted to the salon (like Belinsky a decade earlier), but as representatives of a new social group destined to play an important role in Russia's cultural and social development. Unequipped for even routine forms of salon interaction, the socially unrefined, awkward sons of provincial priests and village doctors faced innumerable social situations that were new to them and that were not covered by any preexisting system of rules. "The rift between the modern man and the environment in which he lives," wrote Herzen, "brings a fearful confusion into private behavior."[51] The new intelligentsia were left with the overwhelming task of making individual decisions and, in the long run, of developing a new code of conduct.[52]

Rigid class divisions were first broken inside the universities. By the 1840s, a university education opened possibilities for distinguished careers even to those who were not born to the gentry. In theory, the universities were open to graduates of seminaries and common schools (institutions of secondary education for the children of commoners), but these schools did not, in fact, prepare students to enter a university; such preparation was done only in gymnasiums and private pensions. For example, the seminaries did not teach modern languages (French and German), an important tool not only for education but also for social interaction. Aimed at preparing students for clerical careers, the seminaries (as well as clergy and petit-bourgeois families) provided no instruction in other skills of *comme il faut* such as art, music, dancing, and athletics, which were an integral part of the upbringing of the gentry. And gentry students still dominated the universities. "Before the reforms," remembered Nikolai Shelgunov, "the Petersburg University student was typically a well-brought-up youth and a young man of good society."[53] As a result, young *raznochintsy* underwent tormenting and humiliating experiences when, first, in the universities and the homes of their gentry classmates and, later, in the salons, they confronted the members of traditional polite society.

To make matters even worse, they were not always welcome. Jokes about ex-seminarians (*seminaristy* or *popovichi*) became a popular genre. Even those of the gentry literati (the first Russian *intelligenty*) who sympathized with the democratization of educated Russian society frequently referred in ideological or literary polemics to the origin and manners of the new *intelligenty* in the most insulting terms. It is remarkable that stylistic considerations (annoyance with their alien style of behavior and general lack of refinement) prevailed over considerations of ideology. The radical Herzen maintained that "*La roture* [the *raznochintsy*] is the only pier onto which one can jump from the sinking ship of the gentry."[54] And yet, perplexed by the style of *What Is to Be Done?*, Herzen commented in a letter to Ogarev: "There are fine thoughts in there, and even fine situations, but all that has been dipped into a Petersburg middle-class-seminary urinal."[55] In a work not intended for publication, he wrote that the style and manner of "these people" had a lot in common "with the mannerisms of court clerks, of store assistants, and of the servants' quarters in a Russian landowner's house."[56] Mikhail Bakunin, the future leader of the anarchist movement, privately referred to the critics of the *Contemporary* as "unwashed seminarians" (*neumytye seminaristy*).[57]

The gentry writers on the staff of the *Contemporary*, A. V. Druzhinin, D. V. Grigorovich, Turgenev, and Tolstoy, nicknamed Chernyshevsky a "bedbug-stinking gentleman" (*klopovoniaiushchii gospodin*).[58] Avdot'ia Panaeva, the wife of one of the *Contemporary*'s editors, Ivan Panaev, and an active participant in the journal, remembered that Turgenev, Pavel Annenkov, and even Vasily Botkin, the son of a wealthy tea merchant and a close friend of Belinsky's, were all skeptical of the "seminarians' invasion of the journal." This snobbery provoked her into saying, "Gentlemen, blame Belinsky: he is the reason that your nobleman's self-esteem is insulted and that you have to work on a journal together with seminarians. . . . As you can see, Belinsky's activity did not disappear without a trace; intellectual development penetrated to other classes of society."[59]

Lamenting the predominance of *raznochintsy* on the *Contemporary*, Afanasy Fet, who was not among those who sympathized with the penetration of educated plebeians into the Russian cultural elite, arrived at a precise formulation of the essence of the conflict: "It is understandable that wherever people of that background, feeling their power, appeared and made themselves at home, they brought their ways of life with them. I am not speaking of pedigrees, but of that gentle upbringing described by the French phrase *'enfant de bonne maison'* compared with its opposite."[60]

The "seminarians" themselves were painfully aware of their social inadequacy. The first to define and analyze this problem was Belinsky, the prototypical *raznochinets*. A person of non-gentry origin and upbringing, he rose to cultural prominence without abandoning the self-consciousness of a commoner. Poverty, chronic ill health, lack of a systematic education, inferior knowledge of foreign languages, and, most notably, an absence of social skills resulted in timidity, shyness, and self-consciousness, which Belinsky recognized as sources of emotional inadequacy:

One thing torments me, and that is the fact that instead of getting better, my timidity and shyness are getting much, much worse at a terrible rate. I can't show myself anywhere because my face is suddenly all aflame, my voice trembles, my hands and legs shake, and I can hardly stand. It's like a curse! It drives me to distraction, almost to suicide. What kind of pathology is this? . . . I am scared of people. I am terrified of social gatherings. And when I see a pretty woman's face, I almost die: my vision blurs, my nerves are paralyzed as if I see a python or a rattlesnake, my breath falters, and I am all on fire. . . . I am afflicted with a terrible disease. Feel sorry for me, friend.[61]

Notably, Belinsky saw his emotional defects as socially determined and traced them to the unfortunate experiences of a childhood in a family afflicted with all the vulgar and ugly habits of the Russian lower-middle class:

I remembered a story of my mother's. She enjoyed dropping in on her friends to chew the fat. Still an infant, I was left with my nanny, a hired serf girl: so that I wouldn't bother her with my crying, she gagged me and beat me. Maybe that's the reason. . . . Then, my father couldn't stand me, he cursed me, humiliated me, picked on me and beat me pitilessly and vulgarly—God rest his soul! I was an alien presence in my family—perhaps that is the cause of this terrible phenomenon.[62]

In a letter to Bakunin, the scion of an enlightened gentry family, Belinsky maintained that essentially they differed in temperament, which depended on heredity as well as on the concrete circumstances of upbringing. According to Belinsky, since Bakunin's father led a life of disciplined moderation and was a man of dignity, Bakunin was endowed with a "harmonious temperament" and a capacity for sublime love for a woman, devoid of sensuality. "Whereas my father drank, led a bad life, although he was a most wonderful man by nature, and that is where I got my nervous temperament" (Belinsky attributed his preoccupation with the bodily to this).[63] Belinsky used this argument, which rested on the positivist belief in the dependence of spirit on matter, as an illustration of the basic difference between a romantic and a realist.

Belinsky, like the intellectuals of the next generation, felt hopelessly inadequate even compared with his close friends of gentry background, who were his intellectual equals and looked up to him as an influential literary critic (in the 1840s he literally ruled Russian letters). Invitations to the aristocratic salons frequented by literary celebrities sent him into a state of panic. A remarkable illustration of this was Belinsky's misadventure at a literary evening at the salon of Prince Odoevsky (Zhukovsky, who held a high rank at court, and Prince Viazemsky, a famous poet and important official, were among the habitual guests there). This is how Herzen described the episode:

One Saturday, as it was New Year's Eve, Odoevsky took it into his head to mix punch *en petit comité* when the principal guests had dispersed. Belinsky would certainly have gone away, but he was prevented by a barricade of furniture; he was somehow stuck in the corner and a little table was set before him with wine and glasses on it. Zhukovsky in the white trousers of his uniform, with gold braids on them, was sitting sideways opposite him. Belinsky bore it in patience a long time, but, seeing no chance of his lot improving, he began moving the table a little; the table yielded at first, then lurched over and fell with a bang on the floor, while the bottle of Bordeaux very deliberately began to empty itself over Zhukovsky. . . . There was a great fuss and to-do . . . While this bustle was going on Belinsky disappeared and, though it was not long before his end, ran home on foot.

Dear Belinsky! How angry and upset he was by such incidents, with what horror he used to recall them, walking up and down the room and shaking his head without the trace of a smile.[64]

This episode became part of the popular lore of the day and served as a source for the scene in Dostoevsky's *The Idiot* in which Myshkin, unused to society, creates a similar incident when he accidentally breaks a vase in the drawing room of General Epanchin and falls down in an epileptic seizure. (According to another version of the Belinsky story, Belinsky fell down fainting after the collapse of the table.) Although Myshkin is not a *raznochinets*, he has many characteristic features of the new men. It has been shown that, through the treatment of the image of Myshkin, Dostoevsky meant to enter into a polemic with Chernyshevsky.[65]

The area of social and personal life most affected was the new intellectuals' interactions with women. Women of the social classes to which the new intellectuals originally belonged remained quite untouched by the new ideas and by the advances in education of the 1840s–50s. They made unsuitable partners for men like Belinsky, Chernyshevsky, and Dobroliubov. The problem was formulated by Dobroliubov in a letter to a friend and fellow *raznochinets*:

If I had a woman with whom I could share my thoughts and feelings to such a degree that she would even read with me my writings (or your writings—it doesn't matter whose), I would be happy and wouldn't wish for more. My only dream now is to love such a woman and to have her sympathy. . . . I am tormented and depressed and paralyzed when I realize that this dream will never come true.[66]

In the absence of such women, the sympathies and passions of the new men were divided between the world of fallen women, whom the idealistic youths tried to save and reform, usually with tragic results, and that of society ladies, glamorous, enticing, and unattainable.[67] Aristocratic society and, especially, aristocratic women had all the magnetism of an alien world. The aristocratic woman was associated with the world of romance and poetry and, in the eyes of young provincial ex-seminarians, had all the attributes of the "ideal woman," for whom one felt "sublime love"—affection on a purely spiritual plane. A remarkable description of this situation appears in a letter to Belinsky from the poet and merchant A. V. Koltsov (another victim of social promotion through literature): "Do you remember walking with me along one of the lanes in Vasilievsky Island one day? We saw a pretty woman, and you said, 'Yes, there are many of them here, but they are not ours [*oni ne nashi*].'"[68]

When entry into fashionable society became possible, the non-noble youths confronted a new obstacle—an emotional barrier called forth by their lack of social and personal ease. Nekrasov, who cultivated the image of a *raznochinets* as his lyrical hero, dedicated a poem to this emotional and social complex and thus introduced it into cultural consciousness. The plot of the poem is the love of a *raznochinets* for a society lady, the title is "Shyness" ("Zastenchivost'"; 1852). It was one of the few poems by Nekrasov that literally made Chernyshevsky weep (14: 322).

In Chernyshevsky's diaries, his lack of social skills figures as a primary motivation for his reticence in approaching women, especially society women. For this reason, he declines invitations to be introduced to young girls despite the value of such occasions:

> I refused to be taken to their house because I was embarrassed. I do not speak French, I do not dance, and after all, I am badly dressed and have little money. (1: 249)
>
> . . .
>
> This Beltsov must be a respectable girl and probably intelligent, and I would have liked to meet her if I had the proper manners. But I can neither speak French nor dance, and above all, I am too clumsy, I am a perfect seminarian. (1: 344)

This is far from being Chernyshevsky's personal idiosyncrasy. Lobodovsky touched on the theme of French in his book of essays (*Bytovye ocherki*[69]), and Dobroliubov, Chernyshevsky's closest friend and "double" in later years, treated it in his diaries and letters in almost identical terms. In a letter to V. M. Peshchurova, a society lady who patronized the gifted young commoner, Dobroliubov complained bitterly of his "shyness, awkwardness, ignorance of society etiquette, lack of social skills." He focused on his inability to dance and draw, his lack of exposure to gymnastics, and, above all, his poor French and German. Because of these gaps in his upbringing, he realized that he did not know things well known to his "current acquaintances" (*tepereshnie znakomye*).[70]

The French language grew to symbolize this entire complex of emotions, revealing the purely semiotic nature of the problem. In fact, many non-aristocratic intellectuals had received an excellent education and acquired (often through independent reading) a good knowledge of modern languages. In society, however, the emphasis was not merely on knowing French, but on having a flawless accent: the wrong accent plagued those who had not learned French in early childhood from French governesses and was the sign of a *parvenu*—a stranger and an impostor. The situation was described in Lev Tolstoy's *Youth* (*Iunost'*; 1855–56):

My favorite and chief division of people at the time of which I am writing, was into the *comme il faut* and the *comme il ne faut pas*. The latter I subdivided into those inherently not *comme il faut*, and the common people. The *comme il faut* people I respected and considered worthy of being on terms of equality with me; the *comme il ne faut pas* I pretended to despise but in reality hated, nourishing a feeling of personal offense against them; the lower classes did not exist for me—I despised them completely. My *comme il faut* consisted first and foremost in speaking excellent French, especially in pronunciation. A man who pronounced French badly at once aroused a feeling of hatred in me. "Why do you try to speak as we do, if you can't?" I mentally inquired with virulent irony.[71]

Chernyshevsky had an excellent reading knowledge of French, German, and a number of other languages, but this did not improve his social standing. He was most fluent in Latin, the language that symbolized a seminary education; in contrast, Tolstoy had a poor command of Latin and received a low grade in it at the entrance examinations to Kazan' University in 1844. The memoirs of contemporaries give accounts of the two attempts Chernyshevsky made to master conversational French. Both resulted in his being considerably embarrassed and humiliated by a female. As an adolescent in Saratov, Chernyshevsky, who had already earned a reputation as a brilliant student, attended French classes in a private pension but, on hearing from a girl that his pronunciation was an object of ridicule for the whole class, he dropped the undertaking. Later, after completing a university degree and becoming a teacher in the Saratov gymnasium, Chernyshevsky started taking lessons in French conversation from a young lady of his acquaintance. When his tutor burst out laughing at the sound of his French accent, Chernyshevsky "grabbed his hat" and fled without a goodbye, never to resume such lessons again.[72]

The theme carried over into Chernyshevsky's fictional writings. The main hero of *The Prologue* (*Prolog*; 1867), Volgin (an autobiographical character), is endowed with a comically bad French accent but a superior knowledge of French grammar and etymology; this combination is exploited in a scene depicting Volgin's confrontation with a young girl from an aristocratic family (13: 48–68). By contrast, the hero of *What Is to Be Done?*, Lopukhov, another educated *raznochinets*, masters French as well as dancing and music, and acquires social ease, much to the surprise and delight of the female protagonist, who had assumed that a student of his background must be an "unsociable savage." Still another projection of the same theme appears in *Gleams of Radiance* (*Otbleski siianiia*; 1879–82). Although the main character receives an excellent upbringing in all the aristocratic skills, he refuses to learn to sing, dance, or draw or to go in for sports (though he did learn French!), in order to make himself a person "unsuitable for salons." He thereby hopes to find protection from the temptation "to feel a desire to fall in love," thus retaining his "purity" (13: 639)—a sentiment shared by Chernyshevsky.

The young plebeian intellectuals saw the consequences of these seemingly trivial drawbacks in upbringing as disastrous. Lack of social skills was a primary reason for social and personal unease; shyness precluded intimacy and was believed to be the ultimate reason for coldness and apathy. Through the notion of shyness, the theme of insensitivity was thus transferred into the social sphere.

Shyness and timidity revealed themselves not only in the drawing room but also on the street, in those situations that showed the ambiguous social status of the *raznochintsy* as members of an educated class without economic power or official rank. Because they did not look or behave like the members of the upper classes, landlords, store proprietors, doormen, and servants, not to mention officials (*chinovniki*) and army officers, looked down on them. Chernyshevsky often discussed such situations in his diaries. He broods over the fact that the owner of a cafe that he frequented for the sole purpose of reading foreign newspapers considered him an undesirable customer (1: 277). He is chagrined and disgusted by his inability to defend himself against the insults of a landlord who caught him defecating in the garden, a not uncommon practice among people of Chernyshevsky's background (1: 295–96). He rejoices at his victory over a cabdriver who pushed a poorly dressed young man with the carriage shaft; Chernyshevsky, in revenge, tore out a bunch of the driver's hair (1: 172), and he related with deep admiration the story of Lobodovsky's triumph in a dispute with an official, a fellow passenger in a boat, who disdained the proud *raznochinets* (1: 307).

These far from trivial situations and the complex of emotions that they evoked found their way into *What Is to Be Done?* Lopukhov calmly throws into the gutter an "important person" who shoved him in the street for not turning aside first. Subsequently, in his polemic with Chernyshevsky, Dostoevsky used the same situation in *Notes from Underground*. The protagonist is involved in a confrontation with an officer over who should move aside; this struggle for equality for a time becomes the sole purpose of his existence.[73]

In the late 1840s, entry into fashionable society and acquaintance with aristocratic ladies were still only remote possibilities for the young Chernyshevsky. In fact, not only had he never been in a salon, he had never even been in the company of women. As he explained to Lobodovsky, in Saratov he could not like women because, being nearsighted, he "could not see their faces, not even one"; in Petersburg, he added, "I did not know anybody, not a soul, and, it should be said, saw absolutely no women" (1: 259). In 1848, at the age of 20, the awkward, withdrawn, and nearsighted priest's son was taken by a fellow student to a small dancing party at his landlady's house. As we have seen, this asocial student experienced the first "ball" in his life as an event of utmost importance for his emotional and social development.

In the diary, Chernyshevsky describes the party with the usual scientific exactitude, with the layout of the rooms and a scheme of the movements of the guests. Chernyshevsky himself spent the evening standing or sitting apart from the dancing couples, involved in a careful examination of the women. Overwhelmed by the closeness of women, tormented by embarrassment and timidity, he nevertheless drew socially significant conclusions from this experience: he contemplated the miserable lot of women of the common class and expressed sympathy for the belle of the ball, a woman married to a crude and vulgar husband, whom he pitied "as a symbol of woman's position in society" (1: 212). The personal problem of relationships with women was thus transformed into the woman question.

This party served as a prototype for a ball in the story entitled "The Story of V. M. Ch." ("Rasskaz V. M. Ch.") in Chernyshevsky's fictional cycle *Tales Within Tales* (*Povesti v povestiakh*), written in prison in 1863–64. The literary version of the ball is remarkably close to the diary account, both in factual detail and in psychological atmosphere. Bearing in mind that the story was written almost fifteen years later in prison, where Chernyshevsky could not consult his confiscated diary, one can only marvel at the firmness and precision with which this seemingly trivial incident remained imprinted on his memory.

In the diary, Chernyshevsky describes the significance of the first ball of his life as follows: "My idea now is to get married . . . and that evening will continue to influence me and will probably further my development. I feel the desire to dance, to frequent social gatherings, etc., I also wish to be able to draw, and being able to speak French and German is also indispensable" (1: 212). For Chernyshevsky, personal realization of love for a woman and marriage depended on the same set of social skills that, for the new men, symbolized the key to society in general and to the heart of women in particular.

A similar treatment of these themes appears in the diaries of the young Dobroliubov. Soon after Dobroliubov's untimely death in 1861, Chernyshevsky prepared a collection, *Materials for a Biography of N. A. Dobroliubov*, which included selections from Dobroliubov's diaries and letters, together with Chernyshevsky's comments. He concentrated on the similarities between himself and Dobroliubov, especially on those character traits and experiences that were connected with their common social background and shared spiritual aspirations. Chernyshevsky illustrated Dobroliubov's first confrontation with women ("the beginning of a desire to love") with long quotations from Dobroliubov's diary, which could have served as a description of his own emotions: "How strange: a few days ago I began to feel that I am ready to fall in love and then yesterday, without any reason, I felt the desire to learn how to dance. What is all this? Whatever it is, it heralds the beginning of my reconciliation with society" (10: 55–56).

Chernyshevsky comments: "N.A. would have been more correct if he had said, 'the beginning of my involvement with life.'" He then resumes with a quotation from Dobroliubov's diary:

How strange this beginning of heart's anxiety is! I felt its first stirring when I heard from B.K. that Countess Trubetskaia, who is a very poor girl, is going to marry Morni. . . . Since then, I have not had a peaceful moment. The thoughts of social problems are interlocked in my head with the thoughts about my own relations to the society of which I am personally destined to be a member. My theoretical aspirations are being replaced by yearning for feverish activity—personal and passionate activity, rather than impersonal, abstract, and theoretical. What is to become of all this? (10: 58)

It is apparent that both young men shared not only a stock of rhetorical commonplaces (such as "stirring of the heart") but also a system of rules bestowed on them by their culture for selecting, connecting, and interpreting certain elements of experience. Thus, concrete love for a woman and the abstract desire to love were equated with sympathy for women's social plight; the capacity for love was associated with the ability to dance and read as a sign of reconciliation with society and involvement in activity.

Such was the psychological reality behind the behavior of non-gentry intellectuals. Remarkably enough, with the growing

prominence of *raznochintsy* on the cultural scene, behavior that
was a natural consequence of their lack of a genteel upbringing
was perceived as signifying. What were originally expressions of
genuine and tormenting shyness turned, in the eyes of society
at large, into ideologically weighted signs of political and social
doctrines associated with the new generation. An interesting illustration of this process is given in the memoirs of Nataliia Tatarinova who, in the late 1850s, was tutored in Russian literature
by Dobroliubov. At that time Dobroliubov already enjoyed a
reputation as a radical. Her tutor, Tatarinova remembered, was
sometimes invited to attend social gatherings at the house of her
wealthy and well-connected family. Although he accepted these
invitations, Dobroliubov did not dance and did not allow himself to be drawn into general conversation; instead, he spent the
evenings leaning against the wall apart from the other guests.
"It would seem," commented Tatarinova, "that he was uncom-
fortable." But in the eyes of his enthusiastic young pupil, Dobroliubov was engaged in deliberate, programmatic activity: "I was
childlishly convinced that he never chattered emptily for enjoyment and never laughed just because something seemed funny
or enjoyable, but only ridiculed something with a moral purpose—to unmask [*dlia oblicheniia*], as it was termed then." [74]

A similar situation is described in the memoirs of the political
activist Petr Kropotkin. In exile in Irkutsk, Kropotkin was for a
time a regular visitor at the soirées in the local club, but eventually, "having work to do" (as he explained), he abandoned
them. This was interpreted by local society as a meaningful action with a specific message—an expression of nihilist disdain
for the world. [75] The reality behind the two episodes—the fact
that Dobroliubov never learned to dance and was, in fact, un-
comfortable, whereas Kropotkin, who was born a prince and
consciously broke the ties with his class, no doubt knew how to
dance and was quite accustomed to society—became totally irrelevant. Concrete personal experience was redefined in terms
of a cultural code.

In depicting Myshkin's misadventure in the salon of the
Epanchins, Dostoevsky penetrated the nature of this situation.
The townspeople in Pavlovsk read Myshkin's behavior as that of

a "young man of good family . . . who had gone crazy over the contemporary nihilism revealed by Mr. Turgenev"; in their interpretation, Myshkin created a scandal in the drawing room deliberately, in defiance of social conventions.[76]

As the next step in the process of the semiotization of reality, curt and awkward manners were, in fact, deliberately cultivated by the younger generation, regardless of their actual background and upbringing; bad manners began to be consciously used as signs. As mentioned earlier, mastering the conventional forms of social interaction with women (the forms of gallantry) was an unattainable desire for the awkward sons of provincial priests in the early 1850s; later, in the 1860s, such forms were deliberately rejected on ideological grounds, as manifestations of inequality between the sexes.

Even poverty and need, in their concrete, material forms, were sought after as positively evaluated social signs. Skabichevsky remembered "the style and gusto with which two young ladies devoured old herring and spoiled ham from the corner store," and commented, "I am sure that no dainties in their parents' homes ever gave them as much pleasure as their plebeian breakfast in a student's garret."[77] The young ladies clearly did not belong to the plebeian strata of society; for them, the diet dictated by the "corner store," which had so tormented and humiliated Belinsky 20 years earlier, was an important sign of their membership in the ranks of the new intelligentsia. Even the ultimate reality of *was man isst* (what one eats) could be entirely absorbed by cultural semiotics.

TWO

Recapitulation: Marriage

By the end of Chernyshevsky's university years, he had, to a great extent, acquired a cultural language. The next stage saw the crystallization of a system of concepts that translated the personal and idiosyncratic into the generally significant and comprehensible.

The final convergence of all psychic and cultural elements into a coherent structure was accomplished in Chernyshevsky's marriage. In personal experience and in literary works written before and after his actual marriage, Chernyshevsky constantly experimented with the marriage arrangement and marital relations; the fruit of these experiments was an original and consistent pattern of marriage that he offered for imitation both in the example he set in private life and in *What Is to Be Done?* and other literary works.

On the Meaning of Marriage

In European culture, marriage serves as the central paradigm for the problems of social and cultural arrangement, in the words of a modern scholar, for the resolution of "the problems of bringing unity out of difference, harmony out of opposition, identity out of separation, concord out of discord."[1] Therefore marriage has not only social but also metaphysical and mythical significance.

In the 1860s in Russia, the experiencing of marriage as an act of self-fulfillment endowed with cultural significance was an innovation. Romantic love, be it sublime affection or fatal passion, is unfulfilled love. In the early 1840s, Belinsky saw unfulfilled love for woman as a source of energy for the fulfillment of love for humanity to be realized through social activity.[2] With the shift to reality and "sociality," the relationship between love for woman and activity was reinterpreted: in the late 1840s, Chernyshevsky saw the gratification of love for woman realized in marriage as a source of energy for activity. Belinsky wrote of the idealists of the 1830s: "Love did not rhyme with marriage or, for that matter, with the reality of life."[3] The "new love," on the contrary, was equated with marriage as the ultimate realization of real life.

Lobodovsky, whose marriage served as a model for Chernyshevsky, married, in Chernyshevsky's interpretation, for the sole purpose of acquiring a stimulus for action. In planning the step himself, Chernyshevsky saw marriage as an act of self-realization that would launch him on the road to important social activity.

In a very concrete sense, Chernyshevsky viewed marriage as a decisive step in the process of maturing and overcoming his emotional deficiency: "One reason why I must marry is that by doing that, I will cease to be the child that I am, and will become a person. Then my shyness, my self-consciousness, and so on, will disappear" (1: 483). Marriage and the personality of the bride he chose, Olga Sokratovna Vasil'eva, were essential for stimulating action: "I must become engaged to O.S. in order to acquire the impetus to act because otherwise—'I do not have the will/To go my heart's way'" (1: 482).

The association between marriage, reality, and activity grew out of a combination of the Hegelian concept of realized love (in Belinsky's words, *deistvitel'nyi brak*) and the conventions of the social group from which the majority of the new men originated. The activities of a clergyman began with marriage: a seminarian was obliged to marry a priest's daughter who would bring him a parish as a dowry. Because the new men thought in the language of the day, in which "woman" was associated with

reality (*deistvitel'nost'*) and activity (*deiatel'nost'*), marriage also ✓
acquired symbolic significance and became an act of reconciliation with reality.

At the same time, the idea of marriage was combined with
dreams of social service and with the whole complex of ideas
that associated the liberation of woman with the liberation of humanity, and equated the rearrangement of the marital relationship with the reorganization of the social order. Although he
stood to gain by his marriage, Chernyshevsky also meant to
help his future wife: he would free a domestically oppressed
woman and develop her mind through education. Becoming the
liberator and educator of a woman was a projection of his aspira-
tion to become a savior and a teacher of humanity. When Chernyshevsky finally disentangled himself from Lobodovsky's family life and planned his own marriage, much more than the
simple fulfillment of personal happiness was at stake: fulfillment
of personal happiness in marriage was the prelude to attaining
universal happiness. That is why, disappointed in his friend's
marriage, Chernyshevsky declared: "Now I have my own idea:
marriage and *perpetuum mobile*" (1: 286).

The immense significance of marriage made it a formidable
task. Chernyshevsky developed a special strategy for each step
of the undertaking: meeting potential love objects, choosing an
appropriate object and evaluating her quality, committing himself to a final decision, and arranging conjugal relations. At each
step, the personal and the cultural were inextricably interwoven.
In the marriage design, the themes and problems encountered
earlier—insensitivity and lovelessness, timidity and shyness,
weakness of will, apathy, and inactivity (in short, the whole
complex of reality)—were restated as part of a final, assembled
pattern.

Teacher

At the very first stage of the undertaking—meeting possible
love objects—the new men encountered a major obstacle: their
social deficiencies. Contemplating the experience of his "first
ball" Chernyshevsky wrote: "I saw that it was necessary to

know many things . . . in order to get close to young girls and women, in order to become accepted among them, and therefore to begin the task of choosing one of them to be my life's companion" (1: 211). For a *raznochinets* who did not have social skills, there were few situations in which he could meet women of good society. Literature, transformed through the experience of his friend and double, Lobodovsky, came to the rescue.

During one of the last intimate conversations between the two friends, when Chernyshevsky confessed his inexperience in love, Lobodovsky revealed the story of his previous love affairs. All three episodes represent the same situation: Lobodovsky lived as a tutor in a gentry house; at the initiative of the wife or daughter of his master, he became her secret lover and, when the affair was discovered, he fled. Chernyshevsky was tremendously impressed by the stories and was fascinated by the potential offered by a position of teacher to a lady pupil in an aristocratic family.

About a month later, Chernyshevsky made an attempt to realize this situation: he obtained an invitation to give lessons to a group of young ladies of gentle birth in a private house. Excited by the opportunity, he indulged in fantasies that involved the pleasures of falling in love as well as those of intellectually influencing the young women while promoting their education and development (1: 270–72). But after the first two lessons, which he spent in anguish over his awkwardness and clumsiness, Chernyshevsky was not invited to resume his teaching, much to his chagrin.

He now developed another project of a similar nature: to become a live-in secretary in the house of an important official. He saw the position as an opportunity to be admitted to society and as a means of acquiring social poise: "I think that gaining access to that respectable house will be a way to enter the circle of respectable people where I will learn proper manners and, in time, will begin to speak French and German, i.e., will become as one should be" (1: 273). At the same time, he welcomed the opportunity to demonstrate his intellectual brilliance and superior education to the members of polite society: "And so one can see in the distance the beginning of being accepted in society, of showing one's intelligence, one's knowledge, one's wit, one's sharp mind" (1: 273). This experience, mused Chernyshevsky, could ensure his future, not only by giving him social status and financial independence but, more important, by allowing him access to female society and equipping him for interactions with women. On hearing that his potential employer's wife was a young woman, Chernyshevsky pondered the opportunities:

And so I expect that she will be sweet and pretty, and intelligent, and so on, and that we will become very close, and that she will like me, i.e., I am not, of course, thinking of love and so on, or anything like that. I am thinking, first of all, of having a pleasant person to be with and, second of all, of an opportunity to learn how to conduct myself with women. (1: 273)

This project was no more successful than the other. The official apparently thought in terms of a different set of social conventions. During the negotiations for the job, Chernyshevsky was frequently made to wait in an antechamber with the servants. He comforted himself with the thought that it was not his personality but the outward signs of poverty and social inferiority that provoked such treatment: "The reason is not me, but my clothes, and the fact that I arrived on foot" (1: 267).

The fulfillment of these plans and desires, unattainable in reality, came in a dream:

I had a long dream about being hired by a noble family to be their little son's tutor. The son is seven or eight, and the reason I was hired was that his mother and I are in love, or rather that she loves me and wants me to be there, and I am also in love with her, though we had hardly known each other before. She has fair hair and is very tall, yes, she is extremely fair-haired, her hair is gold, and she is so beautiful. I kissed her hand two or three times because I was so happy that she will have me live in their house. Her husband is an elderly man. He is dumb, has a large belly, and is somewhat pompous, no, not quite pompous, he is all right. So I was very happy about our love for each other, and I was ecstatic as I was kissing her hand (I think she was wearing a black glove). In fact it was for her sake that I decided to get along with her husband, who wasn't very pleased with me, and I was reluctant to have anything to do with him at first, but then later I brought it up again and told him that I would be living in their house because that's what she told me to do, or just wanted me to do, or maybe she just said, "Live in our house." I had no carnal thoughts (how come? this is strange), not a single carnal thought, only joy in my heart because she loved me, because I was loved. (1: 300–301)

The dream, remarks Chernyshevsky, gave him a feeling of great joy.

The scenario of a non-noble teacher or secretary living in an aristocratic house, admitted to society through the patronage of a noblewoman—a patronage united with tender friendship, which occasionally develops into a love affair—was a well-established cultural tradition that was reflected and codified in the European novel. It depended on the institution of the literary salon and the system of social promotion and elevation through the women who presided over them. The salons cultivated egalitarian principles in polite society: they introduced a system of recognition based on talent, wit, intellect, and education rather than on noble birth or bureaucratic rank. The salon could diffuse revolutionary ideas and promote independent genius in ways threatening to the existing social order.[4] In France, the patronage of society women and the Parisian salon played a major role in furthering Rousseau's career. In Russia, Nicholas I held the salons responsible for the advancement of the Decembrist movement.[5]

Strictly speaking, the Russian situation of the 1850s–60s was not analogous to that of eighteenth-century France. The *raznochintsy* invaded polite society en masse rather than being promoted individually by the salon, and in the long run, they engineered the collapse of a social system based on the rule of polite society. But at the early stages of the process, in search of cultural models of behavior and of guidelines for dealing with the problems of entering polite society, Chernyshevsky treated Rousseau as a fellow *raznochinets*. He could easily identify with Rousseau's concern with shyness and lack of breeding, and with his sexual problems. Numerous situations in the *Confessions* and *La Nouvelle Héloïse* dealing with aspects of the teacher scheme (for example, Mme de Warens teaching her young lover to fence and dance and preparing him for society, or Saint-Preux entering into a love affair with his lady pupil), as well as many other liter-

Fig. 1. Nikolai Gavrilovich Chernyshevsky, 1853. In the year this photograph was taken, Chernyshevsky, age 25, married Olga Sokratovna Vasil'eva in his native town of Saratov. That step, to which he attached great symbolic significance, marked his entrance into public life; in May, only weeks after the wedding, the couple moved to St. Petersburg.

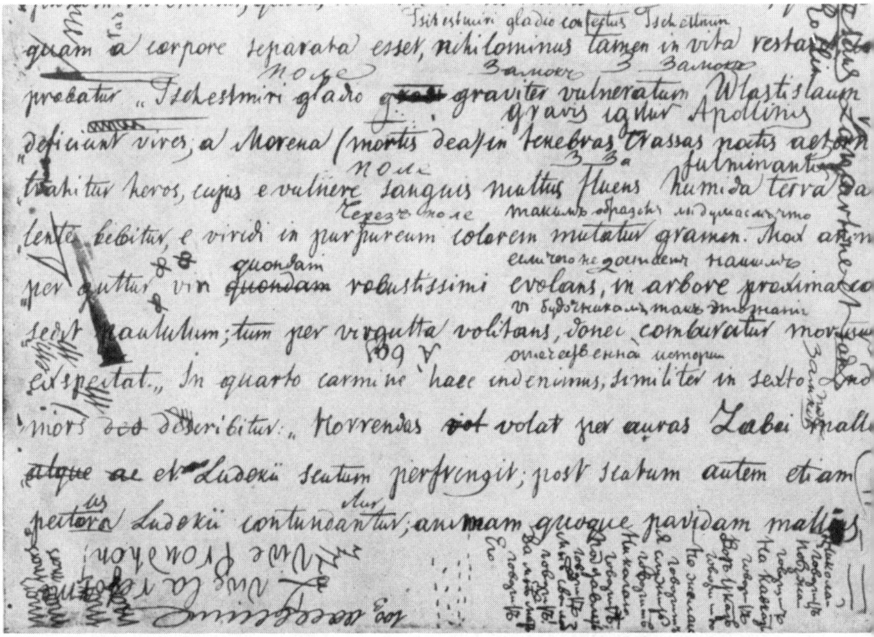

Fig. 2. A sample of Chernyshevsky's notes for a course in the history of Roman literature at St. Petersburg University, ca. 1849

Fig. 3. Diagram from Chernyshevsky's diary for 1848. Chernyshevsky habitually recorded the most minute details of his day. In describing his first dance party, he drew this diagram to pinpoint the position of various guests as they moved around the room. The accompanying entry explains: "At first (i.e., during the first dance) she [the belle of the ball] stood on *l*[л] while Ivan Vasil'evich and I stood at the door, on *b*[б], and I was watching her and almost never took my eyes off her. Then we moved to the doors *v*[в]; she danced at *i*[и] and practically galloped past us; after that the hostess's daughters sat down at *e*[е]."

Fig. 4. Olga Sokratovna
Chernyshevsky, 1860s

Fig. 5. Nikolai Alek-
sandrovich Dobro-
liubov, 1854. Like
Chernyshevsky and
many other radi-
cals of the 1860s,
Dobroliubov, de-
picted here in his
student's uniform,
was the son of a par-
ish priest.

Fig. 6. Mikhail Mikhailov, 1861, and (*opposite*) Liudmila and Nikolai Shelgunov, 1860–61. Prominent members of the radical intelligentsia, the Shelgunovs and Mikhailov were involved in what appears to have been a successful experiment in marital relations—a love triangle that evolved into a fulfilling relationship. The ménage à trois began in 1856 and lasted till 1861, when first Mikhailov and then Shelgunov was arrested for subversive activities.

Fig. 7. Cartoon poking fun at *What Is to Be Done?* from the satirical journal *Osa*, 1863. The caption read:

Woman: What is to be done? Oh god, what is to be done?
Mountain Elder: Do what animals do.
Voice: But even goats fight over a she-goat.
Woman: So what is to be done?
Voice: Throw the stupid book in the trash.

Fig. 8. Eyewitness's drawing of Chernyshevsky's "civil execution" on May 12, 1864. Chernyshevsky was arrested in 1862 on the charge of subversive activities, convicted, and subjected to a ceremonial execution marking the loss of his civil rights. The plaque he is wearing is inscribed "State Criminal."

Fig. 9. Ivan Sechenov, 1861. Sechenov, the author of the physiological study *Reflexes of the Brain* (1863), was seen by his contemporaries as (in his own words) "a philosopher of nihilism"; and for many, even the frogs used as experimental animals in the study of reflexes—like the three victims suspended from the laboratory stand in this photograph, in a manner suggesting crucifixion—became a common symbol of "the new faith." As the contemporary radical critic Dmitry Pisarev commented: "Young people will be inspired with deep respect and ardent love for the dissected frog lying spread-eagled upon the table. . . . It is here, in this same frog, that the salvation and renewal of the Russian people lies."

Fig. 10. Chernyshevsky, 1870. On his conviction for subversion in 1864, Chernyshevsky was sentenced to seven years of forced labor, followed by permanent exile in Siberia. Age 42 at the time this photograph was taken, he was then working in Aleksandrovsky zavod, a silver smelting plant and mine near Irkutsk. Chernyshevsky spent almost 20 years in prison, penal servitude, and exile, mostly in remote areas of Siberia. Revolutionaries made several attempts to free him, but these ultimately unsuccessful efforts only made matters worse for him. Through all these years of harsh privation, near-total isolation, and declining health, Chernyshevsky maintained his dignity and continued his writing.

ary embodiments of this cultural stereotype, provided Chernyshevsky with valuable materials for solving his own problem. The
scheme, however, had to be considerably modified to meet the
needs of a different social situation and a different individual.

The teacher scheme had two basic variants in the European
novel. In *La Nouvelle Héloïse*, social inequality between the male
and female protagonists erects a barrier to their mutual love. In
contrast, in a novel like Stendhal's *Le Rouge et le noir*, a young
and able man of humble origins jumps over the social barrier
and enters polite society by joining the family of an influential
man as a tutor to his children or as a domestic secretary. The
protagonist's ascent of the social ladder is facilitated by his
charm and his talent as a lover, which gains him the favors of the
mistress of the house or the daughter of his master.[6]

Chernyshevsky redistributed the accents and reversed the
whole scheme: the woman is not the means for ascending the
social ladder but the goal of the whole undertaking. For Julien
Sorel, winning the heart of a society woman offered access to
that society. For Chernyshevsky, on the contrary, entry into society was a door to woman's love, a love otherwise unattainable.
Entry into the house of an aristocrat as a tutor or secretary was a
means of acquiring those alien but necessary forms of behavior
associated with opportunities for personal development, which
had been denied Chernyshevsky as a *raznochinets*.

The teacher's employer, a nobleman who is the husband or father of the object of desire, serves as an intermediary between
the protagonist and the woman: he accepts the young suitor into
the household and is instrumental in introducing him to the
woman.[7] But the master's presence and his preeminent position
vis-à-vis the woman protects the young teacher from the necessity of assuming full responsibility for the relationship. Like the
Chernyshevsky–Lobodovsky–Nadezhda Egorovna triangle, the
teacher scheme is another instance of an arrangement giving
Chernyshevsky an honorable excuse for evading the sexual side
of love. The intersection of a literary code that postulated a love
affair between a teacher and a lady of high rank with a social
code that forbade it and rewarded ascetic reticence created an
ambivalent situation that perfectly suited Chernyshevsky's inner
ambivalence.

In the eyes of Chernyshevsky and his contemporaries, several components of the teacher scheme acquired different or additional meanings. The instruction of lady pupils in the 1850s and 1860s became an occupation replete with social significance. The effort to broaden women's intellectual horizons and thus assist the general cause of enlightenment and liberation was the main tactic of Russian feminism after the Crimean War and a common preoccupation of the young people of the time. In the late 1850s, a contemporary recollected, "The entire intelligentsia was seized with an epidemic of mutual self-education." "Mutual self-education" provoked tender feelings:

> That was the only way in which romances began then: suddenly "he" appeared and amazed "her" with the breadth of his knowledge and erudition, with the depth of his ideas and the dizzying novelty of his daring views. [But at that time] the young enlighteners not only did not dare to lead young ladies from the parental estate onto the glorious path of labor and struggle, they could not work up the courage for the tiniest daring step in the sphere of love, and most of their romances ended with the type of cowardly retreat at the decisive moment that characterized Rudin, and the hero of *Asia*, and Molotov.[8]

Becoming the teacher of a lady pupil opened the road to social promotion and personal development for a non-noble intellectual. It also fulfilled a social obligation and served the common cause. A teacher was simultaneously promoting women and being promoted by women, a benefactor and a beneficiary.

Less than four years after his first encounter with the teacher scheme, when Chernyshevsky experienced a brief affection for a woman, Ekaterina Nikolaevna Kobylina, the scheme was immediately put into action: "I decided to tell her that day that I was in love with her, and my head was all astir! She is very beautiful, though not educated. I will offer to teach her, free, of course. So later I will be able to think that she owes me something after all" (1: 408). But Kobylina did not give him an opportunity to declare his love, and the project did not succeed.

Years later the scheme was realized in Chernyshevsky's fiction. It figures importantly in the Siberian novel *The Prologue* in the section entitled "Levitsky's Diary." Nikolai Dobroliubov served as a prototype for Levitsky (the name belonged to a comrade of Chernyshevsky's from his seminary days), and Chernyshevsky used Dobroliubov's diary as a starting point for Levitsky's diary in the novel.

Between 1856 and 1861, Dobroliubov played a role similar to Lobodovsky's in Chernyshevsky's younger days. Chernyshevsky saw Dobroliubov as his double. He realized many of Chernyshevsky's aspirations that, for various reasons, could not be actualized. In his *Materials for a Biography of N. A. Dobroliubov*, Chernyshevsky endowed the image of his friend with those qualities that he himself desired. Among them were remarkable sensitivity and strong passions, social elegance and ease, and a true artistic gift. These were, however, concealed under a disguise of coldness and apathy, claimed Chernyshevsky, and Dobroliubov himself was deceived in regard to his own qualities. Contemporaries saw Chernyshevsky and Dobroliubov as two "comrades-in-arms" who "complementing each other, formed a finished whole."[9]

Among other achievements, Dobroliubov realized Chernyshevsky's dream of entering an aristocratic house: he became a tutor and almost a family member in the house of a wealthy and influential nobleman, Prince Alexander Kurakin. Moreover, Dobroliubov was frequently invited to give lessons on Russian literature to the children of the best families in Petersburg. None of these situations, however, resulted in a love affair. A frequent visitor to brothels, Dobroliubov was more successful with the ladies of the demimonde. Levitsky in *The Prologue* is a "double's double," an idealized image of Dobroliubov. As such, he was designed to bring the teacher scheme to complete fulfillment.

Levitsky, an ex-seminarian with a university education and the son of a provincial priest, is preparing for a career as a public activist and literary critic. In the interim, he becomes a tutor in the house of the extremely rich and distinguished nobleman Ilatontsev. Ilatontsev allows the teacher to become a person of tremendous importance in the household; he seeks the tutor's advice in private matters and state affairs, and grows to depend on him in settling his financial problems and intimate relationships. The nobleman's daughter, a young girl of striking beauty, appears to be in love with the tutor, causing Levitsky's older friend

Volgin (an alter ego of Chernyshevsky's) to consider the possibility of marriage between the young *raznochinets* and this young lady of high rank.

The teacher scheme is repeated at another level. While the tutor is being pursued by the daughter of his master, he falls in love with her maid, Mary. Mary is educating herself to become a teacher, and the young *raznochinets*, in accordance with the moral code of his social group, generously offers to instruct her in various subjects. In accordance with another cultural stereotype, the lessons provoke intimacy between the young pair. However, Mary is loved by Ilatontsev. These plot elements result in a complicated structure based on various components of the teacher scheme. The resulting relationship between the four characters is that of an extended family brought together in a large aristocratic household.

In *What Is to Be Done?*, the teacher scheme is used to bring the male and female protagonists together. Lopukhov, the tutor of Vera Pavlovna's younger brother, makes her acquaintance through him. He then undertakes her education and develops her mind through supervised reading.

Chernyshevsky made an attempt to realize this scheme in his own marriage. He was a teacher, but not a live-in tutor, of Olga Sokratovna's younger brother Venedikt. During the courtship, Chernyshevsky used this position to pass messages and do her small favors. Another component of the scheme was realized in Chernyshevsky's desire to improve his bride's mind by instructing her in various areas of knowledge: "I will become her teacher. I will explain my notions to her and open the encyclopedia of civilization to her" (1: 535). Chernyshevsky dutifully recorded that when he told her this, Olga Sokratovna burst out laughing, but he was not discouraged. His farfetched plans included elevating Olga Sokratovna to the position of Mme de Staël, a woman ruling over the nation's literary society: "This intellect and this grace need only to be developed through serious and scholarly conversations, and then I will perhaps have to say that I have Mme Staël for a wife!" (1: 475–76).

Curiously, Russian feminism of the 1850s–60s, at least in the interpretation of its ardent propagator Chernyshevsky, revived the feminism of the French literary salon of the eighteenth and nineteenth centuries. Apparently, Chernyshevsky took the literary salon as a model of social arrangement in which men and women interact on the basis of equality while women enjoy a position of ethical superiority. It was to woman, who was endowed with a special instinct for literature, that authors looked for inspiration, guidance, and protection.[10] The oppressed Russian petite bourgeoise was to be rehabilitated by being elevated to the position of salon hostess. That is one reason why educating women was so important and why Chernyshevsky put such emphasis on the role of women in the development of Russian literature.

To the end of his life, Chernyshevsky retained a serious belief in Olga Sokratovna's remarkable literary talent and regretted that she had not written any novels. Nevertheless, he claimed, in a letter from Siberia to his wife, that she was a force in Russian literature: "This, my dear friend, is the extent of your influence on Russian literature: Russian society owes you half of Nekrasov's work, almost all of Dobroliubov's, and all of mine" (15: 701). For the other half of Nekrasov's contribution, Russian civilization is apparently indebted to Avdot'ia Panaeva, his longtime mistress and the wife of his friend and co-editor, Ivan Panaev. In a letter to Panaeva, Chernyshevsky maintained: "Your influence on Russian literature . . . promoted the development of honest notions in the Russian public" (15: 757).

In the revolutionary 1860s, when everything from ideas to manners was being rearranged, old cultural patterns and notions seemingly incompatible with the demands of the new era proved to be remarkably vital and valuable once they had undergone the proper reinterpretation.[11]

The Object of Love

Soon after graduating from Petersburg University in 1850, Chernyshevsky, bending to his mother's wishes, returned to Saratov. He became a teacher at the local gymnasium and started to explore the possibilities of social life that Saratov offered to the Petersburg-educated son of one of its most respected members.

At a party on January 26, 1853, Chernyshevsky met Olga Sokratovna Vasil'eva, the daughter of a local doctor, a pretty young girl of boisterous temperament whose uninhibited and carefree manner had marred her reputation. "What was I to talk about?" he asked. "Even before the third dance I realized that she was a fast girl, and that one could make advances. . . . 'What shall we talk about? I shall be frank and say right away that I am consumed by a passion for you, a passion that will continue to be there if you indeed have what I think you have'" (1: 410).

The joke ended seriously: on February 19, Chernyshevsky proposed to Olga Sokratovna. The same day he began a special diary dedicated to his courtship and marriage—"The Diary of My Relations with Her Who Now Makes My Happiness." Chernyshevsky was aware that the casual joke that had started their acquaintance revealed a mechanism of his behavior: "In fact, before I was really in love I liked to pretend that I was in love, in the same way as a sober person sometimes likes to pretend being drunk. But this time the joke turned into the real thing, the impossible—into reality" (1: 548).

Emotion is attached to an object endowed with certain qualities, and the very reality of the experience is proved by the presence of these positively evaluated qualities in the object. Rationalization of emotion takes the place of immediate feeling, as Chernyshevsky explained to his future bride: "But you will see that I was not deluded, or blind, or dreaming. No—I know what I am doing, and I fell for you because you are worth falling for" (1: 425).

In his habitual search for signifiers of reality that proved the validity of emotional experience, Chernyshevsky relied on a positivist conceptual apparatus: the utilitarian idea of behavior's rational motivation (which later became a foundation of his new ethical system) was fused with the romantic notion of the ideal. The main indication of the reality of his feeling for Olga Sokratovna, as had been the case during his relationship with Nadezhda Lobodovskaia, was her superior qualities in relation to all other possible love objects:

> The features of her face are much better than all those girls that I saw in Saratov, and I saw no one in St. Petersburg (except for that pretty girl at the exhibition and Ivan Vasil'evich Pisarev's young landlady whom I saw at that party at the Semenov regiment). (1: 473)

. . .

She is definitely more intelligent than anyone I have ever known!
Her intellect equals that of a genius! Her tact equals that of a genius!
(1: 475)

However, significant changes had occurred in Chernyshevsky
since the time of his first love: he had moved decisively toward
"reality." He had to establish her as the "real" ideal. Idealism in
the sense of the abstract striving for total perfection gives way to
a utilitarian calculus of the desired (ergo, good) qualities:

And so I am in love with her. I do not hope ever to find another woman
for whom I could feel the same fondness, and to whom I would be so
attached. I cannot even imagine a woman more pleasing to my nature
and to my heart. No ideal woman can be superior to her. She is my
ideal, or to put it very simply, I cannot imagine an ideal woman superior to her, or better than she is in any way. She is my ideal, but it is not
because I am being idealistic about her. No, I see her as she is, and even
in my imagination, I do not give her any adornments because she already has everything that is the very best, everything that charms and
captures and fills the heart with joy and happiness. (1: 485)

The reality of his love was proved by the objective qualities of
his loved one, but there still remained a credible cause for doubt:
the object of love could be compared with other perceptible objects, but the emotion itself had no precedents that rooted it in
reality. To be honest with himself, Chernyshevsky declared his
love as follows: "I cannot say that I am in love with you because I
have never experienced this feeling and so do not know whether
my present feeling is love or something else" (1: 436).

Of course, tangible proof of love could be found in physical
expressions of sensuality. Such proof, however, was not to be
found: "Am I in love with her? I do not know. The thoughts of
'possessing her,' as the vulgar phrase goes, does not excite me at
all" (1: 533). In a conversation with his bride Chernyshevsky admitted uncertainty about his capacity to fulfill his nuptial obligations (1: 433), and he discussed the problem in his diary (1: 534).

This feeling of inadequacy prompted Chernyshevsky to take
measures to protect his future wife from possible disappointment. He had decided to seek a bride whose situation would improve by marrying him. While striving for an ideal woman,

Chernyshevsky was also seeking a woman with a blemish: "At first, and until February 15 or 16, I tended to be extreme and wished to marry a very poor girl. This poor helpless girl was supposed to be happy for the rest of her life to possess even the modest means that I could give her and that she had never had before. However, after I got to know O.S., I lost my devotion to that idea" (1: 478).

In Olga Sokratovna, he found a woman disadvantaged in a different sense—morally and not materially (1: 478). Boisterous and coquettish by nature, Olga Sokratovna was careless of her reputation. The moral disadvantage of her position was twofold: her domestic situation was difficult since she was apparently disliked by her authoritarian and unbalanced mother (though adored by an eccentric, overindulgent father), and her status in Saratov society was precarious because her reputation had been stained by rumor.

Therefore, argued Chernyshevsky, Olga Sokratovna was likely to benefit from marrying him because, though eager to leave her parents' house, she could hardly hope to find a suitable partner. He was rather explicit about his motivations and offered his hand in marriage in the following fashion: "Here is what I will tell you. You are being rather careless. If you ever happen to need me, if you ever . . . (again I could not find the words) are insulted by somebody and need me to help, you can ask me to do anything" (1: 416–17). In line with his personal needs, he decided to seek a bride with a handicap that would counterbalance his own inadequacy. This role was filled with culturally appropriate material, and a marred reputation was chosen as the handicap.[12]

The theme of the fallen woman has a long cultural tradition.[13] Idealized in romantic literature, the fallen woman was apotheosized in Goethe's *Faust*, where she acts as an agent of redemption through love. In his student years, Chernyshevsky was deeply moved by the fallen women in Hugo and Balzac, and he wept over the song of Marguerite. The theme was eagerly adopted by the mid-nineteenth-century feminist movement, both in Europe and in Russia, and reinterpreted in terms of the woman question.

For young Chernyshevsky, the position of the fallen woman (or of a woman ostracized by society for less serious crimes against prudence) was a social concern that called for immediate action. Therefore, his choice of such a woman could potentially have broad cultural ramifications. Later, in *What Is to Be Done?*, he devoted considerable attention to the practical means of saving fallen women. The rehabilitation of a prostitute is represented by the story of Kirsanov and Nastia Kriukova. The story of Vera Pavlovna is analogous to that of Olga Sokratovna. Like Olga, Vera has a handicap: the moral disadvantage of her domestic situation.

Not without the influence of Chernyshevsky, marriage to save fallen women, as well as marriage to liberate oppressed women, became a fairly common event among the non-gentry intelligentsia of the 1860s and a popular literary theme. Characteristic parodies of the theme appear in Dostoevsky's novels. In *Notes from Underground*, the protagonist, in the story of his encounter with a prostitute, consciously replays two literary schemes merged into one: the situation of man educating or developing the woman, and that of saving a fallen woman (there are numerous direct references to *What Is to Be Done?*).[14] In *The Idiot*, the "sensible" inhabitants of the town interpret Myshkin's desire to marry Nastas'ia Filippovna, whom he prefers to Aglaia Epanchina, as an act committed "simply on account of nihilism," so that he might have the gratification of marrying a fallen woman in the sight of the world; a fallen woman was, in his eyes, somewhat superior to one who had not "fallen."

Chernyshevsky's choice of a bride with a moral blemish had broad personal implications as well. The unrestrained and audacious manner that disgraced Olga Sokratovna in Saratov and made her a suitable candidate for salvation provided the opportunity for the reticent Chernyshevsky to make her acquaintance and maintain the initial relationship. The situation was described by Chernyshevsky's remote relative Varvara Pypina: "Olga Sokratovna with her easy manner and bold style immediately freed him from the self-consciousness and lack of worldliness that he could never overcome in order to approach a woman."[15]

Shy and awkward, Chernyshevsky tended to attach special value to a natural and easy manner, free of the usual social or psychological restraints on behavior. He associated this with women and specifically with aristocratic women, the traditional exemplars of social refinement. In describing women of gentle birth in his diaries and novels, he consistently stressed such qualities as "simple ways," "natural manner," "ease," "free of ceremony." It is interesting that Chernyshevsky apparently confused the uninhibited and daring manner of women of the demi-monde (like the French courtesan Julie in *What Is to Be Done?*) with the ease and freedom of salon ladies. As far as liberation from shyness and lack of social ease was concerned, Chernyshevsky found in Olga Sokratovna the substitute he needed for the aristocratic woman in his marriage design.

A curious quid pro quo, revealed by comparing scenes from "The Diary of My Relations" with *The Prologue*, will illustrate his confusion. A scene in *The Prologue* aimed at satirizing the mores of a corrupt power elite and of the liberals who court that elite depicts a dinner party at the house of Savelov, an important liberal activist, who is entertaining a group of noblemen and government officials. The well-born and well-connected hostess is concerned to show special attention to the guest of honor, Count Chaplin (a caricature of Count Mikhail Murav'ev, a minister in the government of Alexander II): "There, she moved a piece from her plate to his. . . . But even that was not enough, and she began to cut the food on his plate, leaning toward him. . . . Now she is eating the ice cream from his plate . . . putting half a peach into his mouth" (13: 172–73).

This episode mimics an episode that occurred, not in the salon of the mighty and noble, but in the dining room of Olga Sokratovna's home in Saratov (the first "society" that Chernyshevsky entered) at the time of Chernyshevsky's courtship. In his diary, Chernyshevsky describes the scene with tender emotion:

And then the hors-d'oeuvres. . . . She [Olga Sokratovna] was spoon-feeding Palimpsestov, and I was jokingly trying to take the plate away from him, the plate that he placed on her knees and that she later handed to him. . . . When everybody was eating hors-d'oeuvres and

she reached over to Palimpsestov trying to put some cookie or a bis-
cuit into his mouth, I kissed her hand, and everybody laughed and
shouted. (1: 412)

I. U. Palimpsestov, one of Olga Sokratovna's suitors and a
friend of Chernyshevsky's, even warned him against marrying
this coquette. With this in mind, another detail from *The Prologue* acquires special significance. Savelova's attentions to the
noble guest are only a prelude: after dinner the hostess is expected, by the mores of her circle, to offer herself to Count
Chaplin in her bedroom, with the husband entertaining the rest
of the guests in the living room next door. One can only wonder
what emotions were evoked in Chernyshevsky by the free and
easy frolics of his bride's circle, which he naïvely confused with
the mores of the aristocratic salon (a mistake that Balzac's heroes
made as well).

Among other psychological advantages, choosing a bride with
a blemish provided an external obligation that eliminated the
need to make a free choice. Tormented by indecisiveness and inertia, Chernyshevsky saw the solution in creating a situation in
which marriage, in itself seen as a condition for action, would
become a necessity: "Only one thing left to do—to establish an
opportunity for marrying. Not an opportunity, but an obligation
to marry. The thought of marriage will not have its full effect on
me until I stop thinking 'I want to marry' and begin thinking that
I must marry and cannot escape it" (1: 482). Marrying a fallen
woman was an excellent opportunity: marriage became a matter
of moral obligation, not personal choice. Chernyshevsky was
trying to persuade himself: "I cannot refuse. That would be dishonest" (1: 480); "I would be ashamed of myself if I refused to
give my hand to somebody who needs it in order to escape a
downfall" (1: 481). In many different ways, the choice of a proper
object facilitated action.

A Calculated Marriage

Because of the disintegration of the existing system of cultural
conventions of behavior, people of Chernyshevsky's generation

lived under considerable pressure to develop new principles for the organization of marriage. The starting point of this quest lay in the cultural developments of the late 1830s, in the early stage of realism and Belinsky's views on marriage. Reorientation toward reality revived the idea of a "marriage of convenience" (in Russian, *brak po raschetu*, "marriage by calculation" or "a calculated marriage"). In romantic idealism this idea was not only unacceptable; it simply remained outside the sphere of cultural awareness. Frustrated in his aspirations to achieve ideal love for an ideal woman, the first Russian realist, Belinsky, proclaimed: "Not everyone has it in his destiny to love, i.e., to be in love and to be loved and to marry because of a love that comes before the marriage plans. . . . Not all plans and calculations are a vulgar thing: there is also the humane calculating that is necessary in order to satisfy the best part of human nature." [16]

Projected onto the plane of metaphysics, the new attitude toward marriage was associated with Hegel and his treatment of marriage in *Die Philosophie des Rechts* (marriage as "the direct substantive reality of spirit," a union in which "the accidents of feeling and private inclination" are "rationalized" and receive intellectual and social significance). Without involving himself in the explication of philosophical categories, Belinsky treated Hegel's concept of applying reason to matters of marriage as simple common sense, as a reasonable approach to choosing an appropriate marriage partner and carefully calculating the concrete circumstances of marital relations. [17]

In the early 1850s, Chernyshevsky was thinking along the same lines. A calculated marriage (the calculations having nothing to do with material benefits) was a conscious and desired position, devoid of the negative connotations of the romantic period. He hastened to assure his future bride that his proposal was not a headlong and reckless decision: "Believe me now— and later, when you know me better, you will realize that I am taking a reasonable, well-calculated step" (1: 431). The diary is filled with lengthy passages devoted to weighing the pros and cons and with methodically arranged itemized lists cataloging "reasons for marrying"; for example, "(1) Why Olga Sokratovna

Is My Bride" (1: 472), and "(2) Why I Must Have a Bride" (1: 481). He tried to take every aspect of their future marital life into consideration: a budget worked out to the smallest expenses (two candles for the winter nights, with two extra ones for nights spent with friends); the arrangement of their future apartment and a list of furniture; their future relationships with (1) relatives, (2) friends, (3) acquaintances, and (4) society; and so forth.

The specification of the domestic details of future conjugal re-lations, the logical sequence of motivations for marrying that ra-tionalized every point of the argument, and the sheer number of motivations, dutifully calculated, apparently produced a com-forting effect: they were supposed to facilitate action. But Cher-nyshevsky extended the principle of calculation far beyond Belin-sky's original idea. For him, the main advantage of a calculated marriage was that the calculations abolished the necessity for making a choice. He approached marriage as a test case, with the aim of resolving the general problem of freedom of choice and decision and, in the long run, the issue of freedom of the will. Just as Chernyshevsky sought a concrete external require-ment that would eliminate free choice, he tried to work out some general principles that, when applied to a given situation, would transform the act of decision into a purely technical problem.[18]

He found a philosophical foundation for this strategy in the utilitarian principle of a rational calculus, with its almost mathe-matically exact measurement and evaluation of a human being's behavior vis-à-vis society as a whole. Chernyshevsky became an ardent and extremely effective proselytizer of utilitarian ethics in Russian society; moreover, he extended the sphere of utili-tarian principles beyond the fields of public morals and state leg-islation originally established by Bentham and Mill.[19] Given the emotional appeal that the doctrine had for him, and his ad-herence to what seems to be the peculiarly Russian practice of vigorously applying philosophical categories to daily life, it is not surprising that Chernyshevsky treated the utilitarian cal-culus as a psychological law governing human behavior.

In "The Anthropological Principle in Philosophy" (1860) and

in *What Is to Be Done?* (1863), Chernyshevsky maintained that every act or impulse of individual human beings arises as the direct realization of the calculus of pains and pleasures, which prevails over spontaneity and emotional immediacy of any kind. Thus, determinism rules human life, beginning with perception and ending with action; reason, which is capable of calculating the interplay of pain and pleasure, becomes a governing force in human behavior. The role of free choice is limited, if not eliminated; with it, painful doubts about matters that cannot be controlled or accounted for are eliminated as well.

At different stages in the development of his theory of free will, Chernyshevsky worked with the marriage situation. In 1849, during his involvement in Lobodovsky's marriage, he reached a global metaphysical conclusion from his disappointment over his friend's (and his own) inability to act. He conceptualized concrete emotional experiences in terms of the philosophical categories of "free will" and "man's control over the circumstances":

For a little while, we talked about free will and denied the idea that man can control circumstances and said that "a man with a strong will" is but an absurdity and so on. I do not know what the foundation of his position is. The foundation of mine is his example because any fool, myself included, will tell you that you won't find as firm a person as he is even though he says that he has no will at all. I am made the same way. (1: 226)

In "The Anthropological Principle in Philosophy," among other examples of the interplay of desires and calculations, Chernyshevsky wrote of choosing a marriage partner (7: 231). Three years later, in *What Is to Be Done?*, when he embodied this ethical system in the conduct of the novel's protagonists, he was again working with the marriage situation.

The issues of freedom of will, choice of action, and the limits of human freedom were apparently the major concern of an age in which the Christian ideal of free will was set against the positivist principle of determinism. It tormented Chernyshevsky's great contemporaries and antagonists Tolstoy and Dostoevsky.

At about the time that Chernyshevsky was calculating the

minutest details of his future marriage to Olga Sokratovna, Tolstoy was involved in a similar undertaking. In a series of long and deliberate letters to Valeriia Arsen'eva, with whom he was supposedly in love, Tolstoy indulged in careful discussions of the plans for their future marital relations. These depended, he argued, first, on the man's and woman's inclinations, and second, on their means. The husband's life would consist of three occupations: first, love for his wife, second, concern for her happiness, and third, literature and the management of the household economy. Tolstoy took into account concrete details in the arrangement of the family life, including the minutest details of the budget, up to a hypothetical poplin dress.[20] These deliberations, however, did not assuage Tolstoy's doubts and did not facilitate action. After every detail had been settled on paper, he hastily withdrew from the relationship.

Dostoevsky was, for many years, involved in an intense polemic with Chernyshevsky centering around the issue of freedom of will and action. The polemic began, as is well known, in *Notes from Underground*, whose hero repudiates not only the idea of the rational calculus of human behavior, but even the laws of mathematics itself. He sees the manifestation of his human essence and the ultimate expression of freedom of will in the assertion that "two times two equals five." In *Crime and Punishment*, Dostoevsky puts forth arguments not only of an ethical but also of a psychological nature. For Raskolnikov, a mathematically exact rational calculus does not produce the desired effect of facilitating action: "Grant that there is no element of doubt in all those calculations of mine, grant that all the conclusions I have come to during the past month are as clear as daylight, as straightforward as arithmetic, all the same I shall never summon up enough resolution to do it."[21]

According to Dostoevsky, the principle of utilitarian calculus and the ideal of determinism contradict psychological laws, the laws of the living human heart. Thus, working from different perspectives and drawing both on psychologically concrete personal experience and on a stock of cultural resources, Chernyshevsky's contemporaries sought a metaphysical release from the concerns of their era.

Inversion of Roles

Although Chernyshevsky offered himself in marriage to Olga Sokratovna, he wanted her to take the initiative in deciding whether the marriage would take place. Having expressed his eagerness to marry, he left the final decision to the woman: "The roles were reversed. . . . I was made an offer, and I accepted it" (1: 425). Included in the motif of inverted marital roles was a plan to make his wife the head of the family and to accept, voluntarily and eagerly, a subordinate role: "There will be no doubt that you will be the head of the house. I am a man who would agree to anything and would be prepared to concede everything except, of course, for those few situations when any man would have to be independent" (1: 435).

Chernyshevsky argued that he needed a firm and determined wife to command him in matters of domestic arrangement and relations; this situation, according to his calculations, was needed to force him into action:

I must obey other people and do whatever I am told to do. I can do nothing on my own. Other people must demand things from me, and then I will do everything that is required of me. I must be subordinated to someone. . . . In the family, my role must be that usually played by a wife, whereas my wife must be able to be the head of the family. She is exactly that kind of person. That is just what I need. (1: 473–74)

Olga Sokratovna, with her boisterous and domineering manner, was clearly an appropriate candidate for this role.

According to the memoirs of Chernyshevsky's first cousin E. N. Pypina, the same situation existed in the house of Chernyshevsky's parents, Gavriil Ivanovich and Evgeniia Egorovna: "Gavriil Ivanovich would do whatever Evgeniia Egorovna told him to do. This is all we talked about in the family. 'Evgeniia Egorovna used to do this, Evgeniia Egorovna used to order that.' Gavriil Ivanovich would constantly quote her."[22]

Thus, Chernyshevsky adopted a familiar practice. But he gave it a social interpretation based on the era's current concerns. The inversion of roles in marriage received an ideological motivation:

My notion is that the woman deserves a better position in the family. I am outraged at discrimination in any form. The woman must be equal to the man. But after a stick has been bent for a long time, one has to keep it bent the other way for a long time in order to eventually straighten it out. This is the situation. Women are subordinated to men. In my view, every decent man must give his wife a status higher than his own. This temporary inequality is necessary for future equality. Besides, I was created by nature to be subordinate to someone else. (1: 444)

The personal and the cultural were blended: an act of personal fulfillment simultaneously served an important social function.

The rearrangement of marriage also involved a cardinal rearrangement of sexual relations; this was, again, more than appropriate for Chernyshevsky's private needs. They found a convenient release in the theory of the reversal of sexual roles:

How will it work in our family? I would prefer to have an arrangement that would give her the initiative. So what if this is contrary to the usual arrangement between the sexes? We have done everything contrary to the usual arrangement between the would-be man and wife. She insists on things, whereas I concede. . . . Why not extend the situation to the sexual sphere. Usually the man seeks out the woman, and comes to her, and speaks to her. With me it is the other way round. I always wait for her to come to me and say, "Talk to me, sit with me." And in this sphere it can continue to be so: "You may visit me tonight." "I am very grateful, O.S." (1: 534)

Spatial arrangement, as usual, was of extreme importance for Chernyshevsky, who held onto the reality of a situation with the help of maps and diagrams. He carefully planned the couple's future living arrangements and decided on separate bedrooms. Olga readily agreed to this plan, although Chernyshevsky felt that she was motivated by a commonplace consideration: "She is probably concerned only with her privacy, whereas for me this is a question of the husband's obligation to be extremely tactful in his conjugal relations to the wife" (1: 533).

Viewed in a cultural context, the subordination of husband to wife in marriage and the accompanying concrete details of living arrangements acquired general significance; that is, they could be "read" and utilized by contemporaries. In this capacity, the living arrangement of the Chernyshevskys' household was included in *What Is to Be Done?* The main characters, Lopukhov and Vera Pavlovna, enjoy the privacy of separate rooms, an unheard-of arrangement in middle-class families of the time, although it was quite common in aristocratic families. In the novel, the description of this domestic arrangement is part of the prescription for ideal domestic life, an essential component of the utopian novel. It is echoed in the fourth dream of Vera Pavlovna, in the description of the phalanstery—a building of the type planned by Fourier, with special attention given to provisions for sexual activity. Thus, the idea of the inversion of marital roles had far-reaching implications.

Liberation from the Parental Yoke

For Chernyshevsky, marriage had another significant psychological dimension: it would end his dependence on his parents, a matter of increasing concern after his return home. His parents' reaction to his marriage, especially to his choice of a bride, evoked strong fears and doubts on the part of Chernyshevsky. It was only natural to assume that his conventional and pious parents, especially his mother, would not approve of Olga Sokratovna. And yet Chernyshevsky tried to suppress his doubts:

I am almost certain that my fears that they "may not like her" or that they "may find her flighty and flirty" are quite absurd and in fact are nothing but figments of my horrendously productive imagination. It is much more likely that they will like her. Much more likely. But what if they don't? . . . What is to be done? (1: 494)

Just in case they did not, Chernyshevsky decided to announce his engagement to Olga Sokratovna as a fait accompli and to insist that his parents immediately visit the house of the Vasil'evs to signify their sanctioning of the move. They were to have no opportunity to meet Olga Sokratovna before giving their parental blessing. In the "unlikely" case of their opposition, Chernyshevsky would kill himself. This is how he planned to announce his intention to marry: " 'Say yes or no because if in an hour you are not ready to meet my fiancée's family, I will kill myself.' I'll do that. It would not be hard for me at all. It would not be out of character for me" (1: 479). Chernyshevsky planned the suicide carefully, looking to high cultural examples for his method: "If I do not have time to obtain poison, then I think the best thing is to open my veins. However, I had better find out how the old masters used to do this: I had better read about Seneca, for example" (1: 480).

In this part of the diary, Chernyshevsky expresses extreme bitterness at his parents' despotism. He laments that they (especially his mother) have the temerity to assume that they have the final authority and wisdom to decide what is good and reasonable for him. In an imaginary monologue addressed to his mother, he declares:

I was born to submit and to subordinate myself to others, but I must assume this subordination of my own free will. Meanwhile you have assumed a despotic view of myself as a mere child. [You say:] "Even when you are 70, you will still be my son, as I was an obedient child of my mother even when I was 50." Whose fault is it that you demand too much of me and therefore I have to say, "I have been an obedient child as long as it involved only small, insignificant things—even though in the past these insignificant things were in fact quite important. But in this business I cannot be an obedient child: I have no right to be one because this is an important business. . . . After all I am a man, and I know better what I am doing. And if you continue to be obstinate, I will not argue with you. I will commit suicide." (1: 494)

Liberation from his mother's unbending will was to be achieved by submitting, willingly, to the will of his wife. I must marry, argued Chernyshevsky, so that I can leave my mother (1: 483).

In March 1853, at the time that the couple's relationship entered a decisive stage, Chernyshevsky kept two diaries: one was dedicated specifically to his love for his fiancée, the other to the usual routine of his life, including his relationship with Olga Sokratovna. Both diaries contain an account of his parents' reaction to the engagement. However, Chernyshevsky almost entirely suppressed the evidence of his parents' opposition in the "Diary of My Relations with Her Who Now Makes My Happiness." The second diary contains accounts of dramatic conversations with his father and mother.

Chernyshevsky fulfilled his original plan almost to the last detail. He did not allow his parents to see his fiancée before receiving their formal consent (despite his mother's vigorous protestations) and was almost explicit in hinting at the "horrible consequences" in case of their refusal. He remained determined, if necessary, to assert his will by committing suicide.

The conversation with his parents took place on March 29. The date of the wedding was set according to the wishes of Olga Sokratovna, who insisted on an immediate marriage, for April 29. On April 4, the day after the engagement ceremony, Chernyshevsky's mother fell ill. Her situation rapidly deteriorated. In his daily diary, Chernyshevsky charted the course of his mother's grave illness. The sentence with which Chernyshevsky abandoned his diary starts, "I am going to Mommy . . ." (1: 561). There are no references to his mother's illness in the "Diary of My Relations," which was abandoned on the same day, April 8. Chernyshevsky's mother died on Easter Sunday, April 19, followed two days later by his grandmother.

In spite of this, the wedding took place as planned, one week after the funerals, in violation of all social conventions and standards—a shock for the grieving relatives and a bombshell for the townspeople. E. N. Pypina wrote in her memoirs: "Tuesday, during Easter week, was Mother's funeral, and Thursday, Grandma Anna Ivanovna's. The very day that Grandma was buried, the workers came to decorate the house for the wedding. They upholstered the furniture and hung draperies as Olga Sokratovna liked them. The Chernyshevskys and the Pypins could not abide such draperies."[23]

The memoirs of numerous contemporaries confirm the picture of the marriage as reconstructed from the diaries. The whole process was, apparently, a subject of vigorous discussion around town. Gossip ascribed the sudden illness of Evgeniia Egorovna entirely to her son's engagement.[24] The townspeople saw a deliberate act of defiance in Chernyshevsky's behavior. According to one colorful account, Chernyshevsky "shed not a single tear over the body of his beloved mother"; "quite the opposite, for when the coffin had been lowered into the grave and covered with earth, he, as if nothing had happened, lit a cigarette, took O.S. under the arm, and the two of them started walking home."[25]

Chernyshevsky and his young wife left for St. Petersburg almost immediately after the wedding, leaving his grief-stricken father behind. After the wedding, Chernyshevsky was ill, just as Lobodovsky had been, "before committing the final act" (14: 225). The young couple's traveling companions could not believe that the two were married: Chernyshevsky and Olga Sokratovna addressed each other with the formal *vy* and treated each other with formal courtesy.[26]

Marriage, and the way in which it was conducted, proved to be an important act of self-assertion. In marrying, Chernyshevsky not only defied the authority of his parents, but also openly opposed the conventions and opinions of the local society. The chain of dependence was broken, and the incubation period was brought to a close; he acquired the power to exercise his will and to engage in decisive action:

I feel now that I am a man who knows how to act, who can do something daring if there is a need for that. . . . Oh, I used to be tormented by the thought that I am another Hamlet! Now I can see that I was wrong. I am a man like other men, and even though I may not have as strong a character as I would like to have, I am not entirely without a will. In short, I am a man and not some complete nonentity. (1: 480)

The reference to Hamlet hints at the cultural background of the situation. In Russia of the 1830s–40s, Hamlet stood as a symbol of the idealist generation.[27] Belinsky defined the tragedy and the sin of Hamlet as weakness of the will and indecisiveness in the face of demands for action. Hamlet "fears the feat that he is to perform, grows pale at the challenge, hesitates, and only talks instead of acting."[28] Following the German tradition, Russians of the 1840s endowed this image with political significance: action was understood as social activity.

A symbolic act of personal transformation for Chernyshevsky, marriage was experienced as spiritual rebirth: "I feel like a totally different man, I have become bold and brave, and all my doubts and hesitations are gone. I have will, strength, and energy" (1: 500). The source of this transformation was his wife: "You are the source of my self-confidence, you are the reason why this timid, indecisive, and doubting person became a man with a strong will, with determination, and with the energy to act" (1: 514).

Following the example of Lobodovsky, Chernyshevsky looked for signs of approaching energy. Having discovered them, he felt convinced that his emotion was really love: "O.S.! O.S.! O.S.! No! I love you because there has been a transformation in me. I regret every minute wasted in inactivity. Activity, activity!" (1: 550).

The myth of marriage played itself out, the era of activity followed. "Activity" was of course understood not only in its commonplace sense, but also in a social and a symbolic sense. Chernyshevsky disclosed his plans for revolutionary activity and his expectations of his arrest and confinement to Olga Sokratovna. He pointed to the example of Herzen and his wife, Natalie, and immediately made the connection with Christianity: "Every minute I expect the gendarmes to appear, the way a devout Christian every minute expects to hear the archangel's call. Besides, we are going to have a revolt, and when we do, I must certainly participate in it" (1: 418). He warned his bride about the possibility of a future absence "for God knows how long."

Chernyshevsky replayed all the themes surrounding his account of Lobodovsky's marriage, and in a curious way, his planned absence echoed Lobodovsky's desire to escape marriage by provoking deportation to Siberia. The difference between the two marriages was, however, considerable. From Chernyshevsky's account, Lobodovsky's project to acquire a stimulus for activity in marriage seems to have been based on his almost magic belief in the act of marriage. He otherwise remained entirely passive, and he soon declared the marriage a "miscalculation." For Chernyshevsky, this belief was the starting point for an elaborate conceptual system that tied together various aspects of marital relations and helped to develop their potential for symbolic interpretation and to focus them around the idea of activity/reality. Viewed within the resulting network of associations, almost any aspect of family life could represent the whole model.

Thus, the sexual consummation of marriage—in Chernyshevsky's terms, "a decisive act" (*reshitel'noe deistvie*)—became through a chain of purely linguistic and broad cultural associations (for example, the connection between sensuality and industry) a symbol of activity in general (*deiatel'nost'*). A single detail of their living arrangements—separate bedrooms—stood for social equality in marriage; this became a manifestation of social activity. The same is true of the provision for a prolonged absence; it was connected with the revolutionary predicament and civic duty. The contrast between Lobodovsky and Chernyshevsky demonstrates the difference between a common member of a certain culture and a creative individual capable of transforming his personal experience into a generally significant cultural pattern.

The Third: A Rival-Mediator

Each step in Chernyshevsky's strategy for getting married depended on the mediation of some external agent. Before the marriage, the function of the intermediary was to facilitate the choice of the object. This function could be performed by another person with whom the protagonist identified (a superior friend, a double, an alter ego), or it could be fulfilled by projecting the candidate onto an abstract ideal. The help of an intermediary was also indispensable when Chernyshevsky committed himself to marriage.

The fulfillment of this part of the project already concerned Chernyshevsky at the time of his involvement in the Lobodovskys' marriage. He was planning his own future marriage and was contemplating it as a commitment to certain ideological convictions that were not sanctioned by existing social conventions. The problem was treated in an unfinished story, "Theory and Practice" ("Teoriia i praktika"), written in 1849 concurrently with his diary account of Lobodovsky's marriage. He thought of using Vasily Petrovich as the hero and writing a story about "how difficult it is for any person to realize his convictions in life," about the "doubts, indecisiveness, and inconsistency and, finally, the selfishness that acts more strongly than it does when one has to repudiate it in favor of the generally accepted rules" (1: 325).

In the story, a young man tutors a young lady and her brother, children of an elderly man who has been his benefactor and mentor. One day the teacher witnesses an attack of illness that threatens the life of his benefactor. It immediately occurs to the teacher that he would be obliged by honor, in the case of the old man's death, to marry his daughter and to assume financial responsibility for the family. The prospect alarms the young man, who among other things is financially dependent on his mother. (This situation is clearly related to Chernyshevsky's fantasies about his obligation to marry Nadezhda Egorovna in the case of Lobodovsky's death.)

In order to evade this potential obligation to marry, the hero schemes to arrange a marriage between the young lady and a friend of his, who is also a teacher of the young lady's brother. This friend is inferior to the hero both intellectually and morally (*po umu i razvitiiu*) and is clearly not worthy of the girl. Yet he has one advantage over the hero—the ability to play the piano and sing, "a royal road" to a woman's heart. But at the last moment, the worthless friend shamelessly breaks the engagement. The story is incomplete, but the exposition presents the hero happily married to the lady. One guesses that, after the disappearance of the substitute, the hero had no choice but to offer his hand in marriage in order to save the honor of the cruelly abandoned girl.

The marriage is effected through a long chain of mediating links. The hero is assisted by a man who is simultaneously his rival and an intermediary between him and the woman. On the one hand, in the early stages of the relationship, the self-imposed rival saves the hero from the threatening necessity of marrying. On the other, as events unfold and the rival flees, his disappearance makes the hero's marriage a matter of ultimate necessity.

Some elements of the rival-mediator scheme were dutifully reproduced in Chernyshevsky's marriage. At the first stage of courtship, he declared his intention to offer his hand in marriage in case the need for such a marriage should arise ("I would be prepared, at a word from you, to become your husband"; 1: 414). He made one important stipulation: he would marry Olga Sokratovna only if she had no other suitable fiancé. He then encouraged Olga Sokratovna to look for another fiancé, inquired about possible candidates, and carefully weighed their merits and drawbacks.

The rival-mediator also became an element of the marriage pattern in *What Is to Be Done?* Vera Pavlovna's potential fiancé, Storeshnikov, is totally unworthy of her and is inferior to Lopukhov both morally and intellectually. But, unlike Lopukhov, he is a man of society. Storeshnikov's presence makes it necessary for Lopukhov to offer himself in marriage to Vera Pavlovna. A hypothetical other is introduced into the design, and then removed, in order to catalyze the marriage.

A License for Adultery: Theory and Practice

Among the different potential alternatives of relations with Olga Sokratovna that Chernyshevsky carefully considered was the possibility of adultery. He pictured what would happen if Olga Sokratovna retained her coquettishness after their marriage: "In St. Petersburg, she will collect the best circle of young men that my social status and her connections will allow, and she will flirt with them, and some day some of them will make her go beyond simple flirting" (1: 488).

At first, Chernyshevsky imagined, she would take pains to keep him in the dark, but then, knowing him better, she would abandon every precaution and "do everything openly." He planned his own reaction: at first grief and sadness, then quiet resignation. But what if "there appears a true passion in her life? No matter. She will abandon me, but I will be happy for her if the object of her passion is a worthy man. I will be sad, but I will not feel insulted. And then how happy I will be when she comes back!" (1: 513). Even the joy of reunion after their hypothetical estrangement was planned. Still hoping that his expectations were idle fantasies, Chernyshevsky asked himself: "Suppose I were quite certain that this is the way it is going to happen?

What would I do? I would know that this marriage will make me unhappy, but I would not repudiate it" (1: 489).

When Palimpsestov, a former suitor of Olga Sokratovna's, tried to dissuade Chernyshevsky from marrying a woman whose heart was "worn out," a careless and audacious coquette, Chernyshevsky calmly replied:

If she does more than that: if she remains my wife and still wants to live with another man, I will not object to that. If my children are in fact not mine, I will not object to that. I am not saying that I will welcome that. It will make me very bitter, but I will bear it; I will suffer, but I will still love her and will not say anything. If my wife wants to live with another man, I will say to her, "My friend, when you decide that it is better to come back, please do so without any embarrassment." (1: 451)

As usual, ideological considerations and literary models played a significant role in the organization of real-life events. Chernyshevsky claimed that he subscribed to the principle of "freedom of the heart" advocated by George Sand (1: 444).

George Sand's novel *Jacques* (1834) codified the act of giving a wife a license to commit adultery (a point of honor for the "enlightened man"). *Jacques* offered a way to resolve love triangles based on the principle of "freedom of the heart." Respecting his wife's right to love another man and unite with him in marriage, the hero of the novel liberates her by graciously removing himself from the scene: he commits suicide. The book achieved remarkable popularity in Russia. Druzhinin produced "a Russian *Jacques*"—a novel entitled *Polin'ka Saks*; 1847. (The hero, Saks, not only liberates his wife, but also educates her by reading George Sand's novel with her.) Herzen apparently adopted the title of the preface to *Jacques*—"A qui la faute?"—for his novel *Who Is to Blame? (Kto vinovat?)*, also published in 1847.[29] But, more important, George Sand's novel had far-reaching real-life implications. It would hardly be an exaggeration to say that among the idealists of the forties—the circle around Herzen and Belinsky—a recital of *Jacques* in the manner of a recitation of the Creed became an essential component of a wedding or betrothal ceremony. Thus, Nikolai Ogarev wrote to his young wife, Maria (the letter is dated "6:30 in the morning, March 22, 1839"): "Do you remember how we read *Jacques*? Oh! If, for your happiness, it would be necessary that I be Jacques, then I would be Jacques; I am ready to make any sacrifice. But no! What am I saying! Is it possible that you could love another? Is it possible that you could find happiness with someone other than Kolya? Never, never!"[30] The plot of *Jacques* was soon realized in this marriage (save for the suicide): Maria deserted Ogarev for another man.

Another characteristic episode connected with *Jacques* involved the literary critic Vasily Botkin. According to Herzen's *My Past and Thoughts*, Botkin married to fulfill the moral idea of family expounded in Hegel's *Die Philosophie des Rechts* and for the purpose of "plunging into the gulf of real life." His bride was a "fallen woman," a Parisian grisette named Armance; the wedding occurred after much hesitation on the part of the bridegroom and despite strong opposition from his wealthy but unenlightened family. (The couple was wed by Father Sidonsky, a learned priest and the author of the popular book *Introduction to the Science of Philosophy*.) After the wedding, the couple sailed to France, and on the boat Botkin presented his bride with a copy of George Sand's *Jacques*. Armance, however, disapproved of the novel's philosophy of life; Botkin thereupon informed her that "her criticism wounded his spirit on its deepest side, and that his Weltanschauung had nothing in common with hers." At that, the couple decided to dissolve their marriage and parted for life.[31]

What Herzen described with such irony in 1857 had been performed in all earnestness by Chernyshevsky in 1855. As part of Olga Sokratovna's education in the "new faith," Chernyshevsky recounted the plot of the novel to her as an illustration of his own views on marriage and adultery:

The conversation turned to my notions on marriage. "Do you really think that I might be unfaithful to you?" "I do not think so, and I do not expect you to be, but this situation, too, I have taken into account." "What would you do?" I told her about George Sand's *Jacques*. "Would you kill yourself like he did?" I said that I did not think so and added that I would try to get George Sand's books (she had not read "him" or at least did not remember his ideas). (1: 528–29)

The emulation of George Sand's novel was supported by the popular idea of the unfairness of the double standard in the relations between the sexes. Granting his future wife the right to emotional and sexual freedom, Chernyshevsky declined it for himself, motivating his self-denial by two complementary arguments, personal and cultural:

I am the proponent of certain ideas, but by my very nature I am not capable of using these ideas in my own life, and even if I were, and even if I could take advantage of this freedom, it would be wrong to do so because I think that the proponent of freedom must not take advantage of this freedom lest it appear that he propagates these ideas in order to benefit from them. (1: 444)

Chernyshevsky added an overtone of his own to the popular idea of the double standard: the idea of "bending the stick the other way" (*teoriia peregiba palki*). Women, he argued, had to be compensated for years of disadvantage; he proposed not only giving them the right to infidelity, but making it their exclusive right. Adultery had to become the prerogative of woman. Thus, a new pattern was created at the intersection of an old cultural pattern and an individual psychological characteristic.

An echo of these ideas, which, under the influence of both Chernyshevsky's personal example and his writings, penetrated all strata of the intellectual movement of the 1860s, is found in *Crime and Punishment*. Lebeziatnikov (a caricature of the new man) expects the "rational man" Luzhin to "acquiesce if Dunia were to take a lover a month after marrying."

Chernyshevsky's premarital attitudes could well have played a role in the realization of these hypothetical situations in his own family life. That these patterns *were* realized is well known from the memoirs of contemporaries and from occasional revelations by Chernyshevsky and Olga Sokratovna. Their extraordinary marriage became a subject of widespread gossip, popular not only among contemporaries but even into the twentieth century, when Chernyshevsky became a legendary figure, an object of both reverence and ridicule. Many family stories related by Chernyshevsky's distant cousin Varvara Pypina are understandably critical of Olga Sokratovna's behavior. According to Pypina, in her old age Olga Sokratovna liked to remember the happy times of her youth:

How she would sit here surrounded by young men . . . and many men were in love with her. . . . Ivan Fyodorovich (Savitsky, a Polish emigrant, Stella) was a smart strategist: nobody ever suspected that he was my lover. . . . Only Kanashechka [Nikolai Chernyshevsky] knew: while he was writing at the window, Ivan Fyodorovich and I would be in the alcove.[32]

Chernyshevsky's predictions were realized to the last detail. Rumor held that he had not fathered his children (with the possible exception of his eldest son, Alexander). In addition to casual affairs, Olga Sokratovna apparently had a serious love affair with one of Chernyshevsky's friends—most probably, Savitsky (Sauicki), a member of the revolutionary movement—and a possible separation was discussed. Another cousin, E. N. Pypina, remembered:

I knew from Olga Sokratovna that one of Nikolai Gavrilovich's good St. Petersburg friends asked her to move in with him, and that the three of them had a discussion together. One was insistent, one was hesitant, and the third one said, "Go if you want to. I will bear you no grudge. Everyone should be free in these matters." The hesitant one finally decided not to make any changes.[33]

Olga Sokratovna passed her time in carefree amusements. Lively and cheerful, she led a life full of fun and joy, always surrounded by a crowd of noisy admirers.

Wild amusements were Olga Sokratovna's natural element. In the winter, she loved to go sleigh riding—singing, bells jingling, the whooping. One troika would try to overtake the other ones, everybody would race, and Olga Sokratovna would shout, "We'll catch up and overtake them!" and she would snatch the reins from the driver and standing in the sleigh drive the horses. And in the summer, there would be picnics. . . . Boat riding. . . . Olga Sokratovna saw life as an endless holiday arranged specially for her. She liked to be surrounded by a crowd, but it had to be a crowd of people whom she liked and who admired her and were ready to serve her. . . . O.S. told me that she liked to slip away in the middle of a dancing party and stand outside in the street, admiring the blazing windows of her apartment and saying to the passersby, "See how much fun those people are having? That's a party at the Chernyshevskys'."[34]

Chernyshevsky did not share in the festive atmosphere of his house, nor did he take part in his wife's divertissements: "The house would be full of people but Nikolai Gavrilovich would be standing in the anteroom at his lectern, writing."[35]

These boisterous amusements caused occasional problems; once, at the railroad station pavilion at Pavlovsk, Olga Sokratovna and her sister were approached and insulted by an officer who mistakenly took them for women of easy virtue. The episode had serious consequences: Chernyshevsky insisted that the officer's case be heard in a "court of honor" and wrote repeatedly to the minister of military affairs on the subject. In connection with his complaint, he had an audience with the head of the Gendarmes.[36]

This episode apparently became a popular piece of gossip in the literary circles of Petersburg. As commentators have shown, Dostoevsky used it in *The Idiot* as a model for the scandal scene involving Nastas'ia Filippovna, a "fallen woman," and her deliverer, Prince Myshkin. The scene takes place in the railroad station pavilion at Pavlovsk. In the preliminary notes for the novel, Dostoevsky explicitly referred to the episode involving Olga Sokratovna Chernyshevsky: "In the fifth part the prince's scandal must be overdone. The public insult (Ch[ernyshevsky]'s wife). Words between the prince and the aide-de-camp, almost a duel."[37]

In addition, a scene almost identical to the one involving Olga Sokratovna appeared in *Anna Karenina*. Vronsky is sent to reconcile the officers of his regiment and a titular councilor (*tituliarnyi sovetnik*) whose wife they had offended: she was taken by the officers for a woman of easy virtue. The indignant husband requested that the officers be severely punished. Chernyshevsky was a titular councilor in the civil service.

Chernyshevsky, who was apparently well aware of the state of his family life, accepted it without a word of reproach or complaint. Yet his letters to his cousin Alexander Pypin and to his close friend and patron Nikolai Nekrasov reveal some of the bitter aspects of his situation: his despair during Olga Sokratovna's second, unforeseen pregnancy, which, according to the doctors, was likely to kill her; his doubts that his wife loved him or, at least, "did not hate" him (15: 140). Olga Sokratovna confessed to a total lack of common interests with her husband: she was not interested in the world of books and ideas that was Chernyshevsky's natural element (she made several attempts at reading his articles but, wearied by boredom, could not finish them), nor was Chernyshevsky capable of sharing her life of merriment and "endless holiday." [38]

And yet this peculiar marriage was not a case of an overindulgent husband victimized by an adulterous wife. Chernyshevsky's overwhelming love and concern for his wife are well known from his numerous letters to her. Olga Sokratovna's letters to Chernyshevsky (especially several letters published only recently [39]) show that she responded to these feelings. After his arrest, Olga Sokratovna rejected his generous offer of a divorce and an opportunity to remarry (14: 589). Although Chernyshevsky made several attempts to provoke a quarrel that would lead to divorce, she resisted them all. After Chernyshevsky's release from Siberia, the couple was reunited in Astrakhan', where their life immediately resumed its previous pattern. The situation, it seems, provoked Chernyshevsky into saying: "You think life in Siberia was hard for me? No, that's the only time I was happy." [40]

Nevertheless, in Chernyshevsky's eyes, Olga Sokratovna remained a faithful wife. She upheld his theory of life and turned out to be a perfect partner for the marriage that he had designed to fulfill his ideas and personal needs. Therefore, a seemingly incongruous remark in the diary for 1853, in the middle of a long passage depicting her future infidelities, has a certain reality: "But in essence she will be a very faithful wife, faithful as only few wives are" (1: 513).

Transformations of Reality

The reality of Chernyshevsky's complicated and painful marital situation was transformed in the works of imaginative literature written in exile. A remarkably frank and naïvely direct reworking of biographical events characterizes Chernyshevsky's oral improvisations in Aleksandrovsky zavod. One of these stories, "Old Times" (*Starina*) was related by S. G. Stakhevich. The hero, a young man named Volgin (the name of the autobiographical character in *The Prologue*) seeks the hand of a well-known young lady of a small provincial town. His loved one is involved in charitable activities and sometimes receives visits from women of suspicious appearance, who are taken, by the lady's numerous jealous suitors, to be procuresses. The lady, offended by these suspicions and annoyed by the attention of the suitors, not only refrains from all attempts to clear her name but, in defiance of public opinion, behaves in such a way as to compromise herself still further. Only Volgin, who has a "very special love" for her (a love free of jealousy and demands), is convinced, and rightly so, of her innocence. She can do no wrong, he claims, for she has a "splendid nature."[41]

A variant of this story concentrates on a different aspect of the courtship: a warning from a well-wisher. A recent graduate of Petersburg University takes a position in his hometown and soon becomes engaged to a young lady of scandalous reputation. The hero is warned against this marriage by a friend and replies to the warning calmly and politely. After the friend departs, however, the hero is suddenly overcome by violent hatred for the well-wisher. He forces him into a duel and kills him.[42]

The plot is developed still further in another variant of the same story, retold by V. P. Shaganov, a fellow prisoner. A friend warns the hero against the marriage, claiming that he himself had been one of the young lady's lovers and had abandoned her because of her promiscuity. The hero murders the well-wisher then and there and disposes of the body through a hole in the ice in a river. He marries the lady, and their marriage turns out to be a happy one. The wife, who apparently loves her husband, is faithful, and the murder remains undiscovered. The hero feels no remorse for his crime; moreover, he continues to consider both himself and his victim good, decent people.[43]

Another aspect of Chernyshevsky's situation reworked in fiction was the bride's motivation for marrying. In the diary, Chernyshevsky admits that Olga Sokratovna may have been motivated by a desire for liberation from family restrictions, and that she saw in him a convenient and obedient husband who could be easily manipulated and deceived (1: 488). In a letter to Pypin from Siberia in 1878, he described the situation this way: "My dear, when I married I was quite sure that a woman who would agree to be my wife would certainly never love me. What's more, I was convinced that of all girls my wife-to-be was the least capable of loving me" (13: 138–39).

The situation is presented in quite a different light in *The Prologue*. Volgina, in a conversation with her aristocratic, handsome, and rich admirer, Nivel'zin, justifies her choice of Volgin as a marriage partner:

Uneducated as I was, I realized that from the very first conversations we had, the unimportant conversations about me, about silly little things, about my happiness: I realized the tremendous difference between him and the others. I wasn't wrong, was I? You know what people are beginning to think of him. . . . Back then people thought that he would spend his life on the couch with a book, half asleep. But I realized the full potential of his mind and his will! (13: 90)

The last component of the marriage pattern to be radically transformed in the Siberian fiction was the wife's fidelity. The main female protagonists of the two stories (the one retold by Shaganov and that of Volgina in *The Prologue*) appear to be unfaithful wives. This only seems to be the case, however. The first woman is totally reformed, and the second had been virtuous all along. Though she is always surrounded by a crowd of admirers, her eager partners in noisy amusements, and even though she enjoys the complete freedom granted to her by her husband, Volgina "loves the husband, the husband alone," and remains a faithful wife (13: 95). The diaries were used before the fact to plan future events; the Siberian fiction became a means of reworking the unsuitable reality of their fulfillment.

The Justification of Reality

Chernyshevsky and Olga Sokratovna spent a significant part of their life separated. For the 20 or so years of his Siberian confinement, letters were their only connection. The main theme of his letters to his wife is her health. He constantly inquired about her health, supplied her with endless medical advice, and urged, implored, and demanded that she lead a healthy life, seek diversions and amusements to improve her health, and spend her winters in warm places—southern Italy, Sicily, Portugal, Andalusia. These discussions turned into lengthy scientific treatises on questions of hygiene (physical and moral) and climatology. Although Chernyshevsky kept insisting that his own health was excellent, in reality Olga Sokratovna was the healthy one, while Chernyshevsky's condition was aggravated by the harsh climate and poor diet of eastern Siberia.

The key to the symbolic meaning of these discussions can be found in "The Story of One Girl" ("Istoriia odnoi devushki"), written in Siberia some time between 1864 and 1871. The work is dedicated solely to the issue of woman's health. The treatment of this issue, another aspect of the woman question, once again shows Chernyshevsky's positivist tendency to explain human nature through physiology. The main character, a young girl in a provincial Russian town, decides against marrying because of the lack of suitable candidates and lives happily with her loving parents. She soon develops "malignant paroxysms," which are described in considerable detail (in letters of the Astrakhan' period Chernyshevsky described Olga Sokratovna's hysterical outbursts in similar terms). When her mysterious illness becomes life-threatening, a local doctor diagnoses the condition as one provoked by sexual abstinence and recommends that the patient engage in sexual activity to save her life and restore her health. The prejudices of her family prevent the patient from following this advice.

In the meantime, the young lady moves to Petersburg to live with her brother, who holds more radical views of sexual morality. There she is presented with a dilemma: should she enter into extramarital sexual relationships and thus break the traditional moral code, or should she sacrifice her life to that code and die from the malignant consequences that sexual abstinence causes in the organism of a vigorous young woman? After much hesitation, the heroine gathers her courage and enters into a sexual relationship with one of her brother's friends and then with another; she bears an illegitimate child, and then another.

The native town of the heroine is Saratov, and Chernyshev-sky's family house is easily recognizable in the description of the house of the heroine's parents. Moreover, the brother is en-dowed with characteristics and biographical details that point to Alexander Pypin, in whose household Olga Sokratovna and her two children lived during Chernyshevsky's absence.

The same plot, and the same complex of ideas, is reproduced in another Siberian story, "The Quiet Voice" ("Tikhii golos"), re-told by Chernyshevsky's fellow prisoner, P. F. Nikolaev.[44] The belief that sexual abstinence is damaging for woman's health is expressed in other writings as well (see 1: 403; 13: 574, 661).

The cultural sources of Chernyshevsky's views in this area are the Enlightenment's attitudes toward sexuality, which provided a basis for utopian writings in eighteenth- and nineteenth-century France and later appeared, in modified form, in works on femi-nine physiology connected with women's emancipation. The medical articles on marriage in the *Encyclopédie* maintained that sexual deprivation causes "vapors or hysterical afflictions" in unmarried girls and widows.[45] The farfetched moral conclusions drawn from these medical notions included the idea of allowing women sexual freedom for purely humanitarian considerations.

The idea was a bold one, judging by contemporary standards. Even Belinsky as late as 1840 (the year before he became an ar-dent admirer of George Sand) was outraged by what he in-terpreted as an expression of the social teachings of the Saint-Simonians in George Sand's novels; namely, the proposition to give women the "enviable right to change husbands for reasons of health."[46]

Chernyshevsky carried these principles still further. He main-tained that not only women's health but their lives were at stake. Chernyshevsky's views on physical hygiene, however, grew out of his views on the relations between the sexes: they were domi-nated by the idea of role reversal. Beginning in the diaries, Cher-nyshevsky associated sexual activity by men with an excessive expenditure of physical energy, which would lead to premature physical decline and early death. He apparently retained these beliefs in his old age. Trying to convince Olga Sokratovna that he had enjoyed excellent health in Siberia, he argued: "I am in excellent health and I hope will continue to be so for a long time.

I did not waste it in my youth with the usual diversions of young men. I have not a single time ignored the rules of moral and physical health. Now I can see the good results of that" (14: 502).

The traditional view still dominated public opinion; despite the progress of new ideas, the physical need for sexual fulfillment was ascribed to men and to men alone. This opinion was questioned and attacked by two moralists of the age—Chernyshevsky and Tolstoy, both of whom revealed an intense personal interest in this problem.

Tolstoy expounded his views in the afterword to "The Kreutzer Sonata" ("Kreitserova sonata"; 1890): "A firm conviction, supported by false science, has established itself among all classes of our society to the effect that sexual intercourse is necessary for health, and that marriage not being always possible, sexual intercourse without marriage binding the man to nothing beyond a mere money payment, is quite natural and a thing to be encouraged." [47] This, claimed Tolstoy, was a delusion and a deception perpetrated by pseudo-scientists. As for women, sexual excess was harmful to their health and caused hysteria. One noticed, he said, that no pure maidens were ever afflicted with nerve troubles and hysteria; these were problems of married women living with their husbands, both among Russian peasants and among Jean Charcot's patients in Europe.

Chernyshevsky, however, arrived at the opposite conclusion: abstinence, though beneficial for men's health, was damaging for women's health; female hysteria resulted from sexual abstinence. This conclusion was reached through the fusion of several sources: the popular idea of the Encyclopedists and utopian socialists that women have a physical need for sexual fulfillment, a notion that received additional corroboration in the positivist cult of natural science; Chernyshevsky's theory of "bending the stick the other way," or reversal of the usual sex roles; his own ambivalent attitude toward physical love; and his guilt over a prolonged absence (predicted and programmed before his marriage).

The result was a convenient solution to his family situation. In fact, his requests and demands that Olga Sokratovna take every measure to attend to her supposedly endangered health could easily be interpreted as a license for sexual infidelity. At the same time, he tried to convince his wife that the doctrine of "good morals," which held that "a wife must be faithful," was "extremely stupid" (14: 210). Moreover, his attacks were directed against the double standard of traditional morality: "'When a girl, lacking practical experience, makes a mistake, she loses her honest name.' I think this is a very stupid idea. . . . When a young man makes mistakes that are a thousand times worse, and makes them by the dozen, he does not lose his 'honest name'" (14: 215).

In one letter, Chernyshevsky assured Olga Sokratovna of his fidelity and wrote that he intended to explicate a special "nuance" of his feeling for her in a "scholarly dissertation" that would arrive at the following conclusion: "Take care of your health" (14: 279–80). In another letter, he implored: "Remember, my dove, to follow the rules of personal hygiene. So long as you do, I will be perfectly happy" (14: 284). These rules are explicated in "The Story of One Girl." Adultery on the part of woman is a matter of hygienic necessity prescribed by science.

Another recurrent motif in Chernyshevsky's writings is the opposition of blondes and brunettes as two types of feminine beauty and character. This is undoubtedly related to a cliché of romantic literature: the division of women into virtuous blondes and passionate brunettes. One could treat this motif as a trivial literary cliché, if not for its persistent repetition, for its obvious intimate associations, and for the special importance attached to it in *What Is to Be Done?*, in which this conflict, as well as many others, receives an ultimate resolution.

In most of Chernyshevsky's belletristic works, the main female character, an alter ego of Olga Sokratovna, is a dark brunette (sometimes identified as a "non-Russian type"). The brunette usually has a counterpart: a female character with blonde hair, light skin, and blue eyes. The blonde is usually a young maiden of noble origin. The brunette admires and envies the blonde. This situation is repeated, with minor variations, in all of Chernyshevsky's novels and stories.

The motif is perhaps a fond reminder of Olga Sokratovna's

tastes.* The symbolic meaning of the motif can be illustrated through the use of the image of the blonde in *Tales Within Tales*. Various parts of the novel bear an epigraph from Goethe's poem *Die Braut von Korinth*: "Wie Schnee, so weiss und kalt wie Eis" (Like snow, so white and cold as ice). *Die Braut von Korinth* was frequently quoted in the 1860s (it appeared, for example, in the works of Herzen and Turgenev). Viewed as a treatment of the theme of the struggle between Christian asceticism and pagan hedonism, the poem was used as a projection of the contemporary situation.

The meaning Chernyshevsky attached to the epigraph is made explicit in the part of the novel called "The Daughter of Jephthah" ("Doch' Ieffaia"). The story is directed against the Christian ideal of feminine chastity, which Chernyshevsky calls "inhuman innocence." According to Chernyshevsky, attaching a positive value to purity violates human nature, expecially female nature. The association between the purity of the blonde heroine and death, which Chernyshevsky borrowed from Goethe, can be explicated as another instance of the woman's health motif. Chernyshevsky used Goethe's image of a dead maiden to create a contemporary variant of the romantic myth of love and death. In accordance with the utopian conception of sexuality (with its roots in the Enlightenment), his positivist myth of love associated death not with passion but, on the contrary, with "lovelessness," understood in a physical sense as denial of sexual fulfillment.

Chernyshevsky's brunettes embody a healthy feminine nature, which cannot accept puritanical restrictions on sexual fulfillment. In one letter from Siberia, Chernyshevsky wrote to Olga Sokratovna: "You cannot, my dear friend, become timid just as you cannot become blonde" (15: 293). This motif, which may seem like a trivial, pointless piece of rhetoric, is part of a pattern and a manifestation of Chernyshevsky's central ideas.

*Consider the following from V. A. Pypina, *Liubov' v zhizni Chernyshevskogo*, p. 111, relating a conversation between the aged Olga Sokratovna and a lady friend (Pypina witnessed the episode): "'Oh how I envied your fair locks and your azure eyes,' said Olga Sokratovna. 'Oh no, my dear,' Kapochka objected, 'no woman ever had a chance of being noticed when you were around with your fiery eyes and your wonderful raven black hair.' . . . And the old friends fell to reminiscing about their love affairs in days long past."

Fictitious Marriage: Reality–Literature–Reality

The marriage of the main characters in *What Is to Be Done?* closely follows the pattern developed in Chernyshevsky's life and in his minor belletristic works. As noted earlier, the marriage of Lopukhov and Vera Pavlovna is facilitated by a whole series of mediating steps: the teacher scheme plays an important role; the ability to speak French, play the piano, and dance furthers the process; duty obligates marriage as an act of salvation; the rival-mediator scheme is replayed, and after Lopukhov's attempts to find other ways of liberating Vera Pavlovna end in failure, their marriage becomes a matter of urgent necessity.

Just as in the case of Chernyshevsky's own marriage, the wedding is arranged for the earliest possible date—to the considerable discomfort of the fiancé (Lopukhov leaves the medical academy two months before graduation and gives up his medical career because Vera complains that she cannot endure two more months "in the cellar"). But although the wedding of Lopukhov and Vera Pavlovna is expedited, its consummation is, on the contrary, delayed until it becomes, as it were, a matter of necessity to prevent Vera Pavlovna's seduction by Kirsanov. In short, the marriage is a "fictitious" one.

It is a widespread opinion that one of Chernyshevsky's real-life models was Maria Alexandrovna Obrucheva. The daughter of a general and the sister of a radical activist, Maria Obrucheva developed a serious interest in medicine. She was tutored by Doctor Petr Bokov, who was Chernyshevsky's physician and a close friend. To give her an opportunity to study medicine professionally, a project that her family opposed, Bokov offered her a fictitious marriage. The marriage took place on August 29, 1861.[48] Subsequently the couple fell in love and consummated their marriage, though that was not part of the initial arrangement. Maria Obrucheva-Bokova then fell in love with one of her professors at the medical academy, a friend of her husband's, I. M. Sechenov (the author of the famous *Reflexes of the Brain*). The three parties settled into a ménage à trois, another popular living arrangement of the age. Later, Bokov withdrew from the ménage and eloped with a female patient, Baroness d'Adelheim, wife of the State-Secretary of the State Council T. Izmailov. The marriage between Maria Obrucheva and Sechenov lasted until his death in 1905; it was legalized, however, only in the 1880s.

The misconception that the love plot of *What Is to Be Done?* faithfully depicts the real-life situation of Petr Bokov, Maria Obrucheva, and Ivan Sechenov was, until recently, practically universal. This belief apparently appealed strongly both to contemporaries and to modern students of Chernyshevsky. Many memoirists simply equate Lopukhov and Petr Bokov, Vera Pavlovna and Maria Aleksandrovna Obrucheva, and Kirsanov and Ivan Sechenov. From memoirs, the idea of real-life prototypes penetrated, with few emendations, into annotated editions of the novel and into works of literary and historical scholarship; it became, for example, a stable part of biographies of Sechenov. Bokov, Obrucheva, and Sechenov became firmly associated with their literary shadows: these people of the sixties became the subjects of essays such as "The Heroes of *What Is to Be Done?*" and "The Heroine of the Novel *What Is to Be Done?* in Her Private Correspondence."[49]

Some authors, however, denied a real-life origin for the novel. Vasily Sleptsov (according to Ekaterina Zhukovskaia's memoirs) claimed: "It was not the novel's author who copied the type from him [Bokov], but quite the opposite; the doctor was inspired by the novel and played it out in real life: the chronology is the guarantee of this."[50] However, so strong was the fascination with the idea that the novel was taken from real life that neither Zhukovskaia herself nor the critic who prepared her memoirs for publication (Kornei Chukovsky) believed Sleptsov; the appeal to chronology was ignored.

S. A. Reiser reconstructed a chronology of the events connected with the Bokov–Obrucheva–Sechenov triangle for the 1975 annotated edition of the novel. According to him, only the fact of the fictitious marriage between Bokov and Obrucheva and, possibly, the fact that their relationship had turned into a real marriage could have been known to Chernyshevsky when he started the novel. Chernyshevsky was arrested on July 7, 1862, and worked on the novel in complete isolation in the Peter-and-Paul Fortress between December 1862 and April 4, 1863, whereas the Sechenov-Obrucheva affair, as dated by Reiser, did not start until late 1864 or early 1865.[51]

We are dealing, it seems, with a remarkable case of the mutual influence of life and literature. Chernyshevsky could well have used the case of Obrucheva and Bokov as the starting point for planning the intrigue of the novel. His real-life prototypes, who might well have recognized themselves in the characters of *What Is to Be Done?* and who had every reason to identify with them, might have taken the rest of the fictional intrigue as a model to resolve the conflict that they later encountered in their complicated family life. Even if they acted independently of the novel, their subjective experience and interpretation of events depended on a literary model that elevated the situation, despite its potentially vulgar and ugly aspects (for example, Bokov's involvements with his female patients), to the level of socially significant, and therefore appropriate and meaningful, behavior. It was in this spirit that Bokov chose to inform his mother-in-law of the new developments in his family life:

I beg you to believe me when I say that my dear unappreciated Masha and I live as befits the most peaceful married couple. . . . As an honest man, I assure you that we live in the best of relations, and if her character has brought her closer to that most wonderful of the Russian people, the dear son of our fatherland, Ivan Mikhailovich, this has only strengthened our common happiness. You can imagine the extent to which our life is happy now that Ivan Mikhailovich is a member of the family. Now, I am taking the opportunity to beg you to look on Ivan Mikhailovich as your own offspring, as I have considered myself for a long time, and I beg you not to refuse me.[52]

Having taken a real-life situation as a source of the plot of his novel, Chernyshevsky endowed it with additional meaning. He also had a powerful personal motivation: in fictitious marriage Chernyshevsky found a socially motivated and culturally appropriate form of union that involved no connubial obligations.

By and large, fictitious marriages appeared to be a contemporary—realistic—modification of the romantic idea of chaste union based on brotherly feeling (in imitation of the celibate marriages of the early Christians) that had inspired Granovsky, Herzen, Bakunin, and other Russian romantics of the 1840s. It is notable that the radical youth of the 1860s used the code word "brother" for a fictitious husband.[53] In fact, *What Is to Be Done?* pictures the marital life of Lopukhov and Vera Pavlovna in its early stages (when the marriage is still fictitious) as the ideal family arrangement, based on mutual love and dedication to a common cause and totally free of sensual attraction.

The effect of Chernyshevsky's novel was not only to increase the incidence of fictitious marriages. Subsequent cases, viewed through the prism of the literary model, became endowed with symbolic significance. For the fighters for liberation in the late 1860s and 1870s, fictitious marriage became far more than a legal convenience. It was regarded as the ideal marriage, a union that served not merely to fulfill "individual feelings and sensations" (that is, for reasons of personal happiness), but also to fulfill universal happiness—the realization of the common cause.[54]

Several striking examples of such attitudes are given in the memoirs of Sofia Kovalevskaia and other members of her circle. So strict were the circle's new moral norms that when one of its members married for love, her act was regarded by others as a "fall" and a "betrayal of ideals." The young lady had to refrain from speaking to her comrades about her matrimonial happiness and forbade her husband to show tenderness toward her in their presence.[55] Likewise, the members of the circle viewed Sofia's marriage to Vladimir Kovalevsky, during the period when it remained fictitious, as one based on ideal love, totally free of sensuality, and on shared ideals of freedom, meaningful labor, education, and science. When the Kovalevskys later succumbed, in the vocabulary of the circle, to "sensuality usually misnamed 'love,'" their friends were unanimous in their moral disapproval. Such were the real-life implications of *What Is to Be Done?*, a novel that codified the phenomenon of fictitious marriage as culturally significant.

The Triple Union

At every step leading to Chernyshevsky's marriage, a self-imposed rival played the role of mediator between him and his loved one. Even after intimacy had been established and the couple were married, the function of the mediator did not end. Chernyshevsky saw the continuing presence of a third party as ✓ an integral part of his marriage design. On the one hand, Chernyshevsky left his wife free to give her heart and body to another and even explicitly encouraged her to do so. On the other, the faithful husband planned to remain near her as a member of an "extended family." Memoirists give evidence that this design was realized in Chernyshevsky's family life, but since Chernyshevsky did not continue his diary, there is no personal record of events that could be compared with their literary modification. In his fiction, however, Chernyshevsky elaborated a design of rational adultery. The theme was a central concern in *What Is to Be Done?* In minor fictional works of the Siberian period, the scheme was brought to complete fulfillment: the ménage à trois.

Once again, the starting point for *What Is to Be Done?* was *Jacques.* George Sand's book was used as a blueprint for the plot of Chernyshevsky's novel.[56] In *What Is to Be Done?*, however, the suicide is retained only as a means of forwarding the plot: the husband's suicide leaves his wife free to marry another. But Lopukhov's suicide is faked. In the same way that his marriage with Vera Pavlovna was meant as a fictitious marriage, its dissolution is also "fictitious," a mere device to overcome legal formalities. As far as the law is concerned, Lopukhov is dead, and Vera Pavlovna is free to marry Kirsanov. In reality, Lopukhov shams suicide and flees to America. But his disappearance is only temporary. Critics have frequently overlooked an important aspect of this situation: Lopukhov is forced to this extreme measure against his will.

His original solution is to live quietly in a triple union. Even though he is aware of his wife's love for his friend and of the importance of their union for the satisfaction of those inner needs that remained unfulfilled in their marriage, Lopukhov desires to "remain a person very close to her" and to be "near her" in his daily existence.[57] But Vera Pavlovna's desire for formal social approval of her union with Kirsanov forces Lopukhov to remove himself from the scene. Rakhmetov, who embodies the ultimate positive ideal in the novel, is highly critical of this action.

In a conversation with Vera Pavlovna after Lopukhov's "suicide," he states the optimum solution:

Why all this confusion about such trivial matters? What an embarrassment to all three of you, and especially to you, Vera Pavlovna! Whereas you might all three live as in the past, as you lived a year ago, or take an apartment together, or arrange your life in any other way, according to your choice, but without any upset, and all three take tea or go to the opera together as in the past. Why these anxieties? Why these catastrophes?[58]

Lopukhov had suggested a triple union, and Rakhmetov had ardently supported him. But was it sanctioned by the author? Chernyshevsky's Siberian fiction, in many ways more explicit than his published works, testifies that it was. Several of the fictional works written or improvised in Siberia replay the marriage plot of *What Is to Be Done?*, but what remains a remote possibility in *What Is to Be Done?* is realized in several of these works. For example, in the drama *Forbidden to Others* (*Drugim nel'zia*; 1867–69), known from the accounts of several fellow prisoners, a young lady is engaged to a student. In the absence of her fiancé, she becomes the object of the impertinent attentions of a corrupt landlord. The seducer does, however, offer his hand in marriage (as Storeshnikov does in *What Is to Be Done?*). To save the young lady from an unsuitable partner and to protect her honor, another young man, a close friend of the mysteriously absent fiancé's, enters into a fictitious marriage with her. For a short while they live like brother and sister, but in the end the marriage is consummated. Suddenly the fiancé returns; because of a grave illness in the middle of his trip, he had been unable to communicate with his loved one. Restored to life, the fiancé feels that an emotional tie must still exist with the young woman. The woman returns his affection, and finds herself in love with both young men simultaneously. The husband comes forward with a solution to the conflict: a harmonious union of the three of them that eliminates the conflict without violating any of the relationships.

The solution is obvious. It would not be acceptable for other people because other people should be forbidden to do such things, but you are allowed precisely because you are a nice girl. You are a woman, but your pure feelings are those of a maiden. So please accept my solution, even though we will remember that other people should not be allowed to do such things.[59]

The moral side of the problem is eliminated by proclaiming the woman to be innocent and pure by nature: the adulterous woman is declared to be as pure as an innocent maiden.

The reservation "forbidden to others" might have been a concession to the traditional morality of the majority of his listeners (just as the compromise in *What Is to Be Done?* may have been dictated by censorship considerations). Even the radical community of political prisoners was reluctant to accept Chernyshevsky's ideas. One of his listeners, S. G. Stakhevich, argued against the permissibility of such unions from a utilitarian and positivist point of view. Since the number of men and women in the world is equal, Stakhevish argued, a woman who enjoys the attentions of two "mates" deprives another woman of a mate. Chernyshevsky responded with a counterargument based on considerations of hygiene. Since a significant portion of women were always "in a state of sexual ineligibility" because of menstruation, pregnancy, childbirth, or nursing (a problem that also troubled Tolstoy in "The Kreutzer Sonata"), "for each woman not prevented from sexual relations by physiological reasons, there is not one man in the population, but more."[60]

Another story dealing with the problem of triple unions was related by V. G. Korolenko. The heroine simultaneously loves two men. The rivals are at once similar and complementary: "Each of them, naturally, has his own peculiarities of mind and character, but all of this nature divided between them in such a way that the traits of one person complement the traits of the other."[61] As a result, the woman cannot decide between them. The two friends draw lots to decide who will marry her. The losing suitor then disappears without a trace. The love of her husband, however, does not fully satisfy the woman, and consequently her health rapidly deteriorates. Chance brings the three of them together on a remote island. The situation could develop into a case of mutual suffering and hatred and ultimately provoke murder. Why suffer and die, wonders the author, when the destruction of all three parties (which is otherwise inevitable) can be prevented by a simple and natural solution: "to live for all three, that is, to live *à trois*."[62]

But Chernyshevsky does more than present a new solution: the problem itself has been modified. The classic problem of the adultery novel is: What is to be done when the wife loves another? Such is the conflict of *Jacques*. The novelty of George Sand's treatment of the love triangle is her acknowledgment that emotions can develop over time and her acceptance of a woman's right to change husbands, which is a direct consequence of the "freedom of the heart." The initial conflict in *What Is to Be Done?* and in Chernyshevsky's Siberian stories is different: the woman loves two men simultaneously, and she needs both of them for her happiness. Vera Pavlovna and Lopukhov continue to live as tender lovers; moreover, they are closer than before. In her decisive letter to Lopukhov, Vera Pavlovna writes that although she has never been more attached to him, she cannot live without Kirsanov.[63] The connection between the protagonists is essentially triple. What is to be done in such a situation? There were, of course, literary and real-life precedents.

Triangular relationships are a recurrent and significant motif in Rousseau's *Confessions*. For Rousseau the situation illustrated his basic idea of the plurality of love: different components of an emotion can be separated and directed simultaneously at different objects (Rousseau carried this idea far beyond the traditional dichotomy of carnal desire and pure love). Because of this, the triple love union is a perfectly natural relationship. An example is the ménage of Mme de Warens, Claude Anet, and Jean-Jacques, an alliance that brought blissful happiness to all three. Jean-Jacques acknowledged that Mme de Warens needed Claude Anet for her happiness. Wishing her to be happy, he extended his affection for the woman to her lover. Jealousy and rivalry gave way to a feeling of mutual love. The three lived happily together engaged in various economic projects proposed by the energetic lady:

Thus between the three of us was established a bond perhaps unique on this earth. Our every wish and care and affection was held in common, none of them extending outside our own little circle. Our habit of living together, to the exclusion of the outer world, became so strong that if one of the three was missing from a meal or a fourth person joined us, everything was spoiled; and in spite of our private relationships even our tête-á-têtes were less delightful than our being all three together. All constraint between us was banished by our complete mutual confidence, all boredom by the fact that we were all extremely busy.[64]

But a truly ideal arrangement of relations—an emotional utopia of sorts—is developed in Rousseau's *La Nouvelle Héloïse*. In the fourth part of the novel, the teacher-lover (Saint-Preux), the husband (Wolmar), the cousin (Claire, a sort of double for Julie), and even the father (who originally ruined the union between Julie and Saint-Preux) are brought together around a uniting and harmonizing center—Julie. The harmony between the adults extends toward their children, whom Saint-Preux is to educate. An Edenic emotional harmony is restored against the background of a rationally arranged domestic economy. There follows a lengthy and precise description of how the members of this extended family run their agricultural enterprises and their household, arrange the life of their workers, spend their Sundays, and so forth.[65]

Many components of this picture appear in Chernyshevsky's novel, among them the idea of perpetual activity centered around the woman as the key to harmonious living, the communion of a shared meal as a true celebration of intimacy, and the detailed exposition of the arrangement of the household economy and the family's business enterprises. Rousseau was among the authors whose books Chernyshevsky requested in prison, and simultaneously with *What Is to Be Done?*, he was working on a Russian translation and adaptation of Rousseau's *Confessions*.[66]

But besides established literary models, Chernyshevsky had real-life experiments with marriage as examples. These, in turn, had shaped themselves through literature.

The Triple Union in a Romantic Key: Herzen

The eternal problem of the love triangle concerned Herzen both in literary work and in real life. The early novel *Who Is to*

Blame? (*Kto vinovat?*; 1847) was Herzen's contribution to the literary quest for humane and enlightened ways to deal with a wife's falling in love with another. In *Who Is to Blame?*, a love triangle—made up of Dmitry Krutsifersky, one of the first *raznochintsy* in the annals of Russian literature; his wife, Liubov' ("love"), the illegitimate daughter of a landowner whose children Krutsifersky tutored; and a wealthy gentleman, Beltov—leads to the destruction of all three. Beltov is a Russian "superfluous man": brought up by a teacher from Geneva in the best spirit of Jean-Jacques Rousseau, he has no place or purpose in Russia. Beltov's image was strongly influenced by the hero of George Sand's novel *Horace*, a weak man incapable of action. Herzen saw in him a portrait of his own generation.[67]

"Is love given to a human being by a definite measure?" wonders Beltov, who does not want to see a contradiction in Liubov's love for her husband and her love for him. Liubov' does not believe in loving two men, and yet she is appalled at the unnatural arrangement of human relations: "Were he [Beltov] my brother, I could have loved him openly. . . . How wonderfully we could have arranged the life of our small circle of four." (The fourth member of the "family circle" is the town doctor, Krupov, who serves as an intermediary for the three main characters.) But Liubov' is attached to the traditional idea of marriage, Beltov is incapable of acting decisively, and Krutsifersky is painfully humble and defenseless. As a result, at the novel's end, Liubov' is dying of consumption, Beltov goes abroad to drag out his purposeless life, and Krutsifersky takes to drinking.

Shortly after the novel's publication, the love triangle was realized in the relations between Herzen, his wife, Natalie, and Georg Herwegh, a romantic poet and notable figure in the German democratic movement.[68] The drama opened in 1848 and played itself out against the background of revolution in Europe. In the beginning, a blissful triangular friendship was established. Herzen, Natalie, and Herwegh shared a household in Geneva. Herwegh tutored Herzen's son in natural science, and Natalie gave Russian lessons to Herwegh. The only discordant note was Herwegh's strained relations with his wife, Emma, who was living with their children in Paris. Herzen, with the best intentions, tried repeatedly to harmonize the Herweghs' marriage.

A literary model for the relationship between Herzen and Herwegh (in Herzen's words, "free friendship") was found in George Sand's recently published novel, *La Petite Fadette*. This story of the tender friendship between the twin sons of a simple farmer, who complement each other to form a single inseparable whole, is a model of pastoral happiness in human relations. Having adopted the terminology of the novel, Herzen and Herwegh addressed each other as "my twin" and "my double."[69] Romantically inclined Natalie contemplated the formation of a commune of the two families ("a nest of twins") somewhere "in a quiet corner at the end of the earth" or on Lake Geneva; a project of joint emigration to America was also discussed. These plans, however, were upset by a sudden development in the relationship: Natalie Herzen and Herwegh became lovers. This fact remained unknown to Emma Herwegh for a long time and unknown to Herzen almost until the end of the drama.

Natalie resumed, even more fervently, her attempts to arrange some form of harmonious communal situation for the two families. Both Herzen and Natalie persistently invited Emma to join their triple union. In her letters to Herwegh begging him not to disclose their intimacy to Emma and Alexander, Natalie wrote: "Always, I have desired only one thing—that both families live together."[70] "Just imagine that suddenly Ogarev and Natalie [Ogarev's second wife] came to live with us and swelled our small, our holy commune still more. . . . Oh, that would be wonderful, so wonderful, so wonderful!!!![71] And after that what is the point of destroying the family! Then we would all be one family!"[72] According to Natalie, the interfamilial harmony extended to their children as well (Tata and Sasha Herzen and Horace and Ada Herwegh): "Tata and Horace love each other passionately, Sasha loves Ada, who is adorable."[73] Practical arrangements were made, the economic advantages of living *à quatre* were offered to Herzen as an additional justification for combining the two families.[74]

Of course, "the shadow of Jean-Jacques" (Natalie's words) loomed over the situation; during the life together of the three in

Geneva, with Ile Rousseau in front of their eyes, Natalie was re-reading *La Nouvelle Héloïse*. Natalie apparently saw the experience as a cultural event imbued with cosmic significance. At the height of the drama, she wrote to Herwegh (from whom she was separated because of the birth of her daughter Olga): "Sometime mankind should fall to the earth, blinded by our love as by the resurrection of Jesus Christ."[75]

Eventually, in 1850, the two families (Herzen was still in the dark; Herwegh had informed Emma of his relations with Natalie) settled together, and this immediately led to a catastrophe. Emma was embittered, and Herzen finally became aware of the true nature of the situation. In the course of the dramatic developments that followed, the "harmony" was breached with violent force. Natalie's desire to love both men was not to be realized. Herzen asked the Herweghs to leave the house (in which they lived largely at his expense); in vain Emma begged Herzen to allow Natalie to leave with the heartbroken Herwegh. Herwegh threatened to commit suicide, but Herzen remained unimpressed. In a decisive conversation between the two (related by Herzen in *My Past and Thoughts*), Herzen asked Herwegh whether he had read George Sand's *Horace*. Herwegh, who did not remember the novel, immediately ordered it.[76]

An exchange of monstrously offensive letters followed; financial indebtedness was mentioned. Plans for a duel were discussed, although Herzen preferred that Herwegh be tried in a "revolutionary court of honor" composed of representatives of the international democratic movement of which both men felt themselves to be members. In the midst of all this, in May 1851, Natalie Herzen, who was pregnant and dangerously ill throughout the final stages of the drama, died. It is evident from her letters, which remained in Herwegh's possession, that she was still passionately in love with Herwegh; Herzen, however, chose to ignore the painful reality.

The Herzen-Herwegh affair soon turned into a European-wide scandal. Herzen himself communicated his version of the story to (in his words) "our friends of the Democracy" (*nos amis de la Démocratie*). In his eyes "the Democracy" alone was entitled to judge the participants of what, to a less socially conscious mind, might have seemed a family matter. Moreover, it was obliged to render ultimate judgment. "If the Democracy is not a power, if it does not include the solidarity of all for everyone, then it is not a reality." [77]

With this objective in mind, Herzen related the circumstances in great detail to "the generals of democracy," Jules Michelet and Pierre Proudhon. He also told all to an acquaintance who was living with George Sand at the time, so that he could be judged by "the highest authority on all that pertains to woman," by someone who personified "the revolutionary conception of woman." [78] He wrote to Richard Wagner, a man who was to become in the nearest future (paraphrasing Herzen) the highest authority on all that pertained to the eternal triangle (Wagner took Herwegh's side). [79] Rumors reached Karl Marx; the great economist commented that "Herwegh not only put horns on Herzen's head, but milked him of 80,000 francs." [80] Rumors also reached the representatives of the Russian democratic movement, who allegedly accused Herzen of preventing his wife from joining Herwegh, as he was supposed to do by the democratic code of freedom of the heart. [81]

Herzen's sense of the historical significance of the affair was very strong. He wrote to Proudhon: "This is not purely and simply an individual matter." [82] When he later related his family tragedy in *My Past and Thoughts*, the story opened with a chapter entitled "The Year 1848." The dramatic events of Herzen's private life were thus related to the concurrent events of the European revolution; the personal tragedy of Natalie was presented as a phenomenon of "Christian romanticism."

Around 1857, the "recurrent triangle" replayed itself again in the life of Alexander Herzen. This time the other participants were his best friend and so-called brother, Nikolai Ogarev, and Ogarev's second wife, Natalie Tuchkova-Ogareva. Natalie Tuchkova had once been involved in an exalted, passionate friendship with Natalie Herzen, also patterned on George Sand's fiction (Natalie Tuchkova was nicknamed Consuelo). By the time of their meeting in London in 1856, the three of them, along with the departed Natalie Herzen, were already connected by intimate ties intensified through literary associations. First Herzen and Natalie Tuchkova-Ogareva (a double of his departed wife) formed a bond of sublime friendship; later, they sexually consummated their union. Herzen explained to Ogarev: "In my pure-hearted intimacy with your wife, I saw a new pledge of our trio." He continued:

A friend, a brother, could not be nearer than I am to Natalie; and I will employ all my love for you both to preserve everything. There is no power, no passion, on earth that can part you from me. That Natalie loves me very much is right and proper; that her love has assumed a certain character is not fitting for me. . . . But, My Friend, to eliminate this can be achieved only by great gentleness.[83]

Ogarev, like Natalie Herzen before him, believed in the possibility of a harmonious triple union, even in a situation in which intimacy had assumed a not entirely "pure-hearted" character. Two years later, he wrote to Herzen: "For some time I was carried away by love for you and her. I believed the dream of the union of three in a single love; and even now I believe in that possibility."[84] Ogarev then related a project to save and reform, through love and education, a "fallen woman" and her son. He found consolation in his affair with a prostitute named, in the best traditions of Christian romanticism, Mary. In the course of their relationship, Ogarev gave Mary Sutherland English grammar lessons, taught her the principles of versification, and encouraged her to read the works of Robert Owen. But the triple union of Natalie, Herzen, and Ogarev never came close to realization. The liaison between Herzen and Natalie degenerated into a perpetual drama of mutual accusations, violent emotional conflicts, struggles over children, and petty feuds, which lasted until Herzen's death in 1870. Ogarev and Mary Sutherland lived together until Ogarev's death in 1877.[85]

Regardless of whether or not Chernyshevsky and his friends knew the details of the Herzen affair (and there is very little doubt that they did, for it became common property of the European democratic movement), the ideas and symbols of the 1860s regarding marriage and adultery relied on the traditions set in the marital experiments of the radicals of the 1840s, with their dependence on romantic literary models infused with the ideals of Christian socialism. And yet the radicals of the generation of realists differed from their romantic predecessors in many ways. For contemporaries, the historical shift in the middle of the nineteenth century was a shift from romantic emotional exultation and self-indulgence divorced from reality to rational, disciplined, and carefully calculated action in which passions and desires were subjugated to the claims of shared ideology (the "common cause") and the ideals of revolutionary self-denial. There is ample evidence that, in contrast to the tragedy experienced in Herzen's circle, the model of the triple union was successfully realized by the people of the sixties.

The Triple Union in a Realistic Key: Shelgunov

A real-life example of the "realistic" approach to marriage, adultery, and the multiplicity of love, which resulted in a fulfilling triangular relationship, is the story of Nikolai Shelgunov, Liudmila Shelgunova, and Mikhail Mikhailov.[86] Nikolai Shelgunov was born in 1824 into an impoverished gentry family; an orphan, he was brought up in a closed, semi-military school for boys, educated in natural science and management, and became an officer in the Ministry of Forestry. He grew up with the consciousness of a man of the new generation. (Herzen, the illegitimate son of a wealthy aristocrat, was born in 1812, a fact that for him symbolized a connection with the era of the Napoleonic campaigns.) Shelgunov's calm and rational romance with his future wife, Liudmila Michaelis, who was his cousin, began in 1848 (the year Natalie Herzen met Herwegh). Having chosen his cousin as a suitable marriage partner, Shelgunov settled down to the long and laborious process of developing the mind of his wife-to-be through supervised readings in philosophy and to his own careful deliberations on the problems of love and marital relations.

Before the engagement was formalized, Shelgunov declared his intention to grant his future wife complete marital freedom:

The marriage that bound us might unbind us as well, and you would be free. . . . You could choose yourself a new husband, and could enjoy whatever happiness is possible on the earth with him and not think of me. You will not have to worry about providing for life. I will take care of you, and need will not darken the door of the home in which you live.[87]

If the wife should decide that it was better to return to her husband, she was made to feel that such a move would only make him even happier. Like Chernyshevsky, Shelgunov graciously offered his wife, the weaker party, the dominant position in the family for the sake of equality.

The marriage took place in 1850, but its consummation was delayed. Like Herzen, Shelgunov confessed to his wife-to-be that the "material" bond between spouses had much less attraction and significance for him than the spiritual bond. "What should I do?" he asked himself. "One need not be a prophet to guess that flesh would get the better of the spirit."[88] But Shelgunov withstood the temptations of the flesh much longer than Herzen. Liudmila Shelgunova wrote of the first three years of their marriage, which were spent peacefully in the provincial town of Samara: "Nikolai Vasil'evich and I remained our former idealistic selves; we came out of our rooms completely dressed and continued to use *vy* [the formal form of address]."[89] In the summer of 1853 (at the same time as the Chernyshevskys), the Shelgunovs moved to Petersburg. Like Olga Sokratovna, Liudmila Shelgunova was immediately surrounded by a noisy crowd of admirers and actively participated in the life of the literary salons.

At a masked ball in the winter of 1855–56, she met Mikhail Mikhailov, a young poet and publicist close to the *Contemporary*. Mikhailov soon became her faithful lover and Nikolai Shelgunov's tender friend. In accordance with the cultural code, the woman played a decisive role in Mikhailov's spiritual rebirth and his subsequent social activity and revolutionary martyrdom. What followed was, according to many memoirists and to the letters of the three participants, an idyllic union. The three settled peacefully in one apartment and spent most of their time together; they traveled *à trois* and jointly raised the son of Liudmila and Mikhailov (named after his father, Mikhail, the boy bore the surname Shelgunov).

Selfless social activity accompanied their personal happiness;

the three collaborated politically. A trip to France brought them in touch with current developments in the woman question. On their return to Petersburg, Mikhailov wrote and published in the *Contemporary* an article entitled "Women, Their Education and Their Significance in Society" ("Zhenshchiny, ikh vospitanie i znachenie v obshchestve"; 1860), which, in Shelgunov's words, "produced an earthquake in Russian minds."[90] In this article, Mikhailov argued for equal education and equal marital status for women, and championed the family (he was not sympathetic toward divorce and family dissolution), protesting the practice of vulgar adultery—"Balzacian family life." Mikhailov was thoroughly realistic and practical in his approach to the issue of love, dismissing with dismay the outmoded idea of the role of romantic novels in the education of feelings; he treated George Sand as a transitory phenomenon.[91]

In 1856, during their first trip abroad, the Shelgunovs read Herzen (whom Liudmila's mother had known in Viatka in 1835), and his works affected their whole life. In 1859 in London, the Shelgunovs and Mikhailov visited Herzen and shared a memorable supper with him and the Ogarevs. Liudmila compared the occasion to the pilgrimage of Moslems to the sanctuary of the prophet.[92] On their return to Petersburg, Shelgunov (with the possible collaboration of his wife) composed a pamphlet entitled "To the Young Generation" ("K molodomu pokoleniiu"), which was printed in London in Herzen's *Free Russian Press*, smuggled into Russia, and widely distributed by Mikhailov.

In September 1861, Mikhailov was arrested as the suspected author of "To the Young Generation." He promptly confessed, claimed sole responsibility for the pamphlet to protect Nikolai and Liudmila, and was tried and sentenced to exile in Siberia. At the insistence of Nikolai Shelgunov, husband and wife (and little Mikhail) followed Mikhailov to Siberia (Chernyshevsky approved of their decision). In Irkutsk, the Shelgunovs were arrested and returned to Petersburg. Nikolai was then put on trial, and Liudmila was set free.

With Mikhailov in exile near Irkutsk (where he died in 1865) and Shelgunov imprisoned in the Peter-and-Paul Fortress, Liudmila Shelgunova left the country with her son and settled in Geneva. There, in the circle of the Russian political émigrés, she soon formed a liaison with a member of the revolutionary movement, Alexander Serno-Solov'evich, a reverent follower of Chernyshevsky's, who had been introduced to her in Petersburg by Chernyshevsky. A son was born to them and given the name Nikolai in honor of Shelgunov. Little Nikolai was soon sent to the remote region of Russia where Shelgunov lived in exile and left there under the care of his nominal father. A year later, in 1866, Liudmila Shelgunova decided it was better to return to her husband, and a daughter, Liudmila, was born to the Shelgunovs.

"Whether they lived together or apart," remarked a memoirist, "they always remained the best of friends."[93] On the fifteenth anniversary of their wedding, Shelgunov wrote, from exile, to his wife in Geneva:

> My darling, we really do have some right [to celebrate our wedding day] because, if not in the beginning, then later, when we developed and matured, we were able to separate our lives and to create the kind of happiness that is given to only a few and that never will be given to the many as long as our normal couples continue in that witty Turkish worldview in which they are now to be found.[94]

The New Meaning of Adultery

In developing the marriage pattern in *What Is to Be Done?*, Chernyshevsky relied on many literary sources as well as on real-life attempts at their realization that were widely known in Russia. The blending of different sources, with their different semantic potentials, produced a unique combination. Chernyshevsky joined the plot of George Sand's *Jacques* to the emotional situation of Rousseau's *Confessions* and reinterpreted the starting point of adultery as a situation of emotional ambivalence, proposing the harmonious union of three protagonists as a solution.

Yet another important literary source, which provided an additional justification for such a solution, was found in the sexual utopias of eighteenth- and nineteenth-century France. The utilitarian calculations of the hygienic foundation of adultery in the conversation between Chernyshevsky and Stakhevich echo Fourier's discussion of the "egoist love called fidelity." Women, argued Fourier, have a temperament suited to the fulfillment of the sexual needs of more than one man. His estimation was three to four men at a time, or ten thousand men in thirty years of "philanthropic service." This service was described as a "noble" role.[95] Fourier's ideas were presaged in the eighteenth-century utopian novels that came into fashion after the discovery of the so-called Blessed Isles of the South Seas. Set in a climate that, on the one hand, made hard work unnecessary and provided leisure and, on the other, stimulated passion, these utopias concentrated on the arrangement of sexual relations. Exotic warm countries were depicted as places where polygamous and polyandrous arrangements based on woman's special aptitude for "plurality" were accepted as natural and rational family units.[96]

It was probably through this tradition that the association of warm climates and exotic places with sexual fulfillment became implanted in Chernyshevsky's consciousness. This connection stood behind the woman's health motif of his Siberian letters, in which he urged Olga Sokratovna to improve her health by spending the winter in some exotic southern country (a most improbable concept were one to understand it literally and not symbolically). These novels prompted Chernyshevsky to set a Siberian story about the resolution of a love triangle on an island in a distant sea.

Utopian ideas with a hygienic twist struck a chord with the men of the sixties, who had been brought up on the positivist cult of natural science, and these ideas were combined with the scheme of the adultery novel. Thus Chernyshevsky's marriage pattern is essentially a triple union (or a combination of two love triangles), but he does not give a woman a license to the services of three, four, or ten thousand men.

Chernyshevsky adapted a variety of cultural materials to his own needs—the needs of a concrete member of a specific social milieu in a particular historical era. It is important not to overlook the fact that he reinterpreted the meaning of the various elements of the existing patterns in his sources and redistributed the accents.

Thus, Chernyshevsky, unlike Fourier (and like his contemporary Shelgunov), was concerned primarily with the woman's and not the man's needs. But he was also distressed by the man's inability to form a harmonious alliance with a woman and to satisfy her demands (this was both a matter of personal idiosyncrasy and part of the superfluous man complex). Unlike Rousseau, he was concerned not with the plurality of love but with the inadequacy and weakness of feeling (a problem neither Herzen nor Shelgunov had had to face in their private lives). For Chernyshevsky, the third party is neither an obstacle to the happiness of the two people nor an optional presence. He is an absolute necessity, required to bring two people together and stabilize a marriage. He is the husband's "magic helper," an intermediary between a man and a woman, and, as such, is the husband's mirror image.

This is made explicit in the "island story." Individually, neither of the two men is able to satisfy the emotional and sexual needs of the woman, which, were they to remain ungratified, would eventually cause her death. Being brought together around a harmonizing female, the doubles complement each other and form a single whole. The triple union not only satisfies the woman's desire, it also fulfills the man's need to depend on another.

A closer look at *What Is to Be Done?* reveals the same pattern. Lopukhov is an inadequate husband. The difficulty is described as a difference in "temperament" that makes Lopukhov an unsuitable partner for Vera Pavlovna. The notion of temperament includes a capacity for intimacy, energy, and vivacity; a taste for entertainment (with all the symbolic connotations of this theme); and, last but not least, sexual vigor.

Kirsanov is Lopukhov's double: "In general they acted so much in concert that one meeting them separately would have taken them for men of the same character. But when one saw them together, it then became plain that, although both were very serious and very open people, Lopukhov was a little more reserved, and his companion a little more expansive."[97]

The more sociable and vivacious Kirsanov complements Lopukhov to form a desired whole. At the beginning of Kirsanov's involvement with Vera Pavlovna, he serves as a mediator be-

tween Lopukhov and his wife. The marriage is sexually consummated as a result of his intervention. Kirsanov's passion for Vera
Pavlovna awakens her sensuality and prompts her to initiate
sexual relations with her husband. Kirsanov is proud of the role
he played: "He brought them together. Yes, indeed, he brought
them together." [98] Lopukhov welcomes the intermediary: in
many ways the third party catalyzes the marriage into a fulfilling
arrangement. But Kirsanov also relieves the husband of the burden of unbearable responsibility. In a letter to Vera Pavlovna and
Kirsanov after his disappearance, Lopukhov explains, with total
frankness, how relieved he was to discover that his wife loved,
and was loved by, another. The "rival" released him from the
obligation to give Vera Pavlovna the attention for which his temperament was quite unsuitable: "I saw that I was to be free from
coercion." [99]

In removing himself from the scene, Lopukhov, in turn, serves
as a mediator between Vera Pavlovna and Kirsanov. The two of
them are brought together at the cost of his disappearance. As
always in Chernyshevsky's texts, however, "the third" miraculously reappears. After a period of absence in America, Lopukhov is "reborn"; he returns to Russia under an assumed name,
and soon remarries. The heroes settle together in a single family
unit, though this time not *à trois* but *à quatre*, like the participants in the Herzen-Herwegh affair.

The presence of the third member of the ménage à trois leads
not to the ruin but, on the contrary, to the establishment of a
family unit. Mediating between husband and wife, the lover
fulfills an essential and positive function in their marriage. In a
sense, Chernyshevsky equates the notion of marriage with the
triple (or multiple) union: love relationships unite not two people
but at least three people. Such is, I believe, the meaning of the
adultery theme in *What Is to Be Done?*

Literary Parallels: Tolstoy and Dostoevsky

The reader who saw in *What Is to Be Done?* another adultery
novel and sought in it a solution to the eternal problem of the
love triangle was likely to be disappointed. Herzen was one

such reader. The novel came to his attention in 1867, when it appeared in a second edition in Geneva. "This novel," Herzen wrote to Ogarev, "is a remarkable commentary on everything that happened in 1860–67, and the seeds of evil are also there."[100] Over the next several months, he mentioned *What Is to Be Done?* eleven times in his letters to Ogarev. At the time, Herzen was still looking for a way to resolve the painful relationship between himself and Natalie and Nikolai Ogarev; the novel evoked the strongest emotions in Herzen, but it brought him no consolation. Referring to their situation, he wrote to Ogarev: "Neither you nor Chernyshevsky in his novel has resolved anything in this problem."[101]

Another such reader was Lev Tolstoy. In *Anna Karenina* (written between 1873 and 1877), Tolstoy made many references and allusions to the woman question, to nihilism, and to *What Is to Be Done?*, which he apparently considered a nihilist solution to the problem of adultery and the love triangle. Originally Tolstoy planned a direct polemic with the nihilists, and in the preliminary materials and the drafts of the novel, nihilists and nihilist literature are present at many important junctures in the plot.[102]

During his trip to Moscow, for example, Karenin attempts to find a solution to his personal situation in literature. Reading novels, he engages, in Tolstoy's words, in "a study of the question" (*izuchaet vopros*)—a mocking reference to the peculiar atmosphere of the 1860s, when, in the spirit of positivism, concrete problems of life were approached as matters of "scientific" inquiry and points of public discussion: "Constantly reading novels. Studying the question. Everything is impossible."[103] Karenin then meets a nihilist and listens to his advice; in a variant text, a decisive conversation with a nihilist occurs during Karenin's return trip to Petersburg, in a railroad car (the railroad is a stable symbol of evil in the novel).[104] In the early drafts, after Anna's separation from Karenin, she is depicted as surrounded by nihilists, who are represented by a circle of ill-mannered artists: "badly brought-up writers, musicians, painters, who did not know how to thank her for tea when she served it to them."[105] An obvious allusion to *What Is to Be Done?* appears in the scene of Karenin's visit to the Oblonskys. "What is to be done? What is to be done?" asks Dolly, and Karenin replies: "It's impossible to live *à trois*." [106]

I believe that the final version of the novel also makes reference to Chernyshevsky's novel. At the beginning of her affair with Vronsky, Anna is haunted by a dream that Aleksei Aleksandrovich Karenin and Aleksei Vronsky (the rivals are given the same name) are her husbands simultaneously. Karenin is kissing her hands, saying: "How happy we are now!" And Anna, laughing, marvels that the situation once seemed so difficult to her. The solution is so simple, and now all of them are happy and contented. But this dream torments her like a nightmare, and she wakes in horror.

The scene of "Anna Karenina's first dream" can be viewed as a literary response to the resolution of the love triangle in Chernyshevsky's *What Is to Be Done?*, a response offered by a member of the same generation who took a different ideological position on the same set of problems and themes.

Almost simultaneously with the Geneva edition of *What Is to Be Done?*, which renewed interest in the novel, there appeared in the first four issues of the *Russian Messenger* for 1868 Fedor Dostoevsky's novel *The Idiot*. One of the central conflicts of the novel is the love triangle. In *The Idiot*, the situation of a woman caught between two men, the triangular relationship of Rogozhin, Nastas'ia Filippovna, and Myshkin, provokes murder and results in the ultimate destruction of all three (exactly the outcome discussed as an easily avoided possibility in Chernyshevsky's "island story" written in Siberia). The connection between the outcomes of the love triangle in the two novels must have seemed obvious to the contemporary reader, especially in light of the prominence of the nihilist theme in *The Idiot*. Thus, for Herzen the two novels were somehow connected; reproaching Ogarev for not having reread *What Is to Be Done?*, he remarked that Ogarev preferred to read *The Idiot* instead. [107]

In fact, the affinity between *What Is to Be Done?* and *The Idiot* is closer and deeper than that between *What Is to Be Done?* and *Anna Karenina*: in the first two works, the essence of the conflict is not that of the standard adultery novel. Like Chernyshevsky,

Dostoevsky is concerned primarily with the triangular, mediated structure of love as such and with the triangular structure as a basis for human relations. Rogozhin and Myshkin are both essential for the relationship, as are Lopukhov and Kirsanov. And, as if to affirm the general principle of mediated love, Myshkin is also caught between two women: Nastas'ia Filippovna and Aglaia. "So it seems you want to love both?" asks a bewildered Evgeny Petrovich. Myshkin answers in exultation, "O yes, yes!" As many students of Dostoevsky have noted, in all of his novels either the female protagonist stands between two male protagonists or the male protagonist stands between two female protagonists. This situation has striking biographical parallels in Dostoevsky's relationships with Maria Isaeva and Vergunov, and in his affair with Polina Suslova.[108] The basic principle of the "triplicity of love" is expounded with maximum clarity in *The Eternal Husband* (*Vechnyi muzh*; 1870) for the "eternal husband," Trussotsky, a lover is essential as a guarantee of a love bond. As one scholar has maintained, "the triplicity of human interrelations is affirmed by Dostoevsky as a psychological law."[109] In this sense, *The Idiot* parallels *What Is to Be Done?*

A Russian at a Rendezvous: Collectivity in Love

Far from solving the problem of the love triangle and adultery as a threat to marriage, *What Is to Be Done?* presented the Russian reading public with a possible solution to a different problem of central importance at the time: how to bring a man in contact with a woman. This problem—part of the Russian complex of the superfluous man—was developed in the novels of Turgenev, where, in the words of one student of the adultery novel, the question of adultery gave way to "the basic desire to avoid the whole issue of marriage as a personal confrontation between two people."[110] Indeed, as has been noted, a lack of passion hampered the protagonists of Russian novels of the 1840s–60s in "their emulation of Western romantic love."[111] Chernyshevsky defined and analyzed this problem in his famous article "A Russian at a Rendezvous" ("Russkii chelovek na rendez-vous"; 1858).

The subject of the article is Turgenev's novel *Asia* and its basic conflict: the male protagonist unable to accept the challenge of love. For Chernyshevsky, the hero's main problem is "a malignant weakness of character," the inability to make a decision and act. These qualities are the "epidemic illness of our age." From the level of personal deficiency, which reveals itself in the way Turgenev's hero fails in his confrontation with a woman, Chernyshevsky projects the problem to a social level: "Let us forget the questions of erotic love. The contemporary reader has no time for them because he is involved with the questions of administrative and judiciary reform, the question of finance, and of the liberation of the serfs" (5: 166). On the social level, the question becomes an allegorical representation of the weakness and indecisiveness of Russian society, with its liberal illusions, in the face of the needs of the country and the challenge of social change.

In *What Is to Be Done?*, this theme (and the idea of the complementariness of the personal and social) is developed further. The plot of the novel is an extended allegory of the social question. In accordance with a cultural tradition that associated stability in marriage with the stability of society at large, Chernyshevsky proposed to make the rearrangement of family life into the basis for the rearrangement of society—a point that did not escape contemporary readers. But contrary to the opinion of Chernyshevsky's critics, the form of adultery advocated in the novel was not intended to undermine or destroy society. What appeared as a form of adultery—in the words of one scholar, "a presence of negativity within the social structure"[112]—was for Chernyshevsky the foundation for emotional and social harmony and equilibrium. This equilibrium is reached through the triumph of the principle of mediation. The consistent application of this principle eliminates all personal confrontations and individual responsibilities, reconciles all oppositions in human relations, and diffuses all authority. The key to bliss lies in the presence of a third party between any two people, a triangular structure at the core of any union.

As mentioned earlier, Chernyshevsky found a blueprint for the harmonious arrangement of human relations, with its far-reaching social and economic consequences, in Rousseau's *La Nouvelle Héloïse*, the same book that inspired the ill-fated experiment of Natalie Herzen and Herwegh. The picture of the final union of Vera Pavlovna, Kirsanov, Lopukhov, and Katia Polozova echoes the resolution of the conflict in Rousseau's novel. After his "resurrection," Lopukhov marries Katia Polozova, a double of Vera Pavlovna in the same way that Kirsanov is a double of Lopukhov. The two women mirror each other's qualities. Vera is a brunette; Katia is a blonde. Katia is quiet; Vera is expansive. Katia owes her life to Kirsanov; Vera was saved by Lopukhov. The symmetry is total. The four people complement each other and form a single whole. Their coming together—emotionally, economically, physically (the two couples share a household)—creates harmony and a blissful state of emotional integrity unequaled in any other arrangement of human relations. And unlike the situation in *La Nouvelle Héloïse*, the harmony remains undisturbed by any further developments.

Chernyshevsky intended this arrangement to serve as the prototype of a new social arrangement, a harmonious paradise on earth based on the application of the principle of collectivity to all areas of human life, private and public, as presented in the picture of the communal society of the future in the fourth dream of Vera Pavlovna.[113] Chernyshevsky's critics (among them Dostoevsky) were in error in maintaining that both the family pattern and the social utopia proposed by Chernyshevsky totally disregarded human feelings. On the contrary, the social principle of collectivity had a firm psychological foundation: social harmony was viewed as an extension of family harmony, which was itself the result of the practical realization of the belief that love—a mediated emotion—was essentially of a collective nature.[114]

THREE

The Embodiment of the Model: Texts

The powerful emotional release provided by the "reconciliation with reality" that Chernyshevsky experienced through his marriage was systematically explicated and objectified in Chernyshevsky's writings. The task involved pointing out concrete ways for attaining a sense of conviction about the world and designing mental devices to control reality. The first attempts were connected with Chernyshevsky's master's dissertation, "Aesthetic Relations of Art to Reality" ("Esteticheskie otnosheniia iskusstva k deistvitel'nosti"; 1853), which addressed the issue of reality and treated it in metaphysical terms. In scholarly articles written during the next ten years, Chernyshevsky continued experimenting with various intellectual instruments that could be used to regulate and direct the apprehension of the external world. At this stage, he was also experimenting with different professional roles that would provide a channel to convey his system to society. In the end, his model for dealing with reality was embodied in his main novel, *What Is to Be Done?* (1863).

Dissertation: Ideal and Reality

In May 1853, a few weeks after his wedding, Chernyshevsky returned to St. Petersburg. In full accord with his expectations, he immediately plunged into action and took up preparations for a serious professional career. At this stage, he envisioned an academic career as a professor at Petersburg University, and he started working on his master's thesis, completing it within several months in the fall of 1853.

As far as its philosophical roots are concerned, the work is a product of the Left-Hegelian aesthetic school and was heavily influenced by Feuerbach. Among its other direct sources were the Russian followers of this school: Valerian Maikov, after 1846 the main critic for *Notes of the Fatherland* (*Otechestvennye zapiski*), and Vissarion Belinsky, whose influence, however, was more pronounced later, in the period of Chernyshevsky's work on the *Contemporary*.[1]

The dissertation was intended as Chernyshevsky's philosophical credo and a statement of the new materialistic aesthetics. Its reception as such by enthusiastic radical youth created many problems for the young degree candidate. Reality, Chernyshevsky proclaimed, is superior to the ideal. Therefore, real life is superior to art. From this, it follows that beauty is to be found not in art but in real life: "Beauty is life" (*Prekrasnoe est' zhizn'*).

The dissertation reflects a new stage in Chernyshevsky's relation to reality, attained in the act of marriage. In the dissertation, he re-experienced a reconciliation with reality through a rejection of idealism performed at the level of metaphysical abstraction, but the work was directly related to his personal experience of the preceding period. A comparison of the dissertation with the diaries reveals some striking interconnections.

First, Chernyshevsky's rejection of idealism in favor of reality is expressed through the rejection of the search for the ideal: "The opinion that man must always have 'perfection' is a fantastic one." Striving for absolute perfection, a combination of all possible virtues devoid of any faults, is the sign of a cold or empty heart, Chernyshevsky claims, and can only be regarded as pathological. Fantasy, which sees flaws in everything and is never satisfied with anything, should be regarded as "morbid" (*boleznennaia*); a man of healthy mind (*zdorovyi chelovek*) does not reproach reality for not being "as it should be." When a man is not satisfied, he can indulge his imagination, but in a healthy man, the drive for perfection ceases when gratification is achieved in reality: "Dreaming whips up desire to fever heat only when wholesome, even though fairly simple, food is lacking. This is a fact proved by the whole course of human history and experienced by every man who has seen life and has watched himself" (2: 36; *318*).[2]

This idea, derived from Maikov's interpretation of Feuerbach's epistemology,[3] deeply impressed Chernyshevsky in his student years (1: 248), and he remained true to it in the dissertation. As a true positivist, he appealed to concrete personal experience— experience reflected in his diaries. The diaries held the misery, poverty, and loneliness of his student years, life devoid of sensual gratification, when he indulged in the "feverish" fantasies of an unhealthy imagination desiring a woman who would have a nose and a brow exactly "the way it should be," a woman of genius without equal in history. At the same time, there was his emotional deficiency, which Chernyshevsky blamed on the abnormality of his development; because he had not experienced "that which was experienced by the majority of young men," his development had taken an unnatural course (1: 49–50).

Throughout the dissertation, beauty as an aesthetic category is identified with the notion of feminine beauty. Thus, Chernyshevsky writes: "The sensation that beauty rouses in man is serene joy, like that which fills us in the presence of someone we love. We disinterestedly love beauty, we admire it, it fills us with joy as the one we love fills us with joy" (2: 9; *286*).

The assertion that the sensation beauty aroused in man is comparable to that which fills a person in the presence of someone dear to him is supported by a purely rhetorical argument. Chernyshevsky claims: *"My liubim prekrasnoe"* ("we love beauty"). He then adds: *"My liubuemsia na nego"* ("we admire it"). From this it follows that beauty is love, or even love for woman. At the same time, Chernyshevsky comments that the most general thing that men love is "life." And it "seems" to him that "beauty is also life." Throughout the rest of the dissertation, Chernyshevsky conducts his search for beauty predominantly in the realm of feminine beauty, which stands for life or reality.

For some readers, this identification had a connection to Chernyshevsky's life. Thus, his granddaughter N. M. Chernyshev-skaia commented: "The image of Olga Sokratovna is present between the lines of these pages as the expression of the fundamental thesis 'beauty is life.'" The fact did not escape the attention of young Chernyshevsky's academic adviser, Professor A. V. Nikitenko, who wrote in the margin: "Too much about love."[4]

After rejecting the practice of measuring reality against an abstract ideal, Chernyshevsky proceeds to denounce other mental devices to which he had resorted before his marriage. With a note of bitterness, he admits that looking for a woman of unsurpassed beauty was fruitless: "There is only one most beautiful woman in the world; where could she be found?" (2: 40; 322). He rejects the notion that separate parts could be imperfect in an otherwise ideal face:

As a rule, unless a face is mutilated, all the parts harmonize so well that to disturb them would mean spoiling the beauty of the face. This we know from comparative anatomy. True, one very often hears the remark: "how beautiful that face would be if the nose were slightly tipped, if the lips were a little thinner," and so forth. I have not the least doubt that sometimes all the features of a face may be beautiful except one, but I think that usually, or it would be more correct to say, nearly always, such dissatisfaction is due either to inability to appreciate harmony, or to caprice bordering on lack of true and effective ability and need to enjoy beauty. (2: 56; 340)

This long argument contains obvious allusions to those diary entries in which Chernyshevsky discussed his fears that one or another part of his beloved's face was not perfect (the nose or the line between the chin and the neck seemed "not as they should have been"). In the dissertation, he explains such practices as the result of a deficiency of aesthetic feeling, an emotional handicap he frequently ascribed to himself. He denounces the comparison of a feminine face with a portrait as a sample of ideal beauty. "What, is a painted or a daguerreotype portrait beautiful and a living face not?" (2: 45; 327), he exclaims, as if arguing with himself before his marriage.

That a work of art cannot compare with a living human face in beauty of features can be proved with mathematical exactitude. It is well known that in art, execution is always far below the ideal that exists in the artist's imagination; but this ideal cannot possibly be superior in beauty to those human beings the artist had the opportunity to see. (2: 56; *339*)

The absurdity of the notions he once held is declared to be a fact of common knowledge (*izvestno*), established beyond any doubt and, more important, proved through the objectivity of science (comparative anatomy or even mathematics).

In the dissertation, reality is evaluated as something infinitely superior to the ideal. And yet Chernyshevsky admits that men sometimes "presume" that art impresses them more than reality. This aberration of consciousness he explains away on the following argument: "Reality presents itself to our eyes independently of our will, most often at inopportune times. Very often we go out, to a party, with no intention of admiring human beauty" (2: 74; *361*).

Chernyshevsky himself was one of those rare people who observe reality with the deliberateness of an art critic evaluating a work of art; he would set off on walks for the specific purpose of observing human beauty. And in his opinion, the spontaneity of perception of real life and the fact that emotions exist outside the sphere of volition give art the advantage over reality.

For Chernyshevsky, art represents a sphere of positive assurance, in which quality is guaranteed by the authority of society. By contrast, vis-à-vis reality, man appears isolated, confused, and bewildered; he is disoriented and disarmed:

Life presents special phenomena for each individual which others do not see, and on which, therefore, judgement is not pronounced by society as a whole, whereas works of art are judged by the court of public opinion. The beauty and grandeur of real life rarely presents itself to us with a label on it, and few people can note and appreciate a thing that is not publicly talked about. The phenomena of reality are gold ingots without a hallmark. (2: 75; *361–62*)

The function of art is to provide a seal of quality for the phenomena of reality: to pronounce an ultimate judgment on them, confirming their existence and worth. In the end, Chernyshevsky completes the circle: life is evaluated and subsequently experienced by projecting real-life phenomena onto art.

Circular arguments are not uncommon in the dissertation. For example, Chernyshevsky begins by maintaining that life and not art is the true and ultimate expression of beauty. Then, wanting to demonstrate that the notion of beauty is dependent on real-life experience, he contrasts the peasant and aristocratic ideals of feminine beauty (he is already, without noticing it, operating with the ideal). For the common people, he maintains, the attributes of beauty are a sturdy build and the rosy cheeks associated with hard work and fresh air. For the common people, an "ethereal" society beauty would be decidedly plain and even disgusting: the result of illness or a "sad lot." In short, he declares, in the descriptions of feminine beauty in Russian folk songs one cannot find a single attribute of beauty that does not express robust health. He finds his example not in real life but in art—in folk songs. He then describes society's ideal of beauty and quotes as an example a ballad by Zhukovsky (2: 10–11; *287–88*). Moreover, he uses Shakespeare's characters (Julius Caesar, Othello, Desdemona, Ophelia) to illustrate the notions of the tragic and of the lofty *in reality* (2: 20; *298–99*). Thus, reality merges with literature.

In fact, the circular argument in which reality is declared to be ideal and, by the same token, the ideal is reality is already implicit in the initial thesis of the dissertation: "Beauty is life; beautiful is that being in which we see life as it should be according to our conceptions" (2: 10; *287*). As a result of a whole chain of identifications and substitutions, Chernyshevsky concludes that reality = woman (love for woman) = beauty (feminine beauty) = ideal (ideal beauty) = art/literature.

Life–Literature–Science

According to the doctrine expounded in Chernyshevsky's dissertation, the function of literature is to evaluate (and explain) the phenomena of real life, thereby making them accessible to human understanding and catalyzing action; literature thus serves as an intermediary between man and reality. But by representing and explaining life, literature also serves as a "medium" between living people and the highest authority on the phenomena of reality, "pure abstract science" (4: 5). This idea was introduced in Chernyshevsky's work on Lessing (1856), a person with whom he clearly identified.[5] If the world of belles lettres presented a more secure and accessible field of action than reality, the world of pure abstract science proved to be still another plane of existence on which security and trustworthiness, as well as the ease of action associated with them, could be easily achieved. In science—a realm of relations between actual objects expressed in the clear and unequivocal form of mathematical calculations and formulas—Chernyshevsky found a universal mechanism for resolving conflicts.

Chernyshevsky frequently introduced everyday problems with personal connotations, such as marital relations and even digestion, into his articles. Transformed into extended analogies of scientific problems, these situations were then resolved through a system of scientific arguments. A typical example of this process is the spendthrift wife in a work entitled "Economic Activity and Legislation" ("Ekonomicheskaia deiatel'nost' i zakonodatel'stvo"; 1859). Chernyshevsky starts by listing three measures necessary to establish a just social order. From these three measures, as an example, he picks one ("any one, say, the second"). This randomly picked measure is "abolishing the attraction of vices," and of the many possible vices, one is taken at random—squandering. To illustrate the consequences of squandering for the social order, Chernyshevsky proceeds to discuss a particular situation: the extravagant spending of a vain wife who is killing her indulgent and hardworking husband. The husband of the spendthrift wife, not wanting to "disappoint his wife, works beyond endurance, and is dying of consumption" (5: 585).

This situation is introduced, remarkably, through a reference to a literary text, Nekrasov's poem "Masha," which is then treated as a real-life example. The personal connection is obvious here, for this poem was the object of a painful incident in Chernyshevsky's family life. Olga Sokratovna assumed that Nekrasov had her in mind when he pictured the extravagances of Masha and the suffering of her overindulgent husband. Her indignation was not easily appeased (see 15: 352). Trying to console Olga Sokratovna, Chernyshevsky argued—correctly—that the poem had been written before Nekrasov became acquainted with the Chernyshevsky family. Still, Olga Sokratovna had good reason to believe that she could be identified with Nekrasov's Masha.

In real life, Chernyshevsky was unable to resolve this problem, which continued even after his return from Siberia. However, the solution to the literary modification of the problem was quite clear to Chernyshevsky the political economist. The reasons for the wife's spending are clear in Nekrasov's poem: her envy of a wealthier friend, the bad influence of her corrupt family, and the defects of her upbringing. To solve the problem, the government has merely to abolish these factors, thus gaining control over the vain wives of its subjects:

In order to stop the squandering, all property over a certain amount should be confiscated. In order to abolish family pride, last names should be outlawed, and the subjects should be identified by numbers. In order to improve the upbringing of children, all children should be removed from their homes at the age of five or six and placed in some special military schools for small children. (5: 586)

In this "work of science," Chernyshevsky deals with a painful phenomenon of real life by means of the following strategy. First, he substitutes literature for reality (in a literary text, at the very least, the facts are at hand, and they can be evaluated), and then he regains complete control over reality by transforming the initial problem into an object of scholarly abstraction.

Chernyshevsky also addresses the problem of a spendthrift wife in, among other works of fiction, *The Prologue*. In the sphere of belles lettres, the conflict is resolved simply by reworking the situation in a desirable direction: Volgin is working too hard because he wishes to provide a comfortable life for his wife; his wife, for her part, tries to persuade her husband not to work so much and to take better care of his health.

Another example of the same kind is the problem of the legitimacy of children born in marriage, a situation "randomly" chosen to demonstrate the legal advantages of communally held land. The situation, which had obvious personal connotations (Chernyshevsky had every reason to doubt that he had fathered the children born to Olga Sokratovna), is discussed in the same article. Whether the children born to a wife are sired by her husband (and thus legally eligible to inherit their father's property) or by an adulterous partner is given as an example of a "material fact" whose truth depends on an "innumerable number of facts, circumstances, documents, which are hidden from public knowledge and are frequently unknown to the very person whom they concern" (5: 617).

Chernyshevsky miraculously resolves the problem by applying the "pure abstract" principles of the science of political economy: the principle of communal property eliminates the need to clarify these details by making the issue of whether the children were born in wedlock totally irrelevant.

> The question is not whether Ivan Zakharov is in fact Ivan Zakharov or some impostor or a foundling. The question is not whether Ivan Zakharov is the legitimate son of Zakhar Petrov. The question is not whether Zakhar Petrov was legally married and whether he left a will and had other children. The question is not whether Zakhar Petrov left unpaid debts, etc., etc. Nobody is interested in that. The fact that Ivan Zakharov indeed owns this plot of land is as obvious and unquestionable as the fact that he indeed owns the pair of hard-working hands that keep his family fed. (5: 618)

In a world of abstract Ivans and Zakhars or, better yet, of people-numbers, whose interrelationships are decided by the magic of mathematical formulas and regulated by the universal laws of a utopian social order, the petty and painful problems of daily existence miraculously dissolve.

The use of mathematical calculations is the central device of Chernyshevsky's scholarship. He employed them with such persistence that, even in the context of the period's fascination with mathematical methods and statistics, his use of mathematics became a distinctive feature of his scholarly method and style. The calculations are supposed to prove the validity of the assertions made in an article; the relation between the initial statement and the calculations varies from fairly sensible to completely absurd. What is important is the magic of figures itself; the calculations, which sometimes go on for many pages, lend the argument an aura of objective proof. For example, Chernyshevsky proves his argument that credit depends on budget with these comments:

Let everybody decide for himself whether this can be resolved differently. $2 \times 2 = 4$, and this thing—no, let us use scientific terminology—not this thing, this equation is well known. Let us treat this equation scientifically. Treated scientifically, this equation means that the product of the multiples two and two is four. Let us assume now . . . (7: 555)

The calculations go on and on; the same formula is further presented in the form $2 \times 2 = 1 + 1 + 1 + 1 = 3 + 1 = 5 - 1 = 7 + 2 - 5$ to prove that it always makes 4. These operations, in Chernyshevsky's eyes, prove his point. The arbitrary nature of such calculations is well illustrated by errors in the equations as published. For example, the calculations in two of the examples in the article "Capital and Labor" ("Kapital i trud") are incorrect. Chernyshevsky, who worked very fast and hardly had any time to read proofs, did not notice the errors (they are reproduced in all editions of Chernyshevsky's collected works, with an editor's footnote pointing out the mistake; 7: 20).

The manipulation of figures, which Chernyshevsky used as yet another mental device for attaining reality, was justified by the popular positivist idea ascribing to mathematics the power to universalize human experience. The issue of the applicability of mathematical methods to the problems of human psychology, morality, and social behavior became an object of controversy in Russia in the 1860s. The formula $2 \times 2 = 4$ became a common symbol of the nihilist position. "What's important is that two times two is four. Everything else is trivial," proclaims Bazarov, the hero of Turgenev's *Fathers and Sons*. The hero of Dostoevsky's *Notes from Underground* (an antagonist of the new men), on the contrary, sees a manifestation of his human essence in the assertion that "two times two equals five"—the ultimate affirmation of the freedom of will.[6]

The power of mathematics to provide an "all-encompassing formula" that would explain and govern everything (a typical desire of a utopian mind) symbolized the essence of science for Chernyshevsky. With characteristic bitterness, he wrote in "The Anthropological Principle in Philosophy": "The natural sciences are not ready yet to embrace all these laws under one universal law and to collapse all these equations to one all-powerful equation. What is to be done? We are told that even certain branches of mathematics have not advanced far enough for that" (7: 294).

Throughout his life, Chernyshevsky kept striving to create an instrument capable of an all-inclusive solution to the basic problems of human existence. In his early youth, it was the *perpetuum mobile*. Later, he planned to write an "encyclopedia of civilization," which would encompass the totality of human knowledge and therefore solve all problems and regulate every aspect of life. He was inspired by the traditions of the Enlightenment and their continuation in the attempts of Saint-Simon and his followers to produce a new encyclopedia to replace Diderot's—a synthesis of contemporary science that would contain a formula for social harmony. Immediately after his arrest, free at last from the demands of everyday life, Chernyshevsky decided to undertake this project. In a letter to his wife dated October 5, 1862, from the Peter-and-Paul Fortress, he wrote that he was about to begin the multivolume "History of the Material and Mental Life of Mankind," a history that until that time had not been written. "A Critical Dictionary of Ideas and Facts" based on that history was to follow. There, claimed Chernyshevsky, "all the thoughts about all important things will be taken to pieces and recast, and in every case, the true point of view will be indicated." Finally, after this second multivolume work, he planned to compile a two- or three-volume summary written in such a way as to be comprehensible not only to scholars but to the general public ("The Encyclopedia of Knowledge and Life"). The last stage of the project involved reworking the same material in a popular tone, "practically into a novel with jokes, skits, and witticisms so that everybody who only reads novels will read it." It is necessary, he argued, to explain to people where the truth lies and how they should think and live. He concluded by adding: "No one has done what I want to do since the time of Aristotle, and I will be the good teacher of people for the course of centuries, as was Aristotle" (14: 456).

His belletristic works of the same and later periods were also planned as gigantic cycles whose complicated composition would allow him to unite a variety of small pieces into a single whole. He meant to realize this structure in *Tales Within Tales*

(*Povesti v povestiakh*; 1863–64) and *The Book of Erato* (*Kniga Erato*). Of the latter, he wrote that it would be an "encyclopedia in belletristic form" and added that it would be "colossal" (14: 506–7).

None of these plans was fulfilled, but Chernyshevsky never abandoned the idea. In a way, his translation of Weber's *Universal History* during the last years of his life was a comparable project. In letters to his editor, Chernyshevsky chose to picture this translation as an original study; the name Weber was to serve "merely as a cover" for his own study on universal history, which would then be translated into German, French, and English. Chernyshevsky obviously saw his vocation as scholar and writer in creating a scientific formula or text universal in applicability.

Scholar and Writer

Despite his remarkable talents, Chernyshevsky encountered serious difficulties establishing himself as a scholar and writer; his inability to sustain his professional ambitions resulted in a severe disappointment, which increased his already painful sense of inadequacy. One can recognize traces of this early disappointment in works written long after he established himself as a prominent and influential journalist and public activist.

Chernyshevsky's original plans of becoming a professor at Petersburg University failed because of problems with his master's dissertation. The public defense and publication of the dissertation were delayed for about two years, and three more years passed before his degree was officially conferred. This unusually long period was a result of bewilderment and irritation on the part of academic circles and the university administration with the dissertation's militant style and radical materialist tendencies. Its publication was greeted with almost complete silence; Chernyshevsky, in an attempt to attract attention to it, wrote and published in the *Contemporary* a review of his own work signed N. P——n.

Despite this catastrophe, however, Chernyshevsky did not abandon his academic ambitions until much later. Evidence of these ambitions and of his painful reaction to failure is contained in Chernyshevsky's letters to his father. His tone is sarcastic and flamboyant, and his expectations are totally unrealistic. Thus, on learning that the master's degree had finally been conferred, Chernyshevsky wrote to his father: "I smiled. Once again proposals to take up a chair at the university will be renewed." He then explained that he would accept a chair only if the university waived further "formalities": the doctoral examination, a trial lecture, and so forth, which he considered "unseemly" in his case (14: 370). There is no evidence that he was ever offered a professorship. The whole experience apparently left bitter traces. More than once in his career as a journalist, Chernyshevsky viciously attacked academicians who, he maintained, were not treating him as a colleague, an accomplished scholar of their rank.

The theme of science, his own role in it, and rebukes of the academic establishment are the leitmotifs of Chernyshevsky's Siberian letters. The letters to his sons (whom he had known only as children) are filled with lengthy treatises on mathematics, climatology, philosophy, history, linguistics, and the like, mixed with venomous attacks on "university science" with its meaningless examinations, degrees, and academic titles. He describes himself as a man who was born to be a scholar, who was forced to abandon his research plans temporarily "for lack of time," and who, in exile, was able to return to them and would make a significant contribution to science: "I am a scholar, I am one of those scholars who, in the strongest sense of the word, are men of science, I have been one of them from my youth" (15: 165). He persistently returns to this theme, insisting that the results of the work in which he was supposedly engaged in Siberia "will be greeted with sympathy by the scholarly world" (14: 623).

These ambitions, which reached delusional proportions in exile, were realized by the characters of Chernyshevsky's Siberian fiction. Viazovsky in *Evenings at Princess Starobelskaia's* is a world-famous scholar. So is the young hero of *The Gleams of Radiance*; by the age of 27, he has achieved the status of a leading scholar in each of the many areas of knowledge in which he works (Chernyshevsky submitted his master's dissertation at 27).

Literary accomplishments and literary fame were also never-ceasing ambitions in Chernyshevsky's life. His encyclopedia of human knowledge was to be followed by a "belletristic encyclopedia," and he saw arrest and confinement as an opportunity to accomplish the true mission of his life. He retained his literary aspirations throughout the Siberian exile. In letters to his wife and children, he wrote that he had been a journalist only because he had had "no leisure" to write like a writer or as a scholar. Although Chernyshevsky was obviously aware of the defects in his literary craftsmanship, he was still convinced of the rare merits of his fiction: "My style is a little clumsy, like Gogol's, for example. But this is an insignificant flaw. Everything else that is needed for a good storyteller, like Dickens or Fielding, or, among our writers, Pushkin and Lermontov, I possess in sufficiently good quality and in abundance. Nature has not given me versification. But my prose is good poetry" (15: 390).[7]

Chernyshevsky was unable to complete any of the grand projects he designed to solve the problems of human existence. He abandoned the *perpetuum mobile*, the "encyclopedia of knowledge and life," and the colossal belletristic encyclopedia. He did not discover the "universal formula" in mathematics or the general law of the natural sciences. And yet, in a way, he came very close to his goal in *What Is to Be Done?* The novel is a product of the liberation of creativity that Chernyshevsky apparently experienced after his arrest on July 7, 1862. It was written with remarkable ease and efficiency in less than four months (between December 14, 1862, and April 4, 1863, while he was awaiting trial) and published, in three installments, in the March, April, and May issues of the *Contemporary*.

As a utopian novel, *What Is to Be Done?* offers a model of an ideal living arrangement. We have seen that, among other things, the novel tells the reader how to resolve conflicts with authoritarian parents, eliminate jealousy and possessiveness in marriage, arrange the family's financial affairs, entertain guests, cure a girl dying of love, reform a prostitute, and pay rent on a limited income. Everything is taken into account, from the theoretical foundations of the new order to the arrangement and furnishings of the rooms in the family's apartment, small financial details in organizing communal labor, provisions for the individual desires of household members (bathrooms with hot running water, rich pastries, fresh cream, and comfortable shoes from the fashionable firm of Korolev's), and the price and quality of communally owned umbrellas.

The prescriptive aspect of the novel and the metaliterary techniques for implicating its reader have been commented on and described.[8] However, from a psycho-cultural perspective, *What Is to Be Done?* presents more than a systematic program of action. I believe that the novel also offered a mental mechanism through which reality could be brought under control, and that this mechanism—a system of mental devices for organizing the elements of life—was embodied in the structure of the work. In order to justify this idea, I will analyze the rhetoric of the novel in detail, focusing on narrative techniques and stylistic devices, the organization of the system of characters, and the use of Biblical references and Christian symbolism.

Reconciling Opposites

The basic structural principle of the novel is the organization of its narrative world in terms of contrasting qualities, a world of Hegelian contradictions as it were. Almost every quality discussed in the novel is reflected in the mirror of its opposite: good writer is opposed to bad writer, good reader to bad reader, man to woman, blonde to brunette, passion to coldness, cleverness to simplicity, altruism to egoism. A mechanism that is meant to resolve these oppositions, to reconcile (in Hegelian terms, *aufheben*) the contradictions, is then offered; after a series of formal operations, a quality is identified with or transformed into its direct opposite: weakness turns into strength, ugliness into beauty, vice into virtue, and so forth.

For example, the very first pages of the novel (the dialogue of the writer with his reader) introduce the opposition between good and bad writers. The narrator claims: "I am an author without talent who doesn't even have complete command of his own language" (14; 12).[9] On the negative pole of this opposition is the "author without talent." On the positive pole are "works produced by real talent." A third factor is then introduced into this opposition—the celebrated works of the favorite authors of the general public (publicly accepted great authors). The positive pole is thus replaced by a pseudo-positive one, and the initial opposition is transformed: "I as a talentless writer" versus "authors who are falsely perceived as talented writers." What follows is an inversion of the top and bottom: "As for the celebrated works of your favorite authors, you may, even in point of execution, put it [my book] on their level; you may even place it above them; for there is more art here than in the works aforesaid, you may be sure," says the narrator to the public (14; *13*). Both the merit of popular writers and his own lack of artistic talent appear to be chimerical.

The theme, of course, has personal connotations. In Chernyshevsky's private letters, discussions of ambitious projects and proclamations of his remarkable artistic power go hand in hand with lamentations on the drawbacks of his style and execution. In the novel, Chernyshevsky found a powerful mechanism for resolving this problem and many others. As a result of a series of purely rhetorical operations, gifted writer and ungifted writer turn out to be one and the same thing. The narrator claims that although he has "not a trace of artistic talent . . . it matters little": although he is a bad writer, he is a good writer.

A similar operation is performed with the notion of the reader. In the preface, the "perceptive" or "wise reader" is opposed to the "feminine reader," who is incapable of understanding the book ("thought in man being more intense and more developed than in woman"; 12; *11*). The perceptiveness and wisdom of the masculine reader are then disavowed: comments by the "perceptive reader" reveal a total lack of understanding of the novel's real meaning. In the long run, the feminine reader turns out to be more perceptive than the "perceptive" masculine reader.

The triumph of the feminine intellect over the seemingly superior masculine intellect is echoed in the triumph of the physical characteristics of women. Initially, Chernyshevsky repeats a common opinion: men are physically strong; women are the "weak sex." But later this is proclaimed to be simply a result of "prejudice": "Now, women have always been told that they are weak, and so they feel weak and, to all intents and purposes are weak" (259; 292–93). Feminine weakness is nothing but illusion turned reality; actually, women are physically stronger than men: "the feminine organism is the more vigorous [*krepche*] . . . and better fitted to resist destructive forces" (258–59; 291–92). "But in reality," remarks one of the characters, "the opposite [of the stereotype] seems to be the truth." The causes are clear: "it is the force of bias . . . a false expectation" (259; 292). Ergo, in reality women are stronger than men.

The general scheme then is as follows. An opposition is established having, at one pole, the lack of a certain quality or a negative quality (a talentless writer, an incomprehending reader, feminine weakness). At the opposite pole is the presence of this quality (a talented writer, an understanding reader, masculine strength). A third factor, or an intermediate term, is then introduced into the opposition—a pseudo-quality. It is either an illusory realization of the positive pole (writers who are falsely acclaimed as good, "perceptive" readers who actually misunderstand everything) or an illusory realization of the negative pole (women who, through prejudice, are considered weak). After the empirically perceived quality is demonstrated, or simply proclaimed, to be not real or true, the bottom can be reversed with the top (a bad writer turns out to be a good one, whereas a seemingly good writer appears to be no good; the unperceptive reader turns out to be an understanding and wise one, whereas the "perceptive" reader appears to be inept). Throughout the novel, this mechanism appears either in its complete form or with reductions and variations. Chernyshevsky applied it to those qualities and issues that were a matter of concern for him personally and for his contemporaries, as well as to material that appears to be personally and culturally neutral.

The general scheme is applied to one of the most important themes—insensitivity. The opposition between coldness and passionate love is introduced at the beginning of the novel. At first glance, Lopukhov takes Vera Pavlovna to be a cold girl, and he himself treats her without feeling. At the opposite pole is Storeshnikov's love for Vera Pavlovna; Vera Pavlovna considers it ardent passion. However, Lopukhov disavows Storeshnikov's love as not real: "That is not love." At the same time, Lopukhov's and Vera's coldness and insensitivity prove to be illusory. "No, she is not a cold and insensitive girl," decides Lopukhov (53; 64). Lopukhov's feeling for Vera Pavlovna is then declared to be true love.

The idea that true love, contrary to common opinion, is a calm and tranquil emotion is a leitmotif throughout the whole novel. Vera Pavlovna comes to this conclusion through the experience of her love for Lopukhov, a feeling that "does not excite" and "does not perturb." Vera's love for Kirsanov is also a quiet feeling, but her love for Lopukhov during this period assumes a feverish intensity; it is called *goriachka* ("fever") and dismissed as a disease. At the same time, Lopukhov, who feels genuine love for Vera Pavlovna, remains calm and cold throughout the crisis. Katia Polozova's ardent passion for her suitor Jean, which she mistakes for true feeling, ends in a disease that almost leads to her death; her feeling for Lopukhov-Beaumont, a true love, has every appearance of coldness ("not human beings but fish . . . I am embarrassed by the coolness of their association," the narrator remarks ironically; 325–26; *368*).

In the authorial discussion of the characteristics of the new men, these observations are generalized: the principal trait of the new men is coolness, a quality associated with activity. It is opposed to the romantic exultation of the previous generation, which was accompanied by weakness and inertia. In the long run, coolness is identified with love.

An important part in the novel is played by the opposition between blonde and brunette. Blonde women are supposed to be beautiful, and brunettes ugly. Vera Pavlovna, a brunette with dark skin, thinks, as does her mother, that this makes her ugly. To their surprise, they discover that Vera is admired in the theater (her first public appearance) and is considered a beauty. The beauty of blonde women (a fact of common opinion) turns out to be an illusion. The judgment is pronounced by Julie, a French courtesan and therefore an authority on feminine beauty, at a party after the theater. Julie admires the dark beauty of Vera and proclaims blondes to be ugly as a type: "Colorless eyes, colorless thin hair, plain, colorless face." For Julie, a blonde woman is a Russian (and hence plain and cold) woman, whereas a brunette is a southerner (she takes Vera for a Georgian).

A partial reconciliation of the opposition is offered in a remark by Julie's companion, Serge: "Russians are a mixture of tribes from blondes like the Finns . . . to brunettes much darker than Italians. . . . Our blondes whom you so hate are but one of the local types" (23; 25). Russians are thus proclaimed to be a nation in which different national characteristics, the characteristics of both northern (cold) and southern (passionate) people, are mingled. The distinction between blonde and brunette is thus neutralized.

The opposition between blonde and brunette (like many others in the novel) has a transparent social subtext. Julie's contemptuous judgment about "meaningless blondes" is echoed by a seemingly trivial discussion of the fashion for white pets by the girls in Vera Pavlovna's shop. Some of the girls find that the fashion for white elephants, white cats, and white horses is tasteless; they are obviously physically inferior to colored ones (166; *n.p.*). The conversation then turns to *Uncle Tom's Cabin*: the triumph of the colored pets (= brunettes) over the more popular white ones (= blondes) is the triumph of the black race over the white race. The triumph of dark color over white color (as well as of woman over man) is the triumph of the social bottom over the social top.

Thus, a seemingly trivial topic, the opposition between blonde and brunette, a literary cliché, takes on rich, complex meaning. Behind it stand the themes of woman's beauty, of coldness and insensitivity with the personal associations connected with them, and of the social questions of racial and sexual inequality. The formal resolution of this opposition creates the impression that a solution to these problems has been found.

The ultimate resolution of the opposition between blonde and brunette, Russian and foreigner, beautiful and plain woman, occurs in the description of Lopukhov's bride (a further extension of Vera's image and a symbol of the goddess-revolution). "Is she a brunette or a blonde?" Vera Pavlovna asks Lopukhov. "That is a secret," he replies (55; 67). The secret is revealed in Vera Pavlovna's first dream. In the dream, the woman's appearance and national qualities are constantly in flux, but throughout she retains her remarkable beauty: "Her expression and manner are constantly changing; by turn she is English and French, then she becomes German, Polish, and finally Russian, then English again, German again, Russian again—and yet her features always remain so beautiful" (81; 94). We are dealing here with a variant of the reconciliation of contradictions: a quality is directly transformed or converted into another.

There are many further examples. One of them concerns the opposition "naïve young girl/artful coquette." According to Julie, "Totally naïve young girls sometimes, involuntarily, behave like experienced coquettes" (34; *n.p.*). The actions of "totally naïve girls" are then identified with absolute value ("true coquetry, which is intelligence and tact in the relations between a woman and a man") and are opposed to illusory, seemingly crafty coquetry ("stupid, mediocre imitations"). Thus, the naïve and open Vera manipulates Storeshnikov like an artful coquette, causing her father to comment that "it is thus that the Lord inspires children" (38; 43).

The innocence of a young girl is opposed not only to the ingenuity of a crafty mind but also to the deductions of science. Although Vera Pavlovna could not properly develop her mind within her family, her attitude to marriage shows her to be on the same level as advanced social thinkers. When Lopukhov wonders where she found the ideas that he derived from learned books, she assures him that many young girls and women ("quite as simple as myself") entertain the same ideas. Among them is Julie ("Marriage!" she exclaims, "The yoke! Prejudice!"; 25; 28). An uneducated woman and a fallen woman turn into symbols of wisdom and knowledge. Julie proclaims: "I have a passion for science; I was born to be a Mme de Staël" (23–24; 26). Although this statement may sound like a parody, it has, nevertheless, serious connotations that are revealed by comparing it with Chernyshevsky's diary, where he recorded his youthful ambition to find in Olga Sokratovna a second Mme de Staël.

Whereas wisdom is associated with simple young girls and women (Vera and Julie), the claims of publicly recognized men of knowledge are dismissed throughout the novel as mere semblances of real wisdom. The women overtake the seemingly better informed men by embodying advanced ideas in action. Thus, Vera Pavlovna organizes a workshop of seamstresses

based on progressive cooperative principles. Praising her superior initiative and industry, Lopukhov remarks: "We all talk and
do nothing. And you, who started out later than any of us, are
the first to begin action" (117; *138*). Once again, the last becomes
first, and woman (associated with activity) triumphs over man.

In the same way, a fallen woman triumphs over an honorable
woman and, in the long run, turns out to be "an innocent
maiden." Julie, when she accompanies Serge to visit Vera Pavlovna, introduces herself by saying: "I am not what I appear to
be. I am not his wife, but his mistress. All Petersburg knows
me as the most corrupt woman. But I am an honest woman"
(31; *n.p.*).

In this monologue several layers of semblance are laid bare
and a reversal of values occurs. On the one hand, Julie, who had
seemed to be a respectable and noble lady, admits that she is a
courtesan selling herself to a lover. On the other hand, although
she is known to everybody as a corrupt woman, she is honorable
(in fact, she comes to save Vera Pavlovna from impending dishonor; at the same time, her visit could easily ruin Vera's reputation). While Vera's mother is scheming to sell her own daughter,
this courtesan instructs the young girl that "it is better to die
than to give a kiss without love!" ("Julie, a fallen woman, knows
what virtue is!"; 35; *39*).

In the story of Julie, who was and remains a courtesan, vice
turns out to be virtue. The same transformation, in even more
direct form, occurs in the story of Nastia Kriukova, a reformed
prostitute. When she confesses to Vera Pavlovna that, as a prostitute, she "was so shameless, more than many others," Vera explains: "That was because actually you were timid and were
really ashamed" (158; *186*). Shamelessness is really shame, and a
prostitute is equated with an "innocent young girl" (thus, in her
relationship with Kirsanov, Nastia feels as if she were "an innocent maiden").

At the same time, a woman of easy virtue turns out to be as
pure and dignified as a lady of noble bearing: "Is this the Julie
known to all the rakes of the aristocracy, and whose jokes have
often caused even the libidinous to blush? One would say, rather,
a princess whose ear has never been soiled" (29–30; *33*). Julie is

part of the circle of Petersburg's aristocratic youth; moreover, a brilliant young aristocrat, Serge, strives to marry her, but Julie will not consent (the name Julie le Tellier belonged to Dobroliubov's French mistress). A courtesan is thus equated with an aristocratic lady.

The theme of aristocratism is treated in the opposition "awkward student/well-bred aristocrat." Judging from the report of her brother Fedia, Vera Pavlovna first takes his tutor, Lopukhov, for an "uncivilized savage, with head full of books and anatomical preparations" (48; 57). But the uncivilized student turns out to be a well-bred, graceful, and uninhibited young man who commands a full complement of social skills. At a party at Vera Pavlovna's house, he reveals his talents by playing the piano and dancing. It is also clear that he possesses the most important skill of all: conversational French. The "unsociable savage" turns out to be the opposite: "He is not such a barbarian after all; he entered and bowed with ease" (51; 66).

What is especially important for Chernyshevsky is not the fact that Lopukhov is a person at ease in society but the act of transformation itself. Lopukhov's social ease is presented against a background of false expectations created by his social status. At the party, Vera Pavlovna says to him:

"Monsieur Lopukhov, I should never have expected to see you dance."

"Why? Is it, then, so difficult to dance?"

"As a general thing, certainly not; for you certainly it is." (55; 66)

The pseudo-positive qualities of aristocratic behavior appear in Storeshnikov and his friend Jean, society men with no real sense of honor or refinement. Lopukhov triumphs over Storeshnikov in a verbal duel that Storeshnikov provokes in an attempt to humiliate the tutor. As a result, the *raznochinets* (Lopukhov) is identified with the true aristocrat (Serge): having witnessed the "duel," Vera Pavlovna concludes that the student "behaves as Serge would have behaved." By marrying Vera Pavlovna, who is sought by Storeshnikov, the *raznochinets* Lopukhov wins a woman from a representative of the gentry. Later in the novel, Kirsanov (also a *raznochinets*) triumphs over another pseudo-aristocrat, Jean (Katia Polozova's suitor), and opens her eyes to

Jean's ignobleness. Lopukhov (disguised as the American Beaumont) is then able to marry Jean's former fiancée.

Through his second marriage, Lopukhov enters the wealthy and noble Polozov family. As an American, Lopukhov-Beaumont not only stands outside the Russian social hierarchy, but is also endowed with the magic ability to transform his social status (just as the "bride" in Vera's first dream and Julie were):

> If he had been a Russian, Polozov would have liked it had he been a nobleman, but in the case of foreigners this is not an important consideration, especially when they are Frenchmen and still less when they are Americans. In America one may be today in the employ of a shoemaker or a farmer, tomorrow a general, the day after president, and then again a clerk or a lawyer. (322; 363)

The domain of dream, America and the demimonde, is pictured as a location where free transmutations of social and national status, social role, appearance, and manner occur. Another situation should be added to this list: revolution, the environment in which every possible opposition of the social and emotional orders is resolved. Characters who in one way or another belong to the domain of revolution experience such transformations. For example, Rakhmetov, who (as Chernyshevsky specifies) is a descendant of one of the oldest families in Europe, lives the life of a commoner and never allows himself any luxuries inaccessible to the masses. A special ability to turn qualities into their opposites is one of the most important characteristics of the new men. For example, that which another might consider a sacrifice or privation (like handing one's wife over to another), a new man experiences as a delight. What is generally considered to be altruism is seen as nothing but serving one's own interests, whereas egoism turns out to be a form of altruism (Chernyshevsky based his doctrine of rational egoism on this). Instructing Vera in the art of true altruism, Lopukhov says: "Do not think of me. Only by thinking of yourself, can you spare me unnecessary pain" (196; *n.p.*).

Another important problem that receives similar treatment is the problem of intimacy. Lopukhov and Vera Pavlovna treat each other as it is customary to treat strangers. Thus, they keep separate rooms, do not dare to intrude on each other, and only meet when fully dressed; they have no right to question each other about personal affairs. Living like strangers, however, turns out to be the best way of preserving intimacy. What is universally considered to be intimacy ("always in each other's arms") is only an illusion of real intimacy, a type of behavior that leads to quarrels, jealousy, mutual neglect, and disrespect (we always treat strangers, Chernyshevsky's heroes notice, better than we treat the members of our own family).

For complete clarity, Chernyshevsky generalizes the basic principle of the interchangeability of the two poles of the opposition (in the chapter entitled "A Theoretical Conversation") in a mathematical formula: "A in B's place is B; if in B's place A were not B, that would mean that it was not exactly in B's place" (188; *208*).

The direct transformation of one quality into another is illustrated in a seemingly unimportant scene: a monologue of the author addressed to the "perceptive reader" in defense of women with serious intellectual interests (blue stockings): "'Oh perceptive reader, you are right,' I say to him, 'the blue stocking is truly stupid and unendurably dull, as you have discovered. But you have not discovered who this blue stocking is. Look in the mirror and you will find out. . . . Whose crude image or sleek figure do you see in the mirror? Why, your own, my friend'" (268; *302*). Looking into the mirror, the person sees someone else's image—the image of a person endowed with opposite qualities—which changes into (or simply turns out to be) his own image. Self and non-self turn out to be one and the same person.

This mechanism is employed with remarkable consistency (the list of oppositions could be continued), and it penetrates every level of the structure of the novel, from ideological to rhetorical. It motivates the ethical theories expounded in the novel (the doctrine of rational egoism, and the theory of "bending the stick the other way"), and it appears as a figure of speech: "Kirsanov was the son of a law copyist, that is, a man who often had no meat in his soup [*chasto ne imeiushchego miasa vo shchakh*]— that is, who, on the contrary, often had meat in his soup [*znachit i naoborot, chasto imeiushchego*]" (147; *n.p.*).

In a generalized way, the message underlying such operations can be read as follows: from the fact that a person does not possess a certain quality, it follows that this person does possess that quality. We have seen that such reasoning was already present in the dissertation. However, if in the dissertation such conclusions emerged as a result of flaws in argumentation, in the novel Chernyshevsky offered a carefully arranged series of mediating steps, an algorithm for equating opposites. By using this mechanism consistently, he demonstrated that his method could be applied to practically any conflict and that it therefore provided a powerful mental tool for conflict resolution.

Doubles

The organization of the system of characters in the novel is governed by the same principles that govern the organization of the work as a whole. The characters are paired in many different combinations, and the members of each pair are contrasted to reveal an opposition of human qualities or human types. It is in the context of these oppositions that the operations of inversion and transformation (or "transfiguration") take place.

The two main male characters, Lopukhov and Kirsanov, are almost exact doubles. They share biographical, ideological, social, and personal traits and identical plans for the future; in addition, they share an apartment and work on a joint research project. When met separately (claims the author), they are always taken for men of the same character type. When they are seen together, however, the differences between them are revealed. Lopukhov is cool and reserved, whereas Kirsanov is relatively expansive, and so forth. They complement each other, combining and unifying all desirable qualities and abilities. Each becomes the lover of the same woman, Vera Pavlovna.

Taken together, they fulfill many of the unrealized plans and aspirations of the author himself, thereby jointly functioning as Chernyshevsky's double. Lopukhov, though a *raznochinets*, has all the skills and ease of a well-born young man. Earlier in life, he had favored "high living" and had many "gallant adventures." Kirsanov, on the contrary, realizes Chernyshevsky's academic and scientific ambitions; his international reputation forces the conservative Russian scientists to respect him. Lopukhov, who had identical plans for his future, has to forgo his ambitions, as did Chernyshevsky himself.

Vera Pavlovna and Katia Polozova form another such pair. Although they are very close in spirit and character, Vera is more expansive, Katia more reserved; Vera is a brunette, Katia a blonde. Each is loved by the same man, Lopukhov.

In the final union of the four people, all distinctions between them are neutralized, and some of their qualities are reversed. The cool Katia, for example, turns out to be more ardent than her counterpart, Vera.

Vera Pavlovna, Lopukhov, and Kirsanov (all of them new men) are seen as "ordinary people." As a group, they are opposed to Rakhmetov, who has earned the title of "exceptional person." But Vera Pavlovna and Rakhmetov share many traits, from important ideological ones (they are both "people of action") to trivial ones (both love tea with cream and pastry).

Initially, Vera Pavlovna is introduced as a "common young girl." The author's voice proclaims: "I see nothing extraordinary in you. Perhaps one half of all the girls whom I have known and whom I know, and perhaps even more than one half—for I have not counted them, they are too numerous to be counted—are no worse than you, and some are even better" (61; *n.p.*). In the next passage, however, transformed through the vision of Lopukhov, she is already called an "extraordinary girl."

The transformation of an ordinary girl into an extraordinary being (a female counterpart of Rakhmetov) is complete when Vera Pavlovna is endowed with a divine double—the goddess of her dreams. In the first dream, the goddess calls herself "a bride of your bridegroom" (that is, Vera's double). In the fourth dream, the identity is established beyond any doubt. Vera Pavlovna notices that the face of the goddess is her own. As she looks into this face, as into a magical mirror, she sees herself, but as a goddess.*

Without losing her initial features—those of an ordinary, even plain woman, with the qualities of a real, living person—Vera

---

*The transfiguration of Vera Pavlovna mirrors the transfiguration of Christ; this subject is treated in detail below.

Pavlovna is transformed into an exalted, shining goddess, a woman of ideal beauty. Her ideal attributes are identical to those that Chernyshevsky had dreamed about in his youth. She is more beautiful than the images by great artists, more beautiful than all known beauties. In addition, she is compared with the beautiful women on the streets of Petersburg:

Yes, it is herself that Vera Pavlovna has seen—a goddess. The countenance of the goddess is her own living countenance, whose features are so far from perfection—every day she sees more than one face more beautiful than hers. Yes, this is her own face, glowing with love, a face more beautiful than all the ideals bequeathed to us by all the sculptors of antiquity, all the great painters from the great age of art. Yes, it is she, glowing with the radiance of love, and even though there might be hundreds of faces much lovelier than hers in St. Petersburg—which is so poor in beauty—yet she is more beautiful than the Aphrodite in the Louvre, more beautiful than all the beauties of the past. (281–82; 316)

In the hierarchical chain of characters, Vera Pavlovna is paired, on the one hand, with the goddess, and on the other, with Julie. The two women are endowed with common traits; both, for example, oppose traditional marriage and like noisy gaiety. Yet, as far as status and way of life are concerned, they are opposites. However, they can potentially change places. In her second dream, Vera Pavlovna is shown what her life could have become (and what Nastia's life did become): "On a chair an officer is seated. On the table in front of the officer a bottle, and it is she, Verochka, upon the officer's knees!" (127; 149). For her part, Julie is an honest and even virtuous woman who, were it not for circumstances, could easily have led the life of Vera Pavlovna. By playing a significant role in saving Vera Pavlovna from the dishonorable designs of Storeshnikov and, later, in organizing Vera's cooperative shop, Julie partakes of the life of the new men. But the transformation, which for Julie remains only a potentiality, is realized by Nastia Kriukova. Nastia is, in her turn, another double of Vera Pavlovna (a prostitute with the officer of Vera's second dream on the one hand and a lover of Vera's second husband, Kirsanov, on the other).

In this chain of interchangeable characters (people of different destinies who are potentially capable of changing places), there is even a place for Maria Alekseevna, Vera's corrupt mother. Like Julie, Maria Alekseevna was a poor and honest girl who, by force of circumstances, was forced into a corrupt way of life. Julie's vice is sexual promiscuity; Maria Alekseevna's are greed and deceit. And just as Julie understands virtue, Maria Alekseevna knows what true honesty is. Moreover, in several passages Maria Alekseevna is ironically presented as Lopukhov's double. Their common qualities are practicality and devotion to what Chernyshevsky calls "self-interest" (*vygoda*); the only distinction between them is in the nature of the interest that governs their actions (a reference to the utilitarian ethics propagated by Chernyshevsky). In the "Eulogy of Maria Alekseevna," these observations are generalized in accordance with Chernyshevsky's ideas about the crucial role of social environment in determining a person's actions:

> Now you are engaged in bad business in accordance with the exigencies of your surroundings; but if other surroundings were given you, you would willingly cease to be dangerous, you would even become useful, because, when your interest is not at stake, you do not do evil, and are capable of doing anything that seems advantageous to you, even of acting decently and nobly. (114; *133*)

The transfiguration of Maria Alekseevna is described here in terms of a social theory advocated by Chernyshevsky.

Julie, Nastia, and Maria Alekseevna represent the group of people who, though "bad" (*durnye*), are capable of transformation and change. They are opposed to a group of "worthless" (*driannye*) people, incapable of transformation.

To the group of "immobile" characters, those who cannot change into someone else under any circumstances, belong Storeshnikov and Jean. Each mirrors the other's qualities and functions in the plot (the first is an unsuccessful suitor of Vera Pavlovna, the second of Katia Polozova). They are opposed to Lopukhov and Kirsanov. To this group also belongs a circle of people whom the author addresses as the "public."

Whereas Rakhmetov and the goddess are at the top of the hierarchy of characters, Julie, Nastia, and Maria Alekseevna represent (at least, from the point of view of traditional morality) the bottom. However, each is endowed with the capacity to experience a transformation into a different, worthier person. In contrast, the characters who inhabit the middle ground between the two extremes, Storeshnikov, Jean, and the "public" (those who enjoy the respect of society and are not, as a rule, considered evil), are incapable of becoming something they are not. They are not part of the conversion process and are entirely lost for the new life.

Such a system of characters offers rich potentials for any reader eager to identify with one or more of them (in the same way that Chernyshevsky apparently identified with the Lopukhov/Kirsanov pair). Once readers identify with any of the characters (with the exclusion of those in the middle), they can easily move from one position to another. Moving upward, they have the opportunity to experience vicarious transformations of personality and status, and even to reach the absolute top and identify themselves with the ideal man, Rakhmetov, or with the woman/goddess. The path to the world of the new men and to the divine kingdom of happiness is thus open to everybody, including a poor student, a prostitute, and even a greedy and dishonest schemer.

Double Count

On the level of plot, the basic structural principle is a twofold (and sometimes multiple) organization of narrative sequences. Almost every point of the plot has an alternative—another possible realization of a certain plot movement, another possible interpretation of an event, or another possible motivation for a character's action. Instead of a positive statement or characterization of an event, the reader is frequently offered a network of possibilities, not all of which are realized.

Consider, for example, the discussion of Lopukhov's plans for his future life with Vera Pavlovna. Just as Chernyshevsky tried, in the diary dedicated to his marriage, to take into account all possible developments, Lopukhov thinks of various possibilities: what if Vera Pavlovna feels burdened by the thought that in marrying her Lopukhov is making a sacrifice, or what if he cannot provide for all her wants? Chernyshevsky hastens to forewarn the reader that Lopukhov's monologue does not contain any allusions to the nature of future events. The lives of the characters will take a different course. However, the author also takes these possibilities into account, and they are woven into the narrative. Later, Rakhmetov, in his conversation with Vera Pavlovna after Lopukhov's disappearance, criticizes Lopukhov for failing to consider one more possibility—the possibility of his wife's love for another (a possibility that Chernyshevsky himself did take into account): "He should nevertheless have prepared you at all events against anything like it, just as one would against any accident which is not to be desired and which there is no reason to expect, but which is to be provided for. One cannot answer for the future and the changes it may bring" (225; 254).

"One cannot answer for the future," nor, it would seem, could Chernyshevsky answer for the present. An event exists in the novel as a tree of possibilities that sometimes coexist even though they contradict one another. An example of this narrative device is the reaction of the crowd to Lopukhov's "suicide."

Two variants of the event are immediately presented: (1) the traveler shot himself; and (2) the traveler did not shoot himself. The possibilities are then developed further. If the traveler did shoot himself, he could have done it for different reasons: (1.A) the traveler shot himself because he was drunk; (1.B) the traveler shot himself because he was broke; (1.C) the traveler shot himself because he was simply a fool. The second variant (did not shoot himself) branches out into three main subvariants: (2.A) some drunkard fired the shot; (2.B) a practical joker fired the shot; (2.C) some fool fired a shot. The second branch in turn has two offshoots: (2.B.1) someone fired a shot and fled; (2.B.2) someone fired a shot, mingled with the crowd, and is now laughing at the alarm he caused. Subvariant 2.C is ambivalent, and all the possible variants of the initial event are subsumed in it: "Upon this word 'fool,' all agreed, even those who disputed suicide. In short, whether it was a drunkard or a spendthrift who had blown his brains out or a practical joker who had made a pretense of killing himself (in the later case the joke was a stupid one), he was a fool" (8; 5).

This variant becomes the starting point of a new tree of possibilities. The traveler is a fool to shoot himself on the bridge for "one does not blow one's brains out on a bridge." Therefore, (3) he did not kill himself; or (4) he did shoot himself on the bridge. If he did, then (4.A) he was a fool to do it on a bridge, or (4.B) he was clever to do it on a bridge ("one avoids suffering in case of a simple wound").

The dispute over the reality of the suicide creates a complicated network of possibilities that contradict each other in relation both to the event itself and to its evaluation. This argument ends on a highly ambiguous note: "Now the mystification was complete. A fool, and yet a clever one!" The reality of the event is never established. For the novel as a whole, Lopukhov's suicide continues to exist in its two conflicting variants. On the one hand, the development of the plot is based on the acceptance of the fact that Lopukhov is dead. On the other, the plot depends on the fact that he did not really kill himself and is alive. After his "suicide," Lopukhov is, simultaneously, both dead and alive.

The case outlined above is extreme. Presented as a prologue to the whole novel, it provides a model of narrative organization that is faithfully followed throughout the text.

Many of the important events of the plot, as well as minor points in its development, are offered as paradigms of possibilities. The marriage of Vera Pavlovna and Lopukhov (an important ideological topic) is presented in this manner. Besides the passages quoted above, there is a discussion of the possible paths of development caused by the difference in character between husband and wife, and specifically the possibility of Vera Pavlovna's dissatisfaction:

What form was this dissatisfaction to take? If both, or even one of you, had been deficient in intellectual development and refinement, or if you had been bad people, your dissatisfaction would have taken the ordinary form—hostility between husband and wife; you would have nagged each other, if you have both been bad; or one of you would have been pitilessly tormented. (223; 252)

The same principle is employed in such a decisive episode of the novel as Julie's ultimatum to Storeshnikov: "If you have any objections to make, I am waiting. . . . If you find my aid satisfactory, I will submit my conditions. . . . You can either accept them or refuse to accept them; if you accept them, I will send the letter; if you refuse to accept them, I will burn the letter, everything in the same harping manner" (32–33; *n.p.*).

This principle is also employed as a simple rhetorical device. One of the minor characters, the Lopukhovs' landlady (who is trying to explain the visit of Serge and Julie), casually remarks: "Either he or she is either a brother or a sister to the general or to the general's wife" (121; *n.p.*).

This principle receives allegorical representation in the financial operations of *otkup* and *zalog*. *Zalog* is Maria Alekseevna's main occupation; *otkup* is the occupation of her dreams, the career she envisions for her son-in-law. Maria Alekseevna is a pawnbroker; she lends money on deposited goods (*pod zalog*). The essence of this operation is that the value of the object pawned is defined simultaneously by two different sums. The first is the amount paid to the borrower; the second is the amount the broker receives when the object is redeemed. The same principle stood behind the Russian institution of *otkup*: a private person received a license to collect taxes (for example, on the sale of liquor), and the amount of money he submitted to the state differed from the amount actually collected. Both financial operations presented an opportunity to define one and the same object in terms of two numerical values.

This analogy from the domain of economy and finances (a field that Chernyshevsky frequently used to develop abstract models of conflict resolution) provides a mathematical formula for the double existence of an object and expresses the ambiguity of reality numerically. Such double values are frequently encountered in the novel. For example, a double existence is characteristic of the presents that Maria Alekseevna gives her daughter. Sometimes they are pawned goods that were never redeemed and thus cost her much less than their actual price. Even when she buys the presents, two different monetary values are attached to them: "Both dresses cost 174 rubles, that's what Maria Alekseevna told her husband; however, Verochka knew that the actual expense was less than 100 rubles" (18; *n.p.*).

The same principle of making presents is followed by the family's landlady, the employer of Maria Alekseevna's husband, who says to him: "I make your wife a present of it [a dress]. It cost 150 rubles (it really cost only 75), and I have worn it only twice (she has worn it more than twenty times)" (42; 48).

Chernyshevsky used the same principle of double value in calculating the economic benefits of the cooperative principle employed in the organization of Vera Pavlovna's shop. The main benefit of communal living, according to Chernyshevsky, lies in the fact that a thing costs an individual owner one sum, but each of the communal owners another, smaller sum. An apartment costing an individual tenant 1,675 rubles or a group of unorganized tenants 3,570 rubles can be rented by a commune for 1,250 rubles per person. The same transformation affects the price of dinner and various household items. A bad dinner that cost one person 30 kopeks becomes a good dinner at 16 kopeks per person when it is shared by the 37 residents of the commune.

A still more complicated transformation concerns the price and the quality of communally owned umbrellas. A simple cotton umbrella, the narrator argues, costs 2 rubles: 25 people acting individually will spend 50 rubles for their umbrellas; however, with communal living they can get by with only 5 collectively owned umbrellas, and the price of an umbrella per person is thus reduced to 40 kopeks. In this situation they can afford more expensive silk umbrellas, costing 5 rubles each. Communal ownership of umbrellas and communal living transform the owner of a cotton umbrella costing 2 rubles into an owner of a silk umbrella costing 1 ruble. These and many other numerical operations in the novel can be regarded as a numerical model of the principle of a twofold organization of narrative.

The presentation of an event as a tree of carefully calculated possibilities, a procedure corroborated by numerical analogies, creates the illusion of a scientific method, a guarantee of the trustworthiness of the resulting conclusion. The result, however, proves to be just the opposite: reality is a multiplicity of coexisting possibilities that does not call for an ultimate and absolute judgment and definition.

Illusion and Reality

Chernyshevsky's consistent application of the principle of twofold organization of narrative results in ambiguity: many of the elements of the novel have two or more possible meanings, or two or more possible "realities." The ambiguity of reality becomes a separate theme woven into the narrative. In fact, one of the novel's most important leitmotifs is the gulf between appearance, which is illusory and deceptive, and the real meaning of things, which is hidden or masked—thus, the appearance of ardent feeling and real feeling, the seeming understanding of the reading public and the real understanding of the few, the semblance of artistic talent and the real merit of a writer, and so forth.

The idea that behind outward indications or circumstances there is a second—true—reality, often contradictory to the first, is introduced at many structural levels. The model of the principle of the illusory versus the real is given, as is frequently the case in the novel, in a passage that appears to be a casual digression, merely a figure of speech describing the house in which the main characters live:

This house is now duly labeled with a number, but in 1852, when numbers were not in use to designate the houses of any given street, it bore this inscription: "House of Ivan Zakharovich Storeshnikov, Councillor of State." So said the inscription, although Ivan Zakharovich Storeshnikov died in 1837. After that, according to the legal title-deeds, the owner of the house was his son, Mikhail Ivanych. But the tenants knew that Mikhail Ivanych was only the son of the mistress and that the mistress of the house was Anna Petrovna. (15; *15*)

The operation of revealing the real meaning of things concealed behind appearance is repeated several times in this passage. But not even the last version given here can be taken as the final truth. Later in the novel, it turns out to be nothing but another level of illusion. Inscriptions and documents, which give every appearance of presenting the true state of affairs, do not define the real nature of things: "They both clearly remembered that, in reality, Anna Petrovna was not after all the owner of the house, but only the mother of the owner, and that her son was not the owner's son, but the real owner" (40; *n.p.*). At every stage of this chain of transformations, the apparent state of things turns out to be an illusion. The only thing that points to the true identity of the house is the number attached to it later.

Reality appears as a domain of illusion in which even documents and common knowledge cannot serve as a guarantee of the true nature of things. The principle of relativity established as a result of these operations can be illustrated by another minor episode—the reaction of the Lopukhovs' landlady to the visit of Serge and Julie. Petrovna, the landlady, who was fascinated by the grandeur of their appearance, maintains that the visitor was a general decorated with two "stars":

> How Petrovna could see stars on Serge, who did not yet have them (and even if he had had them, he would not have worn them while accompanying Julie), is a mystery. But the fact that she really saw them, that she was not mistaken and was not boasting, this fact I readily confirm; it is not just her impression. We do know that he did not have the stars, but the officer looked so dignified that from the point of view of Petrovna, it was impossible not to see the stars, and therefore she did see them. I am telling you that she did. (120; *n.p.*)

The authorial voice confirms the reality of an illusion.

Another method of conflating two different meanings (the evident and the hidden) is mistranslation, a narrative device Chernyshevsky uses frequently. For example, an early chapter opens with the text of the French revolutionary song "Ça ira," which is quoted in both French and what appears to be a Russian translation. The Russian, however, departs significantly from the French original. Moreover, this mistranslation is already the second step in the transformation of meaning. The French text, which is presented as a quotation from the well-known song, actually misquotes the original. In this way, Chernyshevsky introduces his own social ideas into the French song.[10] These operations, in the author's eyes, reveal the song's true meaning.

The idea of the basic ambiguity of real-life events is also expressed in many situations of misunderstanding. Through his constant dialogue with the "perceptive reader," for example, the author demonstrates that what appears to be an understanding of the novel is, in fact, a misreading. Maria Alekseevna constantly misunderstands events described in the novel, although she never doubts the truth of her understanding. She misinterprets her daughter's behavior and, seeing a hidden design where there is none, assumes that Vera is skillfully seducing Storeshnikov. Whereas she sees Vera's sincere coldness as an elaborate pretense, Maria Alekseevna understands Lopukhov's allegories in their literal meaning; for example, she takes the story of his rich bride (an allegory of revolution) for real marriage plans.

Another case of misunderstanding is caused by the literal translation of foreign (French) texts. In the theater, Maria Alekseevna misinterprets the intentions of Storeshnikov and his friends because she translates their French conversation word for word. Maria Alekseevna and Storeshnikov, in a different way, misunderstand the nature of the books Lopukhov has brought Vera:

"This one, in French, I have almost made out myself: *Gostinnaia* [*Salon*]. That means a manual of etiquette. And here is one in German; I cannot read it." "No, Maria Alekseevna, it is not *Gostinnaia*; it is *Destinée*." "What then is this 'destiny'? Is it a novel, a ladies' oracle, or a dream-book?" "Let's see." Mikhail Ivanovich turned over a few pages. "It deals with series; it is a book for a savant." "Series? I understand. It treats of transfers of money." (66; 78)

The book in question is Considérant's *Destinée sociale* (1834), and the series discussed in it refer to a form of communal labor. The readings proposed by Maria Alekseevna and Storeshnikov represent several levels of literal understanding, all of which lead to misunderstanding. It turns out that literal translation leads to misunderstanding, whereas pseudo-translation (as in the case of "Ça ira") can reveal actual meaning.

The key events of the plot—the fictitious marriage of Lopukhov and Vera Pavlovna, and Lopukhov's fake suicide—are built on the same basic principle. Vera Pavlovna and Lopukhov, in the strict sense, do not live as husband and wife and are wed purely pro forma. But at the same time, this fiction is more valid than generally accepted reality; the marriage bond between them turns out to be truer than any other form of matrimony.

Thus, what appears to be fiction turns out to be reality in the long run.

The same principle lies behind the device of allegory and, especially, behind the extensive allegories of Vera Pavlovna's four dreams, which convey the author's key ideas.[11] The dreams (which are not without psychological insight) operate with the elements of the characters' real life. The third dream is constructed from the details of Vera Pavlovna's recent experience—the opera, Bosio's performances, Kirsanov's visit. The elements of reality are regrouped and reinterpreted in the dream to reveal their actual meaning. Vera Pavlovna thinks: "Why does ennui sometimes come over me of late?—I have missed *La Traviata* this evening—Can Kirsanov be blamed?—Bosio sings: "Mladye leta otdai liubvi" ["Dedicate your youth to love"]. The chain of associations brings her to a discovery: she is in love with Kirsanov. The dream thus serves as a model of the relation between reality and illusion in the novel: in the dream reality is "translated" to uncover the true meaning of events hidden by the mask of appearance.

All these episodes promote the general idea that the appearance of things points to illusion, or pseudo-reality, and leads to misunderstanding, whereas the true reality is revealed only by a mental manipulation of the elements of experience. Thus, reality becomes accessible to the instruments of mental control.

The New Gospel: The Background

The opinion that, in the nature and degree of its influence, *What Is to Be Done?* was a new gospel (in the words of contemporaries, the "Scriptures" or a "catechism" of "the new faith," a "socialist gospel") has become a commonplace. In the memoirs of contemporaries and in works of Russian literature, testimony abounds that, for the Russian radical youth of the time, the novel was a revelation and became a program of conduct carried out with the kind of piety and zeal inspired in the proselytes of a new religion. However, the intriguing question of how exactly this effect was achieved remains unanswered.

Behind Chernyshevsky's novel stands a long and ample tradition of translating Christianity into utopian social systems. The ideas of social revolution and social reformation have deeply ingrained biblical associations that lie in the public domain of European culture.[12] But Chernyshevsky's novel also had direct and concrete sources in nineteenth-century attempts to translate Christianity into a system applicable to the solution of the concrete social and moral problems of earthly existence in the age of realism. Some of these sources are cited in the novel: in the course of introducing Vera Pavlovna to the world of the new men, Lopukhov gives her two books, Victor Considérant's *Destinée sociale* (1834) and Ludwig Feuerbach's *Das Wesen des Christentums* (1841). In the works of Considérant and other French Christian socialists (positivist offshoots of Saint-Simon's *Le Nouveau Christianisme*), socialism was identified with "true Christianity," that is, Christianity, to use Dostoevsky's ironic formula, "improved in accordance with the century and with civilization."[13] The essence of these improvements lies in the reversal of the theological principle of relations between God and man: in the idea of the adoration not of God, who in his son became man, but of man, who as a son of God created in his image would become God.

A rich complex of biblical associations and metaphors for contemporary social issues arose from these basic ideas. The ideal communist society of the future was seen as a terrestrial realization of the prophetic visions of the Golden Age, the Promised Land, or the New Jerusalem (all three phrases are a stable part of the vocabulary of Dostoevsky's heroes). The New Messiah of the Second Coming would be a true "friend of humanity," like Mohammed, Newton, and the Christian socialists themselves; he would be a "democrat" and a revolutionary. The "heavenly kingdom" would become the "social destiny" of men. Communes or phalansteries were identified with the fraternal communities of the early Christians, and socialists saw themselves as the new apostles. This trend also existed in England, among the followers of Robert Owen, who found a new revealed truth in his *Social Bible* (ca. 1840), an outline of the "rational system of society." (Lopukhov keeps a portrait of Owen, a "holy sage," in his study.)

A parallel system arose almost simultaneously and independently as a left-wing offshoot of Hegelian philosophy in Germany, in the doctrine of Ludwig Feuerbach.* Feuerbach's main objection to Christianity was that its dogmas, though "symbolically true," were not perceptible to the senses and therefore, not "scientifically true." Feuerbach suggested that the notion of God should be viewed as a projected image of the object in reality—man. He systematically treated statements about God as statements about man. In the end, Feuerbach established an absolute identity between man and God.

In Russia the two lines of realistic Christianity converged; French utopianism, with its exalted mystical phraseology and biblical metaphors, and Feuerbachianism, with its abstractions of German philosophy and emphasis on sense experience and science, blended together. They penetrated Russian cultural consciousness in the form of a "not too cohesive or solid amalgam," in the words of a contemporary, Pavel Annenkov. "Treatises of this sort were supposed to bring about a decisive and abrupt change in the philosophical quest of the Russian intelligentsia; and they did so quite thoroughly," he concluded.[14]

In the 1840s, the writing of Feuerbach, Considérant, Félicité de Lamennais, Etienne Cabet, and Pierre Leroux, and the novels of George Sand (in which the doctrine of Christian socialism was blended with romantic love plots) were in everybody's hands. The tradition of positivist revisions of Christianity and romantic *imitatio Christi*, to use George Sand's terms, "extended hands to each other" and smoothed the transition from romanticism and idealism to realism and positivism. Herzen and Ogarev became ardent socialists in the spirit of the New Christianity and almost simultaneously became enthusiastic admirers of Feuerbach.[15] In the 1840s, Belinsky swore by the names of Cabet,

---

*Simultaneously there appeared historical interpretations of Christianity, such as D.-F. Strauss, *Leben Jesu* (1835), and Bruno Bauer, *Kritik der evangelischen synoptiker* (1840); a French counterpart, Ernest Renan's *Vie de Jesus*, appeared in 1863. All these works were popular among the Russian intellectuals.

Leroux, and, above all, George Sand. French Christian socialism and Feuerbach lay at the core of the ideology of the Petrashevsky circle. These ideas became a *profession de foi* of the young Dostoevsky and an article of faith for the young Chernyshevsky in the late 1840s.

In the case of Chernyshevsky, the thin amalgam of Christian socialism and Feuerbachian anthropotheism was infused by the intellectual resources of his earlier development: a priest's son who was being prepared for a clerical career, he had received a solid theological education. He came to Petersburg in the spring of 1846 a devout and well-informed Christian. By the fall of 1848, after two years of voraciously reading the French socialists, he had arrived at a unique blending of Orthodox Christian dogma (expressed in the diary with the precision of the catechism) and the "rationalistic" (Chernyshevsky's word) improvements introduced into Christianity by Pierre Leroux (1: 132). On his twenty-first birthday, on July 12, 1849, he recorded in his diary that he had become a "devout Feuerbachian"; he nevertheless continued to attend mass (1: 297; see also 1: 391). (Chernyshevsky received *Das Wesen des Christentums*, a book banned by the censors, in February 1849 from his classmate Alexander Khanykov, a member of the Petrashevsky circle; a little earlier Khanykov had introduced Chernyshevsky to Fourier.) His version, however, was a Feuerbachianism grown on the spiritual soil of Russian Orthodoxy; in the background of his radical materialist and socialist beliefs lay the ever-familiar wisdom of the Orthodox catechism.

The Catechism of Russian Atheism

Instructing pupils in the purpose of earthly existence, the catechism teaches that God created man in his image, giving him reason, free will, and an immortal soul. Sin is a factor of the freedom of human will. Man's moral nature is determined by the personal responsibility of each man for his own sins, and it ultimately rests on faith in the immortality of the soul and hope for salvation. In his earthly life, man should perfect his own nature so that, in the other life, he may inherit the kingdom of heaven and life eternal. Chernyshevsky's own system of ethics, which was expounded in *What Is to Be Done?* and other writings (most notably, in his famous work "The Anthropological Principle in Philosophy"), results from the systematic and logical revision of these basic principles of the Orthodox catechism.

The starting point is his rejection of personal immortality; it was prompted by the Feuerbachian idea that the hope for eternal life is inconsistent with striving to improve one's earthly life. In 1849, Chernyshevsky recorded in his diary: "It is difficult to say whether I believe in personal immortality—perhaps not; rather, like Hegel, I believe in the merging of my 'I' with the substance of the Absolute, from which it came forth, . . . depending on the merits of my 'I'" (1: 297). The historian Nikolai Kostomarov, who met Chernyshevsky in 1851 in Saratov, described him as an accomplished Feuerbachian who claimed: "The immortality of the soul is a pernicious dream that keeps man from following the straight path of the most important purpose in life—the improvement of his own existence on earth."[16]

Having forsaken personal immortality but still working within the parameters of the Christian definition of the purpose of life, Chernyshevsky logically arrived at the denial of free will ("free will is an absurdity," he declared early in his diary). Of the initial triad of reason, free will, and an immortal soul, only reason is retained, and reason becomes the sole source of truth in Chernyshevsky's system. The notion of free will is replaced by the rationalist notion of determinism (which comes not from Feuerbach, but from the utilitarianism of James Mill and Jeremy Bentham). A person's choice of action is determined by a sequence of causes independent of human will and governed by the fundamental principle of utility. At the same time, the concentration on man himself, which lies at the foundation of the whole system, makes egoism a basic principle of life. According to Chernyshevsky, there is no contradiction between utilitarianism and egoism, and egoism is quite consistent with the principles of Christian morality. The utilitarian calculus of pain and pleasure ensures that man does good deeds, because everything that is good is also enjoyable and useful, whereas everything bad is unpleasant and harmful. Since the exact measurement of utility and a mathematically precise calculus of pain and pleasure create the foundation for virtuous conduct, morality becomes an exact science, comparable to mathematics.

The ultimate limitation of willed acts logically brings Chernyshevsky to the elimination of personal responsibility (replaced by society's responsibility for the happiness of the greatest number) and, further, to the annulment of sin. The negation of sin, an axiomatic assumption of the French Christian socialists, appears in Chernyshevsky's system as a result of a consistent chain of reasoning. In utilitarianism, the notion of wrongdoing is replaced by the notion of "miscalculation," a mathematical error. The denial of sin naturally leads to a revision of the basic Christian notion of good and evil. In Christian socialism, man—the emanation and mirror-image of God—is inherently good, but in Chernyshevsky's system man is neither inherently good nor inherently evil. Good and evil are contextual; they are determined by factors external to the individual. "Under certain circumstances man becomes good," wrote Chernyshevsky in "The Anthropological Principle in Philosophy"; "under other circumstances—evil" (7: 264). Thus, the determinism of human action necessarily leads to the principle of free transmutation of good and evil.

The denial of sin also entails a revision of the ideas of salvation and eternal life. If there is no sin, man is destined for free entry into the kingdom of God. But once sin has been denied, the atonement of sins through suffering and death, following the example of Christ, becomes totally unnecessary and even pernicious. ("In suffering, man denies the reality of the world," Feuerbach maintained.) The notion of sacrifice also becomes absurd. "Sacrifice is a false notion; as absurd as 'soft-boiled boots'; one acts in the way that is most agreeable," reasons Lopukhov as he gives up his medical career to spare Vera two more months of agony in her mother's home (98; *n.p.*). (Parodying the principle of rationality that lies behind this rearrangement of basic Christian principles, Dostoevsky has Luzhin, an epigone of the new men, declare: "Science says: Thou shalt love thyself before all."*) As the logical outcome of the whole chain of reasoning, man—sinless, heavenly man—is reconciled with God and, following Feuerbach, identified with God. The destiny of man is thus to attain celestial harmony in terrestrial life. Man's purpose and obligation are directed to the creation of a heavenly kingdom on earth (the earthly paradise).[17]

The immortality of the soul, which served as a starting point for the whole system, was a stumbling block for several generations of Russian thinkers. Differences over this issue marked the break between the romantics and the realists in the generation of the men of the forties. In *My Past and Thoughts* (Chap. 32: "The Theoretical Difference"), Herzen gives an account of a "historical moment" in Russian intellectual history, an argument over the immortality of the soul between Herzen and Ogarev on one side and Granovsky on the other in the summer of 1846.

The development of science, claimed Herzen, obliges one to accept certain things as truths, such as the connection of cause and effect and the indivisibility of spirit and matter (and hence, of soul and body). But if one accepts the unity of soul and body, Granovsky argued, then the immortality of the soul disappears. "Personal immortality is essential for me," Granovsky claimed; therefore, he found such "scientific truths" far from obligatory. With this theoretical difference, an irreparable rift in the "walls of the temple of friendship" occurred ("How was compromise possible in that realm?" Herzen asked). Granovsky publicly committed himself not only to faith but also to romanticism; Herzen and Ogarev (and with them, the passionate adversary of romanticism, Belinsky) to realism, that is, to left-wing Hegelianism in the "convictions of the heart," and in the sociopolitical realm.[18]

In uncovering the logic of Chernyshevsky's doctrine, one gets an insight into the structure of Dostoevsky's famous refutation

---

*Dostoevsky, *Polnoe sobranie sochinenii*, 6: 116. Vladimir Solov'ev, who was also sensitive to the absurdity of rationality, was more receptive to the inherent contradictions and the generosity of this argument. This is revealed in his famous parody of the confessional writings of the new men: "Man is descended from the ape; let us, *therefore*, lay down our lives for our friends [*Chelovek proizoshel ot obez'iany, a potomu polozhim dushu za grugi svoia*]." Cited in Ovsianiko-Kulikovsky, p. 58.

of Russian atheism. A similar train of thought (the "if . . . then" argument taking the immortality of the soul as a starting point) lies behind the famous paradox of Ivan Karamazov, a character whose ideas not only are closely connected with Christian socialism, but also have direct sources in the writings of Herzen and Belinsky:[19] "If there is no immortality of the soul, then everything is permissible." The denial of immortality for the sake of a social utopia leads Ivan Karamazov to the assertion of the lawfulness of egoism and even of crime, the "inevitable" and "rational" outcome of the initial proposition.[20]

Dostoevsky consistently operated with the same notions as Chernyshevsky, rearranging, in an almost experimental fashion, the catechismal constants (immortal soul, free will, reason, sin) in what appears to be a causal sequence. First, the rejection of immortality led Dostoevsky to reinterpret the limits of human will. But starting with the same basic premise as Chernyshevsky before him and tracing the same course of reasoning, he nevertheless reached a different conclusion. Whereas Chernyshevsky arrived at the determinism of human will, Dostoevsky ended up with unlimited individual volition (*svoevolie*). Several of the characters in *The Possessed* (most notably, Stavrogin and Kirillov) manifest this quality. According to Dostoevsky, the logical results of the rejection of immortality are the malignant hypertrophy of the human will, sin, rebellion (understood also as social rebellion: "Russian rebellion starts with atheism"), and death. (Kirillov, through an expansion of individual will not limited by faith, arrives at the idea of suicide.) Thus, the end product, the rational outcome, of the denial of the immortality of the soul is not earthly paradise, but the destruction of man.

I suggest that Dostoevsky was trying to refute Chernyshevsky not just by attacking his initial premise and final conclusion, but also by attacking his pattern of reasoning itself: the logical sequence of causes and effects. The force of Dostoevsky's rebuttal is directed at the fallacy of rational, deductive, scientific reasoning in matters of personal faith. A character in *The Possessed*, Shatov (quoting Stavrogin), maintains that "if it were mathematically proved that the truth excludes Christ, he would prefer to remain with Christ rather than with truth."[21]

The controversy between Dostoevsky and Chernyshevsky had special emotional poignancy, since for Dostoevsky Chernyshevsky's views represented a logical extension of his own views during his involvement in the Petrashevsky circle in the 1840s, at the time when the theoretical discussion of immortality between Herzen and Granovsky took place. By the 1870s, he had, as it were, sided with Granovsky in asserting that the connections of cause and effect and the positive proofs of science were far from being obligatory, and that personal immortality was essential for personal existence ("God is necessary," proclaims Kirillov). (A direct connection is possible; in the late 1870s, *My Past and Thoughts* was well known and widely read.)

In the final analysis, the famous controversy between Dostoevsky and Chernyshevsky concerning atheism was a continuation of the confrontation between romanticism and realism. It is remarkable that Dostoevsky challenged Chernyshevsky's arguments not as a romantic, as did Granovsky in his dispute with Herzen, but as a "true realist" (it is in Ivan Karamazov, a positivist, that the devil detects a deplorable "romantic streak, so derided already by Belinsky"; the devil himself discloses a special liking for "earthly realism").[22] Whereas, in Dostoevsky's eyes, the positivist mental apparatus that was aimed at obtaining positive proof of reality lacked reality, "pure ideal Christianity," on the contrary, represented reality itself.[23]

Dostoevsky's objections to Chernyshevsky rested on ethical, epistemological, and psychological considerations. According to Dostoevsky, Chernyshevsky's rationalist ideals sharply contradicted the psychological reality of human nature. He saw the essence of his own realism in the fact that he depicted "all the depths of the human soul," including the dark depths of innate human irrationality. Opposing himself to the adherents of realism among the radicals of the 1860s, Dostoevsky maintained that they had "quite different conceptions of reality and realism." "My idealism," he insisted, "is more real than their realism."[24] Thus, the religious differences of the two main ideologists of the age rested on the interpretation of the basic issue of reality.

Although Chernyshevsky's system, as reconstructed above,

begins with a rejection of the immortality of the soul, it is, in a strict sense, not an atheistic system. "What today is atheism," claimed Feuerbach, "tomorrow will be religion."[25] It is true that within Chernyshevsky's system, as well as within Feuerbach's, God as a divine being plays an extremely limited role. But what religion placed in God, Feuerbachian anthropology (or, to be more precise, anthropotheism) placed in man; while reducing God to man, Feuerbach, in his own words, "exalted man to God."* What logically followed from this revolution in God-man relations was a reversal of the spheres of the sacred and profane. Desacralization of the sacred, brought about by the positivist revision of Christianity, involved sacralization of the daily life of ordinary men, especially those who were actively involved in the revolutionary struggle and saw themselves as the new apostles.

In Russia this process was carried to the extreme and was reinforced by an additional factor: the radical intellectuals and revolutionaries of the 1860s typically had a clerical background, and their earliest education was theological. With their arrival and rise to dominance on the cultural scene, Russian intellectual life became permeated with a spirit of the sacred.[26] Christian symbolism pervaded the daily lives of the young radicals, and conflation of the events and roles of sacred history and contemporary life (a recurrent phenomenon in Russian culture, beginning with the Middle Ages) was characteristic of the age of positivism.

An aura of religious fervor surrounded everything connected with the new world of socialist aspirations, beginning with atheism itself. In the words of a contemporary, "Atheism became a kind of religion, and the zealots of this new faith wandered out onto the highroads and byroads like veritable missionaries, in search of living souls in order to cleanse them from the 'abomi-

---

*Feuerbach's ideas fell on ground that had been prepared by the teachings of Eastern Orthodoxy. In fact, a central tenet of Orthodox theology, formed in Greek Patristic thought, is the deification of man: God was made man that man might be made God. This background helps to account for the truly extraordinary influence that Feuerbach had on Russian culture. See Pelikan, *Spirit of Eastern Christendom*, pp. 10–11; and Mantzaridis, *Deification of Man*.

nation of Christianity' [*ot khristianskiia skverny*]."[27] Moreover, as a religion that did not meet official approval and was subject to government persecution, atheism inspired a sacrificial zeal in its proselytes reminiscent of the leader of the seventeenth-century Old Believers, Archpriest Avvakum, and his followers. A radical of the 1860s remarked: "Each of us would have readily mounted the scaffold and laid down his life for Moleschott or Darwin."[28]

The idea that atheism had become "the dominant religion of the educated classes" became a commonplace of Russian nineteenth-century thought.[29] Dostoevsky makes the hero of *The Idiot*, Prince Myshkin, say: "Russians do not merely become atheists, but they invariably *believe* in atheism, as though it were a new religion, without noticing that they are putting faith in a negation."[30] In *The Possessed*, there is a reference to an officer who became "infected with atheism," threw the icons out of his lodgings, and "on three stands placed the works of Vogt, Moleschott, and Büchner, as if they were three altars, and before each of them he would light wax votive candles."[31] Yet, in spite of this mockery, Dostoevsky apparently felt that Russian atheism had an intimate connection with Russian Orthodoxy. "It may be that absolute complete atheism stands closer than anything else to belief," he wrote in his notes for *The Possessed*.[32]

The religious fervor inspired by radicalism can best be illustrated by the example of the sacred aura that surrounded Chernyshevsky in the eyes of his contemporaries. To give but two examples, a member of a revolutionary terrorist organization of the 1860s, Nikolai Ishutin, maintained that history had produced only three great men: Jesus Christ, Saint Paul, and Nikolai Gavrilovich Chernyshevsky.[33] A priest in Saratov, apparently thinking along the same lines but within a different system of values, compared Chernyshevsky with those devils who assume the appearance of angels or of Christ.[34]

The government contributed to Chernyshevsky's sanctification by taking extraordinarily cruel and repressive measures against him and thus creating "a halo of martyrdom," as a contemporary ideological opponent of Chernyshevsky's expressed it.[35] One of these measures, the ceremony of "civil execution" to which Chernyshevsky was subjected after his conviction, had an obvious symbolic quality. On May 12, 1864, amid a weeping and cheering crowd, Chernyshevsky was secured to a pillar in the middle of a public square with a plaque bearing the inscription "State Criminal" attached to his chest.[36] Herzen, in his journal *The Bell* (*Kolokol*), called this pillar "a comrade of the cross."[37] This mock crucifixion inspired Nekrasov's poem "The Prophet" ("Prorok"; 1874):

> He has not yet been crucified,
> But the hour will come when he will be on
>   the cross,
> He was sent by the God of Wrath and Sorrow
> To remind the earthly kings of Christ.

For many, the scene became a crucifixion of the "Russian democratic Christ." It is no wonder that when Chernyshevsky died, his son Mikhail was struck with the resemblance of his father's dead body to representations of the deposition of Christ from the cross, and Chernyshevsky's widow, who was a religious person, reported witnessing "miracles after death."[38]

The Theology of 'What Is to Be Done?'

Curiously enough, we cannot say conclusively, from Chernyshevsky's personal documents or from the memoirs of his family members and friends, whether or not he had lost his faith. (Dostoevsky, as we know, in many ways remained a believer throughout his involvement in Christian socialism and Left-Hegelianism.) But one thing is beyond doubt: in accord with the spirit of the age, Chernyshevsky maintained a belief in the validity of Christian symbolism and Christian texts. A copy of the Bible (one of the few books he took with him to Petersburg in 1846) was in his library during the last years of his life. Chernyshevsky's last words, said in delirium (they were transcribed by a secretary), were: "Strange: in this book there is no mention of God." "It remains unknown," commented Chernyshevsky's son Mikhail, who published the record, "which book he meant."[39]

God is indeed mentioned in *What Is to Be Done?* A rich network of allusions to the Bible and Christian tradition permeates the novel and alerts the reader that it is a text aimed at global solutions to the problems of human existence and the organization of human spiritual and earthly life. The very title of the novel, *Chto delat'?*, among other associations,[40] recalls the episode of the baptism in Luke (3: 10–14) and the question that "the multitude that came forth to be baptized of him" asked of John: "What shall we do?" (*Chto zhe nam delat'?*). (Tolstoy took this formula, further reinforced, for the title of his treatise, *Tak chto zhe nam delat'?; And Yet, What Shall We Do?*, 1880s.) The subtitle—*Iz rasskazov o novykh liudiakh (From Tales About the New People)*—refers to the call for a spiritual renewal of the world and its people underlying the novel's demand for the reorganization and reform of society and mores.

The new men—"men of goodness and strength, justice and ability," as they are introduced to the reader—are seen as the apostles of a new creed, a renewed and improved Christianity. "You are the salt of the salt of the earth," the author says of them, reinforcing the words that Christ addressed to his disciples in the Sermon on the Mount. Their cause is "the cause of mankind" and "the cause of progress." The neglect of this cause, or even the neglect of the concrete duties connected with supervising Vera Pavlovna's commune, is tantamount to "committing a sin against the Holy Ghost." Petrovna, the landlady of the newlywed Lopukhovs, impressed by the chastity of their marriage ("as if they were brother and sister"), takes them for members of a religious sect.

The figure of Rakhmetov is especially charged with Christian symbolism. Just before a decisive episode in the development of the plot (Rakhmetov is going to announce to Vera Pavlovna that Lopukhov is alive), Rakhmetov is presented reading Newton's *Observations on the Prophecies of Daniel and the Apocalypse of St. John*, a book that, by blending the scientific point of view with the prophetic, treats apocalyptic prophecies as predictions of future historical events. For the Christian Socialists, Newton was a symbol of science (the man who presented the world as measurable), and the Newtonian revolution in natural science was seen as analogous to future social revolution.

From this point in the novel (Rakhmetov's reading of Newton's exegesis of the Apocalypse), the author starts to calculate the time that must pass before the realization of certain mysterious events prerequisite for the glorious finale of the novel (this obviously hints at revolution). The calculations, as is always the case with apocalyptic predictions and as is typical for Chernyshevsky, play an important role. Rakhmetov subsequently disappears from St. Petersburg, and his impending return is discussed (in the scene of the winter picnic at the end of the novel) in terms of the Second Coming; it is somehow connected with expected fundamental changes in society.

In the image of Rakhmetov, the symbolism of French Christian socialism is blended with that of the Russian Orthodox tradition.[41] Rakhmetov is portrayed in full accord with the hagiographic canon. Chernyshevsky was intimately familiar with Orthodox hagiography; in his autobiography he recalled that his first and favorite reading (between the ages of eleven and fifteen) was the collection of hagiographic tales *Chet'i minei*, a set of which could be found in every household at that time. A little later, those tales were followed by the novels of George Sand, which regularly appeared in the popular literary magazines to which the family subscribed (1: 632–34). It has been suggested that the story of Rakhmetov's life follows a particular hagiographic text, *The Life of Aleksei, the Man of God* (*Zhitie Alekseia, cheloveka bozhiia*), which pictures a wealthy young man who gives away his property, abandons worldly success and the love of a woman, and dedicates his life to faith, subjecting himself to extraordinary self-mortification (Rakhmetov, to test his endurance, sleeps on a bed of nails).[42] And, as though he wanted to reach even the "unperceptive reader," Chernyshevsky makes the woman whom Rakhmetov risks his life to save (a blending of the canons of hagiography and George Sandian romance) see him in a dream "surrounded by a halo."

The key symbol of the novel—the wedding—goes back to the persistent New Testament image of the union between bridegroom and bride as a symbol of redemption. In the novel, the wedding (*svad'ba*) stands for liberation in its various aspects— the immediate liberation of a woman, Vera Pavlovna, from family and social tyranny through her marriage to Lopukhov, and the ultimate liberation of humanity through social revolution.

The evangelical roots of these symbols are obvious—the Kingdom of Heaven is likened in the Gospel to the arrival of the bridegroom, a stable symbol of Christ ("Behold, the bridegroom cometh"). In *What Is to Be Done?*, however, the coming of the new world is associated with the advent of a female messiah; not the bridegroom but the bride cometh. Behind this stands the feminism of George Sand's novels (and the tradition that ascribed to her the title of "female Christ"), as well as a symbolic interpretation of women's liberation. The idea also has another specifically Russian connection: the popular symbolic image of Russia as a woman.

The image of the bride first appears in Lopukhov's conversation with Vera's mother; in order to dispel her doubts about his association with Vera, he announces that he is already betrothed. What he refers to as his "bride" is actually the revolution, the cause to which he has committed himself. Vera, in her first dream, sees Lopukhov's bride performing one of Christ's miraculous cures. Vera dreams that she is paralyzed and immobile (an allegory of her oppressed condition); suddenly she hears a voice commanding her to "arise and walk" (a "*Talitha cumi*" of sorts): "'As for you, you will be well, if I touch you with my hand. You see, there you are, cured; arise.' . . . Verochka arose" (81; *94*). From this point on, almost any situation connected with a wedding or marriage in general is endowed with symbolic meaning.

The same is true of the disappearance and return of the characters: they are projected onto the Christian death-and-resurrection pattern and the idea of the Second Coming. The two motifs (wedding and resurrection) intersect in the scene where Katia Polozova informs Vera Pavlovna of her betrothal. In Katia's description of her bridegroom Beaumont, who has recently arrived from America (a recurring symbol of the otherworld in the Russian and European utopian tradition), Vera Pavlovna recognizes her ex-husband Lopukhov, who had disappeared and is generally believed to be dead. Rejoicing, she says to Kirsanov: "It is Easter today, Sasha; so say to Katenka: 'He is risen indeed'" (332; *375*). And the three of them embrace and kiss each other.

The climax of the whole line of biblical allusions comes in Vera

Pavlovna's fourth dream, which is also the culmination of the whole novel. The lady of the dreams (the "tsaritsa" or "goddess") reveals her kingdom to Vera—the kingdom of God, which is simultaneously the socialist society of the future. The land in which it is situated is described as the biblical Promised Land, in Chernyshevsky's words, "the land that was described in the old days as 'flowing with milk and honey.'" It is called the "new Russia," and its location is specified with a precision of suggestive geographical detail. This is what Vera Pavlovna sees from a certain elevated point to which the lady of the dreams has taken her:

> Far away to the northeast are two rivers, which unite and flow together straight to the east from the place where Vera Pavlovna is standing. Further to the south, in the same southeast direction, there is a long and wide bay; to the south the land stretches into the distance, growing wider between this bay and the long thin bay that forms its western boundary. Between this narrow bay on the west and the sea, which is far away to the northwest, there is a narrow isthmus. (286; *n.p.*)

Although the location is not named, it is easy to recognize from this meticulous description. The two rivers form the valley of the Tigris and Euphrates, the biblical Eden. And the elevated point from which Vera and the lady of the dreams look down on it is Mount Sinai, where Moses received the Ten Commandments.

Vera Pavlovna's Fourth Dream: The Kingdom of Heaven

Vera Pavlovna's vision of the Kingdom of Heaven (the domain of the "bright tsaritsa" or "goddess") is a combination of the prophetic and the scientific characteristics of utopia in the age of positivism. The economic and biological foundations of prosperity in this paradise are discussed with "mathematical" stringency and the minutest precision of detail (many details have easily recognizable prototypes in Chernyshevsky's real-life environment, most notably in the domestic habits of Olga Sokratovna). The social arrangement is based on communal principles similar to those advocated by Fourier, Considérant, and Owen, as well as to the system of the rational organization of labor advocated by Louis Blanc, one of Chernyshevsky's favorite authors. The domicile of the members of the commune, a building of crystal and iron, is patterned after the Crystal Palace built for the Great Exhibition of 1851 in London, a contemporary symbol for the advance of science and technology (after Dostoevsky's *Notes from Underground* appeared, it became a symbol of socialist utopia).

The biological foundations of utopia lie in the "theory of the functions of the nervous system," advocated in the novel by Doctor Kirsanov. The theory is a scientific justification of Chernyshevsky's favorite idea that love for a woman stimulates activity and brings involvement in real life. The connection between love and activity, a matter of direct identification with clear mythological overtones in Chernyshevsky's earlier writings, is elaborated in the novel in terms of positivist physiology. Kirsanov explains that love is a continuous, strong, and healthy excitement of the nerves that necessarily develops the nervous system. Consequently, intellectual, moral, and physical forces grow in proportion to love, and the excitement aroused by passion gives one energy to work. The men of the future—the communitarians in the fourth dream—are pictured as people with an organic predisposition for love. The strong physical constitution of working-class people is combined with the refinement of the educated classes. The combination of energy and sensitivity produces a new human being, with a different nervous system, characterized by a natural, powerful, and healthy thirst for pleasure, a man who is by nature endowed with a passion for dancing and singing, with social ease and energy, and with a capacity for sexual enjoyment. Love provides extra energy for work, and by working hard all day, the people prepare their nervous systems for the raptures of true joy.

The climax of this cycle of love and labor is a daily ball, described in the fourth dream with the usual precision of detail (including specifications of spatial organization). "A normal weekday evening" in the socialist community of the future "resembles a court ball of contemporary times"; it also resembles young Chernyshevsky's first ball, as well as the dancing parties given by Olga Sokratovna. This communal entertainment of noisy movement, enjoyed with energy "beyond our experience," is accompanied by intimate sexual delights; these are provided for by

the arrangement of living conditions and furnishings. The dancing hall is surrounded by private rooms into which one or another couple discreetly disappear. The tsaritsa explains the arrangement to Vera Pavlovna:

Half of them are now enjoying themselves at the party in the hall,
but where is the other half? "Where are the others?" says the bright
tsaritsa. "Why, they are everywhere . . . but as for the most of them—
well, that is my secret. You saw in the hall how people's cheeks burnt
and their eyes shone? You saw people going off and people arriving?
They left because I enticed them away. The room of every man and
woman here is my sanctuary, and in them my secrets are inviolable.
Over the doors hang sumptuous carpets which muffle all sounds, and
behind those doors is complete privacy." (289–90; 327–28)

(Herzen, impressed by this scene, wrote to Ogarev: "[Cherny-
shevsky] ends the novel with a phalanstery, a brothel. A bold
work."[43])

The resplendent ball in the fourth dream is only the apogee of
a series of scenes of noisy merriment and high jinks that seem to
define life in the households of the new people (dancing and
singing, shouting with joy, chasing each other in jest, leaping
over chairs; in the summer boat rides and picnics, in the winter
racing troikas).[44] Many of these scenes have easily recognizable
prototypes in the scenes of perpetual gaiety and merriment that
surrounded the life of Olga Sokratovna. But in the novel the
theme of gaiety has a symbolic significance. It has obvious biblical connections (as well as a connection to the Schillerian notion
of "joy"). In the Sermon on the Mount, the disciples of Christ
receive a commandment to "be glad and rejoicing" (their Old
Testament predecessors, "the children of Zion," were described
as "dancing and playing," "leaping with joy," and "making a
joyful noise unto the Lord"). "Rejoice and be exceedingly glad
for great is your reward in heaven: for so persecuted they the
prophets which were before you. You are the salt of the earth"
(Matthew 5: 12–13).

The idea of prophetic vision also has a long cultural tradition.
Such a vision is a staple of novels in the utopian genre, borrowed from Early Christian texts and therefore a matter of literary convention. And yet, curiously enough, Vera Pavlovna's

dreams, which presented carefully elaborated solutions to contemporary social problems (such as the woman question, or the issue of the communal labor), have an actual counterpart in the real life of the Russian socialists. Nikolai Ogarev apparently had dreams comparable to the literary visions of Chernyshevsky's heroine (Ogarev recorded the most interesting of them in his diary). In one dream, he saw himself in his village in Russia discussing with the peasants, in considerable detail, the advantages of communal land tenure; in another, he had a conversation with a "fallen woman" on the backwardness of common views of the matter; and in yet another, he puzzled over the appropriate arrangement of a commune:

Sept. 10 [1873] Wednesday. Today a question came to me as I dreamed: how can a commune be arranged? What is the difference between the concept of a commune and that of equality? What means can equalize the ownership of land and that of all other goods? What means can bring the labor of separate individuals into common labor? Can it be done by equal divisions per family or per head, or should only the labor, i.e., the profit, be split?
The question is not easy, it would seem.[45]

Since Ogarev experienced these dreams in the 1870s, after the publication of Chernyshevsky's novel, it is difficult to say whether we are dealing with a case of art borrowing from life or life borrowing from art. Did Chernyshevsky reflect the real-life habits of his milieu, or did his readers transform the literary dreams of the novel's heroine into the reality of individual human consciousness or, rather, subconsciousness? The question, as Ogarev might have said, is not easy.

Christian Mysteries in a Positive Key

Perhaps the most important aspect of the novel's Christian symbolism relates to the "rational" interpretation of the persistent New Testament pattern of transformation, which reaches its apogee in the mystery of transfiguration, a concept of overwhelming importance in Orthodox theology. Transfiguration is the appearance of Christ to his disciples in divine glory during his earthly life: "And he was transfigured before them: and his face did shine as the sun, and his raiment was white as the light" (Matthew 17: 2). It is interpreted as a revelation of the image that human beings will assume in their future life in the heavenly kingdom, when the whole earthly world will be transfigured.

In the novel, the miracle of transfiguration is enacted in the evolution of the image of Vera. As shown above, Vera, who is initially presented as an ordinary human being, confronts a divine being (a female god) in her dreams. The goddess introduces herself to Vera as a "bride of your bridegroom"; that is, as Vera's double. (The name Vera, meaning "faith," stands for one of the most important saints in the Orthodox tradition, a maiden dedicated to Christ, or Christ's bride.) In the fourth dream, the identity between Vera and the goddess is established beyond any doubt. This mysterious being had revealed herself earlier in such glory and radiance that her human form could not be comprehended ("Although you revealed yourself to me before, you were surrounded with such radiance that I could barely see you"). Her countenance is now altered and the human face of the deity is revealed to Vera: "For your sake I shall dim for a moment the brightness of my aura. . . . For one moment I shall cease to be a tsaritsa" (281; 316). But the human face of the goddess is Vera's own face. The goddess thus undergoes a transfiguration in reverse (reveals a human image in a divine being), while a human being is transfigured and exalted to divine glory and shining beauty. "Yes, it is herself that Vera Pavlovna has seen—a goddess. The countenance of the goddess is her own living countenance, whose features are so far from perfection . . . yet she is more beautiful . . . than all the beauties of the past" (281; 316).

Although the general principle is that of transfiguration, the "double transfiguration"—the humanization of God and the deification of man—is a realization of Feuerbach's principle. In the fourth dream, Feuerbach's philosophical formula of identity, "God is man, man is God," was joined with the exalted biblical phraseology and imagery of French Christian socialism. The resulting synthesis was infused with George Sand's feminism: "There is nothing nobler than a man," says the goddess to Vera Pavlovna; that is, she continues, "there is nothing nobler than a woman" (281; 361).

However, Chernyshevsky departs from the canon established by the positivist revision of Christian dogma on one important point. One of the main components of Feuerbach's critique of religion was the rejection of miracles, phenomena that are not perceptible to the senses and that are contradictory to the laws of science. The essence of Christ's turning of water into wine, he maintains, lies in the implication that "two absolutely contradictory predicates or subjects are identical." This seems conceivable, since the resulting transformation—the visible appearance of the identity of two contradictories—can be perceived. And yet there is an inherent contradiction: the miracle itself, that which makes the water suddenly wine, is not a natural process, hence it cannot be an object of the senses or of any real or possible experience.[46]

Chernyshevsky amends this point in Feuerbach's critique of Christianity. In his novel, he offers a scientific explanation of miracles: the transformation itself is presented as a natural process. The encoding of the idea of transfiguration in its broad sense (miraculous transformation of quality) into the language of positivism and science takes place in Vera's second dream. Vera dreams that a long discussion between Lopukhov and a friend about "analyses, identities, and anthropologisms" takes place in a field. The principle under discussion is the following: "Let the disposition of the atoms be a little changed, and something different will result" (123; *145*). And that is all that transmutation (or transfiguration) is—a chemical rearrangement of atoms that results in the conversion of one chemical compound into a different compound of a higher order.

Chernyshevsky illustrates this principle with an extensive analogy from agricultural chemistry: the sun warms humid soil, and the heat displaces the elements and forms them into more complex chemical combinations (combinations of a higher level); then an ear of wheat, which is white and pure, grows out of rotting black soil. Destruction turns into production, black becomes white. (This principle recalls Chernyshevsky's theory of good and evil: "under certain circumstances man becomes good, under other circumstances—evil.")

Extending the agricultural allegory, Chernyshevsky elaborates and specifies the notion of transformation and, in the long run, correlates it with the notion of reality. There are two types of soil: one that, "in the language of our philosophy," is called "real soil," and one that is "fantastic" or "rotten." The real soil, although it is a product of decay, produces vegetation; the fantastic soil is barren. The cause of this abnormality is the absence of motion. Fantastic or rotten soil is fruitless because the waters in it do not move and therefore provoke further decay; when water moves and flows away, it makes the field healthy and productive. The concept of motion is then developed further. The fundamental form of motion is labor, or activity, which is the basis for all other forms—distraction, amusement, gaiety, and so forth. Without motion, there is no life, no reality. According to Chernyshevsky's argument, reality is those phenomena of life that can, when motion-activity is applied to them, be transformed into different, opposite phenomena (rotting, black soil that can become living, white wheat).

The conversation between Lopukhov and his friend is an adaptation of Justus Liebig's theory of agricultural chemistry, which was of extreme importance for the ideology and concrete social program of Russian radicals.[47] However, throughout the metaphorical use of the concepts of contemporary natural science, which are blended with metaphysical concepts, symbolic elements from the New Testament are transparently present. Among them is the Christian symbolism of the field and the tilling of the land, as well as the specifically Russian symbolism of Mother Earth, the Humid. More important, the New Testament pattern of transmutation, which implies the inherent identity of opposites and instant transvaluation, stands behind the whole principle.

Thus, in Chernyshevsky's novel the miracle of transformation receives a scientific corroboration consistent with the spirit of the age of positivism—with general scientific principles (the rearrangement of elements in a chemical compound) and with concrete theories in natural science (Liebig's theory of agricultural chemistry). Contrary to Feuerbach's critical argument, the transformation itself (that which makes water wine, or black white, or the dead alive, or the human divine) is presented as a natural process and explained in terms of chemical science.

What was a Christian miracle and a concept of idealistic metaphysics—Hegelian qualitative transformation—is turned into a phenomenon conceivable from the point of view of science and therefore (in Feuerbach's terms) an object, if not of actual, then of possible, experience.

The pattern of transformation that arose at the intersection of the mystical and scientific is then translated into a literary structure and appears as a narrative pattern. The basic structural principle governing the organization of the whole novel and penetrating the text on many levels, from the ideological to the rhetorical, is the reconciliation of opposites. What it ultimately entails is the transformation of a quality into a contradictory or opposite quality—lack of artistic talent turns into true giftedness, weakness becomes strength, coldness of heart is transformed into passionate love, clumsiness and shyness turn into social ease. The transformation is mediated through an algorithm of concrete operations arranged with almost mathematical precision. And yet the persistent New Testament pattern of transformation—making water into wine, turning the dead into the living, and exalting the human into the divine—is recognizable in it. In fact, the reversal of the positive and negative poles of the opposition (successful authors declared to be giftless, and an inept writer truly talented; an aristocrat shown to be ignoble, and a commoner noble) follows the New Testament inversion of values: "Many that are first shall be last, and the last first" (Matthew 19: 30); "Whosoever exalteth himself shall be abased; and he that humbleth himself shall be exalted" (Luke 14: 11). Thus, Christian symbolism affected every element of the novel—from its scientific allegories to its narrative strategies and rhetorical devices.

What is the pragmatics of the rhetorical arsenal outlined above?

Feuerbach provided a psychological explanation of the power of religion based on the miracle of transformation: "It sets aside all limits, all laws which are painful for the feelings, and thus makes objective to man the immediate, absolutely unlimited satisfaction of his subjective wishes."[48] In *What Is to Be Done?*, Chernyshevsky, a faithful disciple of Feuerbach, in accordance with the specifically Russian tradition of substituting literature for religion, attempted to use a literary text and its structural properties for this very purpose. Concerned with his novel's proselytizing power, he made his model accessible and acceptable to a wide range of contemporary readers, especially to those whose activity he saw as decisive for the cultural development of his day—the radical avant-garde of the Russian intelligentsia. By encoding the Christian miracle of transformation into the language of contemporary positivist discourse, Chernyshevsky seemed to give a scientific justification of the miracle.

Embodied in the narrative structure of the novel, the pattern became truly all-pervasive. As Chernyshevsky planned, his model was accessible both to radicals who read and trusted nothing but scholarly treatises and to those who "read only novels." It also had a special emotional appeal for minds nurtured on modern ideals of positive science, yet cast in the mold of the Russian Orthodox tradition. Through the novel, a *raznochinets* was invited to free himself from a sense of social inadequacy and inferiority and undergo a mental transformation into an aristocrat; a woman was offered superiority over a man; a fallen woman was invited to identify with and triumph over an honest woman. This model apparently had the power to liberate a whole generation of the new Russian intelligentsia from the burden of the culturally motivated inadequacy that they shared.

Conclusion

My principal task in this study has been to trace the transformation of personal and cultural experience into a literary structure. In order to accomplish this task, I have followed the course of Chernyshevsky's life, trying to show, at every point, the concrete mechanisms by which the individual and the cultural interacted and ultimately converged to create a generally significant model. This discussion has been supplemented by a detailed analysis of the structure and symbolism of Chernyshevsky's most important novel, *What Is to Be Done?*, in which his model was embodied. In short, the solution that I bring to the initial problem is empirical; rather than a universal formula or abstract definition, it is a systematic description of the process by which personality intervenes in the historical development of literature.

But although this book is an empirical study concerned with concrete historical material, it can throw some light on two general methodological problems: how to introduce considerations of active human agency and broad historical context into structurally oriented literary analysis, and how to integrate structural analysis with the study of literary pragmatics. And yet the question remains: How can the structural properties of the novel account for the power of its influence?

In art, Chernyshevsky saw the possibility of a global organization of reality, an all-encompassing guide to life enabling humanity to resolve all the basic problems of its existence. He not only developed a theory of art that expounded this idea, but also tried to create a work of art that would equip his contemporaries with an instrument for dealing with reality. In doing this, he did not ignore or minimize the importance of formal structure, as some critics have suggested. On the contrary, *What Is to Be Done?* productively utilizes the active creative energy of artistic structure.

Like any work of art, the novel offers its own model of reality. On the one hand, the world is structured in terms of oppositions of two contrasting qualities, notions or personages; on the other hand, the possibilities of transforming one quality, notion, or personage into another inherent in this structure are practically unlimited. In this sense, it can be said that in its constituent parts the novel is structured as a myth. The general conception of the world projected by the novel is that reality consists of those things that can at any point be transformed into something different. Thus, the fundamental principle advanced in the novel is the transformation (be it rearrangement, transmutation, or revolution) of a certain way or form of being.

But the reader can find more than a model of reality as potentiality for transformation in *What Is to Be Done?* The "perceptive reader" is offered concrete mechanisms for transforming and mastering reality and, in the long run, means for liberating himself from reality's constraints. Projected onto the realm of individual experience, the literary structure organizes both the individual's vision of the surrounding world and personality itself. Thus, the carefully arranged arsenal of structural devices contained in the novel can be utilized as a mental instrument to bring about the symbolic resolution of conflicts. All oppositions can be resolved, all contradictions can be reconciled, all painful aspects of reality can be exposed as illusory (and thus symbolically canceled); the second, "true" reality, even though it might be contradictory to the first, can be uncovered behind the mask of appearance.

There are several reasons for the power of this system. First, its power lies in the coherence and flexibility of the structure described above. Second, the system's power also lies in its potential to be projected onto the manifold situations of everyday life. The novel abounds in concrete details reflecting daily life ("ordinary life of ordinary people"), and contemporary readers promptly recognized such details. Because they were seen as the elements of the artistic structure, and because that structure had the properties of a mythological scheme, commonplace ways of living were experienced as having symbolic significance and universal meaning. The teleological order of things was revealed in seeming trivia.

The final secret of Chernyshevsky's influence lies in the unique blending and integration in his thought and in his novel of diverse traditions that were of crucial importance for his time: Russian Orthodoxy, French Christian socialism, left-wing Hegelianism, English utilitarianism, positivist scientism, the aesthetics of realism, and the remnants of idealism and romanticism. This creative synthesis assured both continuity and revolutionary change, and accounted for both universalism and national specificity in the development of Russian culture.

Behind Chernyshevsky's creative efforts lies a belief in the unlimited power of human reason to arrange the world, individual lives, and even human nature itself by independent, "rational" principles, a belief characteristic of the age of realism. But behind it also lies a romantic belief in the unlimited power of art; it is after all a work of art that was chosen as the main vehicle of "reason." But in the age of realism a work of art was no longer seen as an object of aesthetic cultivation. Unlike romantic literary models, which relied on the aesthetic for their expressive power, Chernyshevsky's model relied on the anti-aesthetic.

The idea of a bad writer, that is, a writer who is aesthetically inept and whose role is not that of the poet, but that of a practical man (a man of action), a political activist and popularizer of science, became an integral part of the epochal model. Chernyshevsky's novel fulfilled its role not in spite of its artistic faults, but rather because of them. In this sense, he was right when he declared in the preface to his novel that his lack of artistic talent was of no importance and that his novel could be placed above the celebrated works of famous authors.

In fact, *What Is to Be Done?* turned out to be a more appropriate medium for conveying a symbolic model of reality and the man of reality than novels modern readers consider to be works of genius, such as those of Dostoevsky and Tolstoy. All of the above reasons, taken together, account for the tremendous emotional appeal that Chernyshevsky and his novel had for the generation of the 1860s and for the novel's impact on, to use the language of the day, the rearrangement and transfiguration of all life.

Reference Material

The Russian Texts

Listed below are the original texts of the quotations from Russian given in translations. All quotations from Chernyshevsky are included, as well as substantial (one sentence or more) quotations from other authors.

Introduction

The New Man

Everything that...
Все, традиционно существовавшее и принимавшееся ранее без критики, пошло в переборку. Все, — начиная с теоретических вершин, с религиозных воззрений, основ государственного и общественного строя, вплоть до житейских обычаев, до костюма и прически волос.

I once worked up...
Я однажды отважилась сказать моим подругам, что не люблю Некрасова; что не люблю Герцена — не отважилась бы. [...] мы имеем теперь две цензуры и как бы два правительства, и которое строже, — трудно сказать. Те, бритые и с орденом на шее, гоголевские чиновники отходят на второй план, а на сцену выступают новые, с бакенами и без орденов на шее, и они в одно и то же время и блюстители порядка и блюстители беспорядка.

Writers mostly...
Писатели в своих романах и повестях большею частию стараются брать типы общества и представлять их образно и художественно, —

типы, чрезвычайно редко встречающиеся в действительности целиком и которые тем не менее почти действительнее самой действительности.

Literature predicts...
Литература провидит законы будущего, воспроизводит образ будущего человека. [...] Типы, созданные литературой, всегда идут далее тех, которые имеют ход на рынке, и потому-то именно они и кладут известную печать даже на такое общество, которое по-видимому всецело находится под гнетом эмпирических тревог и опасений. Под влиянием этих новых типов современный человек, незаметно для самого себя, получает новые привычки, ассимилирует себе новые взгляды, приобретает новую складку, одним словом — постепенно вырабатывает из себя нового человека.

Never, neither earlier...
Никогда, ни раньше, ни после, писатель не занимал у нас в России такого почетного места. Когда на литературных чтениях (они начались тогда впервые) являлся на эстраде писатель, пользующийся симпатиями публики, стон стоял от криков восторга, аплодисментов и стучанья стульями и каблуками. Это был не энтузиазм, а какое-то беснование, но совершенно верно выражавшее то воодушевление, которое вызывал писатель в публике.

Creative writers...
Беллетристы составляют ариергард направления, авангардом же дружно движущихся литературных полчищ являются публицисты.

It turned out...
Вот какое страшное, если не прямое обвинение, то подозрение в нашем обществе могло возникнуть из такой пустой вещи, как красиво написанная легкомысленным человеком повестца, и какою оно тяжестью обрушилось и на ни в чем не повинный журнал, и на ни в чем не повинных работавших в нем сотрудников, и тем более на ни в чем не повинную учащуюся молодежь, и, наконец, также на не повинную ни в чем либеральную партию.

I don't care...
Верно ли понял Писарев тургеневского Базарова, до этого мне дела нет. Важно то, что он в Базарове узнал *себя* и *своих* и добавил, чего недоставало в книге.

All the prominent traits...
Все резко выдающиеся черты их [«новых людей» в романе] — черты не индивидуумов, а типа [...] Эти общие черты так резки, что за ними

сглаживаются все личные особенности. [...] Недавно зародился у нас этот тип и быстро распложается. Он рожден временем, он знамение времени, и, сказать ли? — он исчезнет вместе с своим временем, недолгим временем. [...] И он возвратится в более многочисленных людях, в лучших формах [...] тогда уже не будет этого отдельного типа, потому что все люди будут этого типа [...]

This mutual interaction...
Странная вещь — это взаимодействие людей на книгу и книги на людей. Книга берет весь склад из того общества, в котором возникает, обобщает его, делает более наглядным и резким, и вслед за тем бывает обойдена реальностью. Оригиналы делают шаржу своих резко оттененных портретов, и действительные лица вживаются в свои литературные тени. В конце прошлого века все немцы сбивали не-много на Вертера, все немки на Шарлотту; в начале нынешнего — университетские Вертеры стали превращаться в «разбойников», не настоящих, а шиллеровских. Русские молодые люди, приезжавшие после 1862 года, почти все были из «Что делать?», с прибавлением нескольких базаровских черт.

What Is to Be Done? was a prophet
«Что делать?» в своем роде пророк. Многое, что представлялось ему [Чернышевскому] как греза, свершилось воочию: новые люди разо-шлись [...] по городам и весям, тщаться на практике осуществить уроки учителя, далеко уже превзойдя его надежды, еще запечатленные некоторой сантиментальностью [...] И теперь, как прежде, беда именно в том, что Кирсановы могут быть профессорами, Мерцаловы иереями, их приятели мировыми судьями, членами судов, полковни-ками генерального штаба, тайными советниками [...]

The desire to look...
Желание ни в чем не походить на презренных филистеров простира-лось на самую внешность новых людей, и, таким образом, появились те пресловутые нигилистические костюмы, в которых щеголяла моло-дежь в течение 60-х и 70-х годов. Пледы и сучковатые дубинки, стриженные волосы и космы сзади до плеч, синие очки, фра-дьяволь-ские шляпы и конфедератки, — боже, в каком поэтическом ореоле рисовалось все это в те времена и как заставляло биться молодые сердца [...]

[The] elder looked at my...
[...] заметил [...], глядя на мои длинные волосы, очки и толстую палку: «ну, видно вы проглотили всю бездну премудрости нигилизма».

Aristocratism...
Аристократизм с его внешним благообразием, изяществом, блеском
и величием,   был высшею формой нашей тогдашней культуры. Но
этот красивый цветок вырос на почве крепостного права, которое
совершенно перепутывало все понятия.

Nikolai Chernyshevsky

There are names...
Есть имена, которые покрывают собою духовную работу целого
поколения, деятельность огромного числа лиц, иной раз лиц очень
самостоятельных и сильных. Имя одного человека становится вы-
разителем массового движения — движения не темной массы, а целых
интеллигентных групп [...] Для молодого поколения 60-х годов, в его
радикальных группах разных оттенков, имя Чернышевского было
таким условным именем [...]

There was a time...
Было время, когда Россия стояла на здоровом и много обещавшем
пути: это были первые годы царствования Александра II. Но потом
началось революционное брожение, и все спуталось, и так идет до
сего дня. Всему виновник Чернышевский: это он привил революцион-
ный яд к нашей жизни.

Informers tell me...
Мне доносят, что подготовляется движение, я посылаю за Чернышев-
ским, говорю ему: «Пожалуйста, устройте, чтобы этого не было». Он
дает мне слово, и я еду к государю и докладываю, что все будет
спокойно.

It's time for toasts...
являются тосты — за Н.Г. Чернышевского первым долгом, потом
мы воспеваем вольность, свободу, браним все и всех без пощады,
начиная с Н.П. [Николая Павловича, т.е. Николая I] — ну, да ты, я
думаю, догадываешься с кого... потому что не может быть, чтобы
тебе в душу не запали слова Николая Гавриловича, нашего просвети-
теля.

Chernyshevsky had a strong...
Чернышевский имел на нас [...] сильное и прямое влияние. Его мы
знали наизусть, его именем клялись, как правоверный магометанин
клянется Магометом, пророком Аллаха.

had opportunities to see...
случалось видеть семидесятилетних стариков, для которых «Совре-

менник» был «учебником жизни» и руководителем для правильного понимания разрешавшихся тогда вопросов.

regarded themselves...
[...] считали себя [...] какими-то Жаннами д'Арк, призванными к пересозданию человечества, в сопровождении своих поклонников, разумеется.

such a perversion...
[...] что такое извращение идеи супружества разрушает и идею семьи, основы гражданственности, что то и другое прямо противно коренным началам религии, нравственности и общественного порядка и что сочинение, проповедующее такие принципы и воззрения, в высшей степени вредно и опасно.

Katkov and I...
Мы с Катковым не могли прийти в себя от недоумения и не знали только, чему удивляться более: циничной ли нелепости всего романа или явному сообщничеству существующей цензуры.

It would not be an exaggeration...
Я нимало не преувеличу, когда скажу, что мы читали роман чуть не коленопреклоненно, с таким благочестием, какое не допускает ни малейшей улыбки на устах, с каким читают богослужебные книги.
    Влияние романа было колоссально на все наше общество.

Manna from heaven...
Никакой манне небесной не обрадовались бы так люди, погибающие от голода, как обрадовалась этому роману молодежь, доселе бесцельно шатавшаяся по Петербургу. Он был для нее точно озарением, посланным свыше. Они начали делать именно то, что должны были делать по прямому смыслу романа в настоящем.

We made the novel...
мы сделали из романа какой-то Коран, в котором искали и находили не только общее руководство правильной жизни, но и частные указания как поступать в отдельных случаях.

From the time...
С тех пор, как завелись типографские станки в России и вплоть до нашего времени, ни одно печатное произведение не имело в России такого успеха, как «Что делать?».

What Is to Be Done? is not only...
«Что делать?» — не только энциклопедия, справочная книга, но и кодекс для практического применения «нового слова».[...] Под формой

романа (формой неуклюжей, крайне аляповатой) предложено полное руководство к переделке всех общественных отношений, но главным образом — к переделке отношений между мужчинами и женщинами. [...] За 16 лет пребывания в университете мне не удалось встретить студента, который не прочел бы знаменитого романа еще в гимназии; а гимназистка 5-6 класса считалась бы дурой, если бы не ознакомилась с похождениями Веры Павловны. В этом отношении сочинения, например, Тургенева или Гончарова — не говоря уже о Гоголе и Пушкине — далеко уступают роману «Что делать?»

Producers' and consumers'...
всюду начали заводиться производительные и потребительные ассоциации, мастерские, швейные, сапожные, переплетные, прачечные, коммуны для общежития, семейные квартиры с нейтральными комнатами и пр. Фиктивные браки с целью освобождения генеральских и купеческих дочек из-под ига семейного деспотизма в подражание Лопухову и Вере Павловне сделались обыденным явлением жизни, причем редкая освободившаяся таким образом барыня не заводила швейной мастерской и не рассказывала вещих снов, чтобы вполне уподобиться героине романа.

I grew up on...
я воспитывался на Чернышевском, и один из героев его романа «Что делать?» Рахметов был идеалом. Конечно, я не решался спать на гвоздях, но на голых досках спал год. Мало того, я старался есть как можно меньше и пищу выбирал самую простую.

There were cases...
Были примеры, что дочери покидали отцов и матерей, жены — мужей, некоторые шли даже на все крайности, отсюда вытекающие [...]

It would have been a crime...
Это было бы преступлением, посягательством с моей стороны на ее свободу, так как я был ее законный муж.

the conversation began...
разговор начался с разных моральных и общественных тем, свелся по ассоциации идей и на вопрос любви, и закончился признанием.

The life described...
Жизнь, описанная в ней, перекликалась с нашей.

My life and yours...
Наша с тобой жизнь принадлежит истории.

1 Exposition

In our immediate...
В ближайшем кругу не было человека, имевшего какое-нибудь понятие о Петербурге. Это была неведомая, отдаленная страна, пребывание всех властей, с особенными нравами и великими житейскими трудностями [...]

I feel...
и ничего не чувствую, ровно ничего. (1: 113)

Starting with Hegel...
Начиная Гегелем и Фейербахом и кончая лубочными французскими романами, Чернышевский прочитал все.

The Diaries: Attention to Pennies

Everything in reality...
Все *в самом деле* непосредственное, всякое простое чувство было возводимо в отвлеченные категории и возвращалось оттуда без капли живой крови, бледной алгебраической тенью. [...] Самая слеза, навертывавшаяся на веках, была строго отнесена к своему порядку, к «гемюту» или к «трагическому в сердце [...]».

I sit down...
Я сажусь за дело, перевожу с немецкого или делаю что-нибудь другое, — и что же? я дрожу от холода, руки мои не в состоянии держать перо, животная сторона моя громко дает о себе знать. Я бросаю перо и иду — куда-нибудь, иногда в лавку Глазунова, где часов шесть сряду болтаю черт знает что. В другое время, только что разделаюсь, то есть разохочусь делать, пользуясь гармоническим состоянием души, — и вдруг получаю записку, где мне напоминают, что за взятые мною 500 р. надо заплатить за месяц 30 р. асс[игнациями], а в ответ пишу, нельзя ли этих денег за меня заплатить, да еще достать мне сот восемь за такие же проценты [...]

2 [December 1848]...
2 [декабря 1848 года], 11 [часов]. — Было менее холодно, чем вчера, и я сумел, особенно, когда шел в университет, весьма хорошо закутаться, так что уши нисколько не озябли. Теперь во второй раз зимою ходил без калош, между прочим по экономии: не достанет ли этой пары сапогов и старых калош до лета? Конечно, нет, но все-таки. В

университет пошел в 10 1/2; не пошел к Грефе, как и хотел, а в библиотеку, где читал «Revue d.d. Mondes» критические статьи Limayrac'а — пошлость, так же, как и замечания о бездушии, непостоянстве и проч. отсутствии принципов у Бенж. Констана. Чудаки, — они думают, если человек в негодовании говорит: «я не верю, люди подлы и глупы», так это в самом деле потому, что он менее их одарен душою, жаждущей верить, любящей человека, а не потому, что, напротив, у него эти силы жаднее ищут удовлетворения и что горше для него несообразность действительного с разумным? (1: 185)

At first...
Сначала я стоял у двери, которая ведет в их комнату, где стоят фортепьяна, после у двери у входа; во все это время танцевали шесть или во всяком случае четыре пары [...] Сначала (1 кадриль) она стояла на месте "л", мы с Ив.Вас. в дверях "б" — я все смотрел на нее, почти не спуская глаз. (1: 210)

The time...
Я ходил всего: от Максимовича к Булычеву и назад около 100 минут, после к Ал.Фед. 16 мин., оттуда домой снова 16, оттуда к Булычеву еще 50 или 48 хотя, всего 180 мин. = 3 часа — и оттуда на дачу пришел без 1/4 9, между тем как у Булычева был в 6, — по крайней мере 2 1/2 часа — итак, 5 1/4 часа, 32 версты. (1: 278)

As we walked...
Когда шли (у угла на повороте с проспекта во 2-ю линию, когда идешь мимо казармы), мне мелькнуло чувство, что не хороша у нее походка. (1: 71)

feelings are determined...
[...] чувствования зависят не от места, а от времени. (1: 99)

perhaps the quickening...
[...] вообще верно чувствительность изнутри, а не извне [...] так и волнение сердца не от событий, а так от чего-то беспричинного. (1: 99)

Three to four...
выкатилось 3-4 слезы. (1: 53)

Living Merged with Writing

Oh Lord...
Боже мой, как подробно писано! Все, решительно все с стенографической подробностью! [...] Ведь целых 44 простых и 10 двойных страниц! [...] написал целых 64 страницы! Ведь это выйдет: 64 x 27 (строк) x 80

(буквы в строке) = 138 200 букв! Ведь это 140 страниц обыкновенной печати! ведь это, наконец, целая повесть. Вот плодовитый писатель! (1: 471)

I keep writing...
Я пишу все романы. Десятки их написаны мною. Пишу и рву. Беречь рукописи не нужно: остается в памяти все, что раз было написано. И как я услышу от тебя, что могу печатать, буду посылать листов по двадцати печатного счета в месяц. (15: 87)

Sometimes he would...
Бывало и ночью проснется, вскочит и начнет писать.

Two tables...
Между эстрадой и передним полукругом аудитории, несколько правее и левее эстрады, стояли два стола, за тем, который был налево перед эстрадой (если смотреть из середины полукругов к эстраде), сидели шесть стенографов, все шестеро были молодые люди, за другим пять стенографисток и мужчина лет тридцати пяти или несколько побольше, он, очевидно, был главой этого общества стенографисток и стенографов. (13: 788)

capturing the dramatic transition...
[...] уловление драматических переходов одного чувства в другое, одной мысли в другую. [...] о таинственном процессе, посредством которого вырабатывается мысль или чувство [...] [...] нам представляются только два крайних звена этой цепи, только начало и конец психического процесса. [...] едва уловимые явления этой внутренней жизни, сменяющиеся одно другим с чрезвычайною быстротою и неистощимым разнообразием. (3: 425-26)

The Intermediary: Lobodovsky

In late April...
В конце апреля 1848 г. сказал мне Василий Петрович Лободовский, что он женится. (1: 29)

I love you...
Люблю Василия Петровича, люблю. (1: 68)

At last we began to talk...
Мы, наконец, стали говорить о переворотах, которых должно ждать у нас; он [Лободовский] воображает, что он будет главным действующим лицом. (1: 363) [Лободовский] говорил мне, чтобы я был вторым Спасителем, о чем он не раз и раньше намекал. (1: 281)

V.P. is...
В.П. истинно великий человек. Велик по сердцу, может быть, еще более, чем по уму. (1: 115)

The main reason...
[...] главная причина жениться: это существо, которое я буду обязан сделать счастливым, будет для меня необходимым побуждением к деятельности. (1: 29)

I am becoming an active person...
Начинаю быть деятельным. (1: 33)

Only the physical side...
Если пробудилась во мне, то только физическая сторона. (1: 30)

This may initiate...
может быть из этого выйдет перемена моего характера, и, кажется, я довольно чувствую в себе что-то похожее на понимание сладости любить в смысле любви к возлюбленной, между тем как раньше я серьезно не думал об этом: бредни были физические, а потребности любить не было. (1: 37)

Before carrying out the ultimate act...
[...] перед совершением окончательного действия. (1: 36)

When I did not...
не любил Вас.Петр. и думал, что вовсе нет у меня любви. (1: 59)

I suppose...
Я верно после буду привязан к ней и из-за нее самой, вместо того, чтобы быть привязанным из-за Вас. Петровича. (1: 35)

I looked...
смотрел [...] собственно в надежде и желании убедиться, что Вас.Петр. должен быть очарован этим, особенно когда она будет образована. (1: 148)

I can strengthen...
я могу много содействовать его любви к ней, и поэтому, хотя мне самому незаметно это, чувство долга и желание счастья ей (оно зависит от любви его), — т.е. ему, потому что и он не выдержит со своим характером, если не сделает ее счастливою, — заставляет меня беспрестанно думать о ней. (1: 36)

He is no longer...
он уже не в силах, т.е. не хочет понять это простое, милое создание, которое досталось ему законным образом. (1: 83)

The reason...

это, конечно, оттого, что охоты нет, а охоты в нем нет почти ни к чему. (1: 286)

We were walking...

Переходим мы по камням от Введенской церкви к мосту, он [Лободовский], оглянувшись, сказал: «Право, если найдет слишком тяжелая минута, я узнаю, у кого есть 1 000 р. сер[ебром] в кармане, и украду; половину отдам Наде, половину домой, а сам пойду в Сибирь». (1: 98)

This is...

«Это с материальной стороны, а кроме того, есть и нравственная, сердце». (1: 99)

Resources of Culture: Love and Reality

Do you want...

Хочешь ли ты жить с ним в абсолютной любви? Это тоже интересно. Скажи же мне, ты нашла, что твой муж живет в абсолюте, но чем же он связан с ним — картошкой или изрекаемыми им глупостями? Нет, Варенька, он стоит вне абсолюта, он и абсолют это — две крайности, которые никогда не соприкоснутся.

Our love...

Наша любовь, Мария, заключает в себе зерно освобождения человечества [...] Наша любовь, Мария, будет пересказываться из рода в род; все последующие поколения сохранят нашу память, как святыню.

everyday, household...

ежедневные, домашние, так сказать, будничные отношения людей [...] которые только для поверхностных наблюдателей могут казаться ничтожными, а которые в сущности играют самую важную роль в вопросе человеческого счастья.

I have never loved...

Я никогда не любил. Любовь у меня всегда была прихоть воображения, потеха праздности [...] Действительность есть поприще настоящего, сильного человека, — слабая душа живет в Jenseits.

A new epoch...

Наступила новая эпоха [...] Новый мир нам открылся. [...] Не могу описать тебе, с каким чувством услышал я эти слова — это было освобождение [...] Слово «действительность» сделалось равнозначительным слову «Бог».

Reality...
Действительность — вот лозунг и последнее слово современного мира! Действительность в фактах, в знании, в убеждениях чувства, в заключениях ума — во всем и везде действительность есть первое и последнее слово нашего века.

Rush into life...
Спешите жить, пока живется. Любите искусство, читайте книги, но для жизни (т.е. для женщины) бросайте и то и другое к чорту.

A knowledge of...
знание Гете, особенно второй части «Фауста» [...] было столь же обязательно, как иметь платье.

In Eniseisk...
в Енисейске одна купчиха любила повторять: «Наш ученый профессор Сеченов говорит, что души нет, а есть рефлексы».

Realization of Metaphor: Head and Heart

The day passed...
День прошел ничего, чувствовал только головою, кроме того, когда был у них [Лободовских] было несколько приятно сердцу. (1: 51) [...] я думал, но без сердца, только головою, и о нем и о ней [...] (1: 137) Во время разговора [с Лободовским] я сидел как будто в другом месте, совершенно бесчувственно сердцем, хотя головою чрезвычайно [...] Но сердце ничего не чувствовало и не чувствует — странно — как раньше было перед женитьбою его. (1: 100)

It is strange...
Странно, сердце снова при постоянных мыслях о Над.Ег. неспокойно, как это бывало в первые дни после их свадьбы; снова есть чувство, странно — что это такое? [...] И мне приятно это биение сердца или, лучше, не биение, а как-то особенным образом оно сжимается или расширяется и что-то в самом деле чувствуешь в нем. (1: 80)

The truth is...
Ведь я только жду первого повода, первой возможности и врежусь, и сердце этим стало шевелиться: в самом деле, я чувствую боль или приятное чувство в сердце, в физической части тела, как, напр., чувствую это и в наружных частях тела и в половых органах, и т.д. (1: 270-71)

Almost no sensations...
Ничего почти нынешний день сердцем не чувствовал, и когда говорил

с Вас.Петр., только тогда чувствовал несколько, но не так сильно. А он когда говорил, то дышал даже так тяжело, что было видно, так весь колышется. (1: 96)

The Ideal

I kept comparing...
все сличал хорошеньких с Надеждой Егоровной — все хуже [...] (1: 49) Воротился домой через Невский, смотрел картины и женщин: ни одной лучше Над.Ег. (1: 111) Должно сказать, что я постоянно сравниваю всех — и картины, и живых — с Над.Ег. (1: 116)

I looked closely...
Я смотрел внимательно, старался отыскать что-нибудь, что было бы не так, как следует в ее лице, и не мог найти ничего; оно мне показалось весьма, весьма хорошо, обворожительно, и мне показалось (однако не могло истребить сомнения у меня), что мои сомнения насчет ее красоты, решительной красоты, — вздор; что грубого у нее в лице ничего решительно нет, следовательно, однако я еще колеблюсь сомнением. (1: 76)

the sides of her nose...
нос по бокам показался не так, как должен был бы быть. Я думаю, это ошибка с моей стороны. (1: 134)

I was walking...
шел по Невскому смотреть картинки. У Юнкера много новых красавиц; внимательно, долго рассматривал я двух, которые мне показались хороши, долго и беспристрастно сравнивал и нашел, что они хуже Над.Ег., много хуже, потому что в ее лице я не могу найти недостатков, а в этих много нахожу, особенно не выходит почти никогда порядком нос, особенно у этих красавиц, у переносицы, и части, лежащие около носа по бокам, где он подымается, да, это решительно и твердо. (1: 83)

I noticed...
Лоб у Над.Ег. показался каким-то слишком выпуклым посредине и в лице показалось что-то простонародное. (1: 205)

Rather tall...
довольно высокого роста, по крайней мере, много выше Над.Ег., тонкая, весьма стройная, весьма белое лицо, глаза прекрасные, черты чрезвычайно правильные, умные, несравненно лучше всего, что было тут. (1: 290)

Quite obviously...

Они были, очевидно, очень знатные люди, что видели все по их чрезвычайно милым манерам. (15: 177)

That girl...

Красавица, дивная красавица была та девушка, — иначе не могла ж бы она понравиться мне. (15: 203)

Shyness

The rift...

Разрыв современного человека со средой, в которой он живет, вносит страшный сумбур в частное поведение.

Before the reforms...

В дореформенное время петербургский студент был по преимуществу благовоспитанный юноша и светский молодой человек.

La roture — единственная гавань, в которую можно спрыгнуть с тонущего дворянского судна.

There are fine...

Мысли есть прекрасные, даже положения, и все полито из семинарски-петербургски-мещанского урильника [...]

with the mannerisms...

[...] с приемами подъяческого круга, торгового прилавка и лакейской помещичьего дома.

Gentlemen, blame...

Вините, господа, Белинского: это он причиной, что ваше дворянское достоинство оскорблено, и вам приходится сотрудничать в журнале вместе с семинаристами [...] Как видите, не бесследна была деятельность Белинского, проникло-таки умственное развитие и в другие классы общества.

It is understandable...

Понятно, что туда, где люди этой среды, чувствуя свою силу, появлялись как домой, они вносили и свои приемы общежития. Я говорю здесь не о родословных, а о той благовоспитанности, на которую указывает французское выражение: «enfant de bonne maison», рядом с его противоположностью.

One thing...

Одно меня ужасно терзает: робость моя и конфузливость не ослабевают, а возрастают в чудовищной прогрессии. Нельзя в люди показаться: рожа так и вспыхнет, голос дрожит, руки и ноги трясутся, я боюсь упасть. Истинное Божие наказание! Это доводит меня до смертельного отчаянья. Что за дикая странность? [...] я просто боюсь людей, общество ужасает меня. Но если я вижу хорошее женское лицо: я умираю — на глаза падает туман, нервы опадают, как при виде удава или гремучей змеи, дыхание прерывается, я в огне. [...] я болен, друг, страшною болезнию — пожалей меня.

I remembered...
Вспомнил я рассказ матери моей. Она была охотница рыскать по кумушкам, чтобы чесать язычок; я, грудной ребенок, оставался с нянькою, нанятою девкою: чтоб я не беспокоил ее своим криком, она меня душила и била. Может быть — вот причина. [...] Потом: отец меня терпеть не мог, ругал, унижал, придирался, бил нещадно и площадно — вечная ему память! Я в семействе был чужой. Может быть — в этом разгадка дикого явления.

Whereas my father...
А мой отец пил, вел жизнь дурную, хотя от природы был прекраснейший человек, и оттого я получил темперамент нервический.

One Saturday...
Раз в субботу, накануне Нового года, хозяин вздумал варить жженку en petit comité, когда главные гости разъехались. Белинский непременно бы ушел, но баррикада мебели мешала ему, он как-то забился в угол, и перед ним поставили небольшой столик с вином и стаканами. Жуковский, в белых форменных брюках с золотым «позументом», сел наискось против него. Долго терпел Белинский, но, не видя улучшения своей судьбы, он стал несколько подвигать стол; стол сначала уступал, потом покачнулся и грохнул наземь, бутылка бордо пресерьезно начала поливать Жуковского. [...] сделался гвалт [...] во время этой суматохи Белинский исчез и, близкий к кончине, пешком прибежал домой.

Милый Белинский! как его долго сердили и расстраивали подобные происшествия, как он об них вспоминал с ужасом — не улыбаясь, а похаживая по комнате и покачивая головой.

If I had...
Если бы у меня была женщина, с которой я мог бы делить свои чувства и мысли до такой степени, чтоб она читала даже вместе со мною мои (или, положим, все равно — твои) произведения, я был бы счастлив и ничего не хотел бы более. Любовь к такой женщине и ее сочувствие — вот мое единственное желание теперь. [...] сознание полной бесплотности и вечной неосуществимости этого желания гнетет, мучит меня, наполняет тоскою, злостью, завистью.

Do you remember...
Помните, мы шли как-то с Вами по линии Васильевского острова, с нами повстречалась хорошенькая, вы мне сказали: «да, их здесь много, да все они не наши».

I refused...
не согласился быть введенным к ним в дом, потому что [...] неловко: не говорю по-французски, не танцую, наконец, нехороша одежда и мало денег [...] (1: 249) Эта Бельцова должно быть порядочная девушка и должно быть умная; мне бы хотелось познакомиться с нею, если бы я был в состоянии держать себя в обществе, как должно, а то ни говорить по-французски, ни танцовать, да и, главное, слишком неуклюж, семинарист в полной форме. (1: 344)

My favorite...
Мое любимое и главное подразделение людей в то время, о котором я пишу, было на людей comme il faut и на comme il ne faut pas. Второй род подразделялся еще на людей собственно не comme il faut и простой народ. Людей comme il faut я уважал и считал достойными иметь со мной равные отношения; вторых — притворялся, что презираю, но в сущности, ненавидел их, питая к ним какое-то оскорбленное чувство личности; третьи для меня не существовали — я их презирал совершенно. *Мое* comme il faut состояло, первое и главное, в отличном французском языке и особенно в выговоре. Человек, дурно выговаривавший по-французски, тотчас же возбуждал во мне чувство ненависти. «Для чего же ты хочешь говорить, как мы, когда не умеешь?» — с ядовитой усмешкой спрашивал я его мысленно.

I did not know...
Я не одну не мог видеть в лицо [...] я решительно не знаком был ни с кем, решительно ни с кем, и должен сказать, совершенно не видел женщин. (1: 259)

My idea...
жениться теперь моя дума [...] и этот вечер будет иметь большое влияние на меня, и кажется, что он двинет меня намного вперед: мне сильно хочется и танцовать, и бывать на вечерах, и проч., хотелось бы также и рисовать, и говорить по-французски и немецки для этого необходимо. (1: 212)

How strange: a few days...
Странное дело: несколько дней тому назад я почувствовал в себе возможность влюбиться, а вчера ни с того ни с сего вдруг мне пришла охота учиться танцевать. Чорт знает, что такое. Как бы то ни было, а это означает во мне начало примирения с обществом. [...] Точнее

выразился бы Н.А., если бы сказал: «Начало того, что я вовлекаюсь в жизнь». (10: 55-56)

How strange this beginning...

Как странно началось во мне это тревожное движение сердца! В первый раз шевельнулось оно во мне, когда я услышал от Б.К., что кн. Трубецкая, очень бедная девушка, выходит за Морни... С тех пор я не знаю покоя и социальные вопросы переплелись в моей голове с мыслями об отношениях моих к обществу, в котором мне именно суждено жить. Вместо теоретических стремлений начинается какая-то лихорадочная жажда деятельности, — и деятельности живой, личной, а не книжной неопределенно-безличной и отвлеченной. Что-то будет?.. (10: 58)

I was childlishly...

Я же по-детски была убеждена, что он никогда не болтает пустяков для забавы и никогда не смеется просто, потому что ему смешно или весело, а только насмехается с нравоучительной целью — для обличения, как говорилось тогда.

the style and gusto...

Я помню с каким шиком и смаком две барышни уписывали ржавую селедку и тухлую ветчину из мелочной лавочки, и я убежден, что никакие тонкие яства в родительском доме не доставляли им такого наслаждения, как этот плебейский завтрак на студенческой мансарде.

2 Recapitulation: Marriage

On the Meaning of Marriage

love did not...

[...] любовь нисколько не рифмовала с браком и вообще с действительностию жизни.

One reason...

Мне должно жениться уже и потому, что через это я из ребенка, каков я теперь, сделаюсь человеком. Исчезнет тогда моя робость, застенчивость и т.д. (1: 483)

I must...

Я должен стать женихом О.С., чтобы получить силу действовать, иначе — На путь по душе/ Крепкой воли мне нет. (1: 482)

Now I have...

Теперь у меня своя мысль — жениться и perpetuum mobile. (1: 286)

Teacher

I saw...

[...] я увидел необходимость знать много вещей [...] чтоб сблизиться с девицами и молодыми женщинами, чтобы проложить себе путь в общество их и, следовательно, путь к тому, чтобы избрать одну из них в подруги жизни. (1: 211)

I think that...

Сближение с этим домом порядочным введет меня в круг порядочных людей, думаю я [...] приучусь быть как следует, держать себя как следует, стану через несколько времени говорить по-французски, по-немецки, одним словом — стану, как должно быть. (1: 273)

And so one can...

Итак, рисуется светская жизнь, блистание некоторое умом, знаниями, языком острым, остроумием, некоторая перспектива приятного общества, приятного существа, с которым несколько раз в день видеться и говорить, некоторые виды на обеспечение будущности и т.д. (1: 273)

And so I expect...

Вот я и ожидаю, что миленькая, хорошенькая, умная и т.д., что я сближусь с нею, понравлюсь ей — т.е., само собою разумеется, не что-нибудь вроде любви и т.д., а, во-первых, буду иметь приятное общество, во-вторых, приучу держать себя как следует с женщинами, приучусь знать их и т.д. — о любви у меня в мыслях нет и помину. (1: 273)

The reason...

ведь это не я, а моя одежда, и то, что пришел пешком. (1: 267)

I had a long dream...

мне снилась долгая история о том, что я поступил в какое-то знатное семейство учителем сына (лет 7 или 8), и собственно потому, что мы с этою дамою любим друг друга — или собственно она любит меня и хочет этого, я тоже люблю ее, а до этого почти мы не знали с ней друг друга. Она белокурая, высокая, волоса даже весьма светлорусые, золотистые, такая прекрасная. Я у нее целовал 2-3 раза руку в радости, что она заставляет меня жить в их доме. Муж ее человек пожилой, глупый довольно, с брюхом, несколько надутый или собственно не то что надутый, а так. Итак, я чувствовал себя весьма радостным от этой любви с нею, с наслаждением целовал ее руку (которая, кажется, была в перчатке и еще темного цвета). Собственно для нее уладил я с мужем, который не слишком-то тянулся за мной, но я сначала был разошедши с ним, после сам завязал снова дело и сказал ему, что я-таки поселяюсь у них, потому что она так велела или желала, или просто сказала: живи у нас. Никакой мысли плотской не было (каким образом? это странно), решительно никакой плотской мысли, а только радость на душе, что она любит меня, что я любим. (1: 300-301)

That was the only way...
Романы иначе и не начинались тогда, как вдруг появлялся «он» и поражал «ее» обширностью знаний и начитанностью, глубиной идей и головокружительной новизною смелых взглядов [...] [Но в то время] молодые развиватели не только не дерзали еще увозить барышень из родительских усадеб на славный путь труда и борьбы, но не отваживались и на мало-мальски смелый шаг в любовном отношении, и большинство романов оканчивались таким же малодушным отступлением в решительную минуту, каким отличались и Рудин, и герой «Аси», и Молотов.

I decided...
Я решился в этот день высказать ей свою любовь и какие тут мысли вертелись у меня в голове! Она весьма хороша, но не образована. Я предложу ей давать уроки; конечно, без платы. И я буду иметь потом удовольствие думать, что она обязана мне кое-чем все-таки. (1: 408)

I will become...
Я буду ее учитель, я буду излагать ей свои понятия, я буду преподавать ей энциклопедию цивилизации. (1: 535)

This intellect...
Нужно только развить этот ум, этот такт серьезными учеными беседами, и тогда посмотрим, не должен ли я буду сказать, что у меня жена Mme Staël! (1: 475-76)

This, my dear...
Вот каково было твое влияние на русскую литературу, моя милая подруга: половиной деятельности Некрасова, почти всею деятельности Добролюбова и всей моей деятельности русское общество обязано тебе. (15: 701)

Your influence...
развитию честных понятий в русской публике [...] так много содействовало ваше влияние на русскую литературу. (1: 757)

The Object of Love

What was I...
О чем было говорить? До третьей кадрили я увидел, что она девушка

бойкая и что с ней можно любезничать. [...] «О чем нам говорить? Начну откровенно и прямо: я пылаю к вам страстною любовью, но только с условием, если то, что я предполагаю в вас, действительно есть в вас». (1: 410)

The Diary...

Дневник моих отношений с той, которая теперь составляет мое счастье.

In fact...

Действительно, раньше, чем я в самом деле влюбился, я любил уверять, что я влюблен, как трезвый иногда любит притворяться пьяным. А вот вышло из смеха дело, из невероятного — действительное. (1: 548)

But you will...

«Но вы увидите, что я не увлекался, не ослеплялся, не обманывался, что я понимаю, что делаю; что я увлекся вами, потому что вы достойны того, чтобы увлечься вами». (1: 425)

The features...

[...] по чертам лица она гораздо лучше всех, кого я видел в Саратове — в Петербурге ведь я никого не видел (кроме той хорошенькой девушки на выставке и молоденькой хозяйки Ив.Вас. Писарева в Семеновском полку на вечере). (1: 473) Она решительно умнее всех, кого только я не видывал! Это гениальный ум! Это гениальный такт! (1: 475)

And so I am...

Итак, я люблю ее. Я не надеюсь найти другую, к которой я бы мог так сильно привязаться, я даже не могу представить себе, никак не могу представить себе, чтобы могло быть существо более по моему характеру, более по моему сердцу, чтобы какой то бы ни было идеал был выше ее. Она мой идеал, или скажу просто: я не в состоянии представить себе идеала, который был бы выше ее, я не могу даже вообразить себе ничего выше, лучше ее. Она мой идеал, но идеал не потому, чтобы я идеально смотрел на нее: я вижу ее, как она есть, я не украшаю ее в моем воображении, нет — потому что в ней все, что может быть лучшего, все, что может пленять, обворожать, заставить биться радостью и счастьем мое сердце. (1: 485)

I cannot say...

«Я не говорю, чтобы я был в вас влюблен, потому что никогда не испытывал этого чувства и не знаю, то ли это, что я испытываю теперь, или что-нибудь еще другое». (1: 436)

Am I in love...

Влюблен ли я в нее или нет? Не знаю, во всяком случае мысль об «обладании ею», если употреблять эти гнусные термины, не имеет никакого возбуждающего действия на меня. (1: 533)

At first...

Сначала, и почти до самого 15 или 16 февраля, во мне преобладала крайность, я хотел жениться не иначе, как на весьма нуждающейся девушке, на девушке, которая была бы весьма бедная и беспомощная, чтобы она всю жизнь радовалась и тому немногому довольству, каким бы пользовалась со мною и какого никогда не видывала раньше. Но когда я узнал О.С., эта мысль у меня ослабела. (1: 478)

Here is what...

«Вот что я скажу вам. Вы держите себя довольно неосторожно. Если когда-нибудь вам случится иметь надобность во мне, вы если когда-нибудь... (я снова не знал, как сказать) вы получите такое оскорбление, после которого вам понадобился бы я, вы можете требовать от меня всего». (1: 416-17)

Olga Sokratovna with...

Своим свободным обращением и лихим нравом Ольга Сократовна сразу освободила его от гнета застенчивости и отсутствия светскости, мешавших ему подойти к женщине.

There, she moved...

Вот, она переложила кусок со своей тарелки [...] И этой любезности мало: она сама стала резать ему кушанье, на его тарелке, склоняясь к нему [...] Она ест мороженое с одной тарелки с ним [...] Кладет половину персика прямо ему в рот. (13: 172-73)

And then the hors-d'oeuvres...

Наконец закуска. [...] Она [Ольга Сократовна] кормила со своей руки Палимпсестова; я шалил, отнимал у него тарелку, которую держал он на ее коленах и которую после отдала она ему [...] (За закуской, когда она протянула руку Палимпсестову, чтобы положить ему в рот какое-то пирожное или сухарь, я поцеловал эту руку — общий смех и крик.) (1: 412)

Only one thing...

остается одно — приобретение возможности жениться. Да не просто в части возможности жениться, а *по необходимости* жениться. Мысль о женитьбе только тогда подействует на меня, когда я буду думать не «я хочу жениться», а когда я буду знать, что я должен жениться, что мне уж нельзя не жениться. (1: 482)

I cannot...
Я не могу отказаться. Это было бы бесчестно. (1: 480) [...] мне совестно перед собою не дать руки, которую хотели взять, чтобы выйти из пропасти. (1: 481)

A Calculated Marriage

Not everyone...
не всем суждено любить (т.е. *влюбиться*), быть любимым и жениться по любви, почувствованной и сознанной прежде, чем вошла в голову мысль о женитьбе [...] Кроме пошлого расчета есть еще расчет человеческий, имеющий в виду удовлетворение лучшей стороны своей человеческой природы.

Believe me...
«[...] Но поверьте — и впоследствии для вас, когда вы меня более узнаете, это будет понятно, что я поступаю рассчитано и совершенно благоразумно». (1: 431)

Why Olga Sokratovna...
(1) Почему Ольга Сократовна моя невеста. (1: 472) (2) Почему я должен иметь невесту. (1: 481)

For a little while...
Мы толковали с ним о свободной воле, весьма немного, и отвергали возможность человеку управлять обстоятельствами; говорили, что нелепость «человек с твердою волею» и проч. — у него основание было не знаю что, у меня главным образом его пример: всякий дурак и я скажет, что тверже его нельзя найти человека, а он говорит, что решительно не имеет никакой воли. И сам тоже я. (1: 226)

Grant that...
Пусть, пусть даже нет никаких сомнений во всех этих расчетах, будь это все, что решено в этот месяц, ясно как день, справедливо как арифметика. Господи! Ведь я все же равно не решусь!

Inversion of Roles

The roles...
[...] роли были наоборот против обыкновенного [...] мне делали предложение, я принимал его. (1: 425)

There will be...
«Нечего говорить о том, что вы будете главою дома. Я человек такого характера, что согласен на все, готов уступить во всем —

кроме, разумеется, некоторых случаев, в которых нельзя не быть самостоятельным». (1: 435)

I must obey...

Я всегда должен слушаться и хочу слушаться того, что мне велят делать, я сам ничего не делаю и не могу делать — от меня должно требовать, и я сделаю все, что только от меня потребуют; я должен быть подчиненным [...] Так и в семействе я должен играть такую роль, какую обыкновенно играет жена и у меня должна быть жена, которая была бы главою дома. А она именно такова. Это-то мне и нужно. (1: 473-74)

Gavriil Ivanovich...

Что Евгения Егоровна скажет, то Гавриил Иванович и выполняет. У нас в семье только и было разговору: «Евгения Егоровна делала то-то, Евгения Егоровна распоряжалась так-то». Гавриил Иванович постоянно приводил ее слова.

My notion...

«По моим понятиям женщина занимает недостойное место в семействе. Меня возмущает всякое неравенство. Женщина должна быть равной мужчине. Но когда палка была долго искривлена на одну сторону, чтобы выпрямить ее, должно много перегнуть ее на другую сторону. Так и теперь: женщины ниже мужчин. Каждый порядочный человек обязан, по моим понятиям, ставить свою жену выше себя — этот временный перевес необходим для будущего равенства. Кроме того, у меня такой характер, который создан для того, чтобы подчиняться». (1: 444)

How will it work...

Как это будет совершаться у нас? Я желал бы, чтоб это устроилось так, чтоб обыкновенно я бывал у нее по ее желанию, чтоб инициатива была не так часто с моей стороны. Но это противно всем обычным отношениям между полами? Что ж такого? У нас до сих пор все наоборот против того, как обыкновенно бывает между женихом и невестой: она настаивает, я уступаю [...] Почему ж не быть так и в половых отношениях? Обыкновенно жених ищет невесты, подходит к ней, заговаривает с нею — я наоборот, я дожидаюсь, чтоб она подошла ко мне и сказала: «Говорите со мною, сидите со мною». Так и тут — может быть и будет так: «Вы можете ныне быть у меня». — «Покорно благодарю, О.С.». (1: 534)

She is probably...

она понимает, вероятно, только то, что не хочет, чтобы я надоедал ей, а я понимаю под этим то, что и вообще муж должен быть чрезвычайно деликатен в своих супружеских отношениях к жене. (1: 533)

Liberation from the Parental Yoke

I am almost...

В одном я почти совершенно уверен, — что мысль «не понравится», покажется «слишком верченою, слишком кокеткою», что эта мысль одно из тех нелепых произведений моей фантазии, которые рождает она в таком огромном количестве. Скорее понравится. Гораздо скорее. А если не понравится? [...] Что делать? (1: 494)

Say yes or no...

«Да или нет, и через час или вы поедете знакомиться с родными моей *невесты*, или я убью себя». Это я сделаю. Это для меня вовсе не трудно даже. Это в моем характере. (1: 479)

If I do not...

Если яда не успею запасти, думаю, что лучше всего будет разрезать себе жилы. Однако, предварительно прочитав, как древние поступали в этом случае, напр., Сенека. (1: 480)

I was born...

Я создан для повиновения, для послушания, но это послушание должно быть свободно. А вы слишком деспотически смотрите на меня как на ребенка. «Ты и в 70 лет будешь моим сыном и тогда ты будешь меня слушаться, как я до 50 лет слушалась маменьки». Кто ж виноват, что ваши требования так велики, что я должен сказать: «В пустяках, в том, что все равно, — а раньше этими пустяками были важные вещи, — я был послушным ребенком. Но в этом деле не могу, не вправе, потому что это дело серьезное. [...] Я мужчина, наконец, и лучше вас понимаю, что делаю. А если станете упрямиться, — извольте, спорить я не стану, а убью себя». (1: 494)

Tuesday...

Во вторник на святой хоронили мать, а в четверг — бабушку Анну Ивановну. Похоронили бабушку, вернулись с похорон, и в тот же день пришли обойщики украшать дом к свадьбе: перебивали мебель, повесили занавески по вкусу Ольги Сократовны, а их не выносили ни Чернышевские, ни Пыпины.

shed not a single...

не проронил ни одной слезинки над трупом любимой матери [...]

Напротив, когда гроб опустили в могилу и зарыли землей, он, будто ни в чем ни бывало, закурил папиросу, взял под руку О.С., и оба пешком отправились домой.

I feel now...
Теперь я чувствую себя человеком, который в случае нужды может решиться, может действовать [...] О, как мучила меня мысль о том, что я Гамлет! Теперь вижу, что нет; вижу, что я тоже человек, как другие, правда, не так много имеющий характера, как бы желал иметь, но все-таки человек не совсем без воли, одним словом человек, а не совершенная дрянь. (1: 480)

fears the feat...
робеет предстоящего подвига, бледнеет страшного вызова, колеблется и только *говорит* вместо того, чтобы *делать*.

I feel like...
Я чувствую себя совершенно другим человеком [...] Я стал решителен, смел; мои сомнения, мои колебания исчезли. Теперь у меня есть воля, теперь у меня есть характер, теперь у меня есть энергия. (1: 500)

You are the source...
Ты источник моего довольства самим собою, ты причина того, что я из робкого, мнительного, нерешительного стал человеком с силой воли, решительностью, силою действовать. (1: 514)

O.S.!
О.С.! О.С.! О.С.! Нет, я люблю вас, потому что во мне в самом деле перемена. Я не теряю времени ни минуты без сожаления. Деятельность, деятельность! (1: 550)

Every minute...
«я жду каждую минуту появления жандармов, как благочестивый христианин каждую минуту ждет трубы страшного суда. Кроме того у нас будет скоро бунт, а если он будет, я буду непременно участвовать в нем». (1: 418)

The Third: A Rival-Mediator

how difficult...
[...] о том, как трудно всякому человеку следовать своим убеждениям в жизни, как тут овладевают им и сомнение в этих убеждениях, и нерешительность, и непоследовательность, и, наконец, эгоизм действует сильнее, чем в случаях, когда он должен отвергать его для общепринятых уже в свете правил и т.д. (1: 325)

I would be prepared...
«всегда буду по одному вашему слову готов стать вашим мужем». (1: 414)

A License for Adultery: Theory and Practice

In St. Petersburg...
Окружит себя в Петербурге самою блестящею молодежью, какая только будет доступна ей по моему положению и по ее знакомствам, и будет себе с ними любезничать, кокетничать, наконец, найдутся и такие люди, которые заставят ее перейти границы простого кокетства. (1: 488)

there appears a true...
А если в ее жизни явится серьезная страсть? Что ж, я буду покинут ею, но я буду рад за нее, если предметом этой страсти будет человек достойный. Это будет скорбью, но не оскорблением. А какую радость даст мне ее возвращение! (1: 513)

Suppose I were...
Но если бы я был решительно уверен, что так будет — что бы я делал? Я знал бы, что через брак с ней буду несчастлив, но я не отступил [бы] от своего обязательства. (1: 489)

If she does...
«если она, моя жена, будет делать не только это, если она захочет жить с другим, для меня все равно, если у меня будут чужие дети, это для меня все равно (я не сказал, что я готов на это, перенесу это с горечью, но перенесу, буду страдать, но любить и молчать). — Если моя жена захочет жить с другим, я скажу ей только: „Когда тебе, друг мой, покажется лучше воротиться ко мне, пожалуйста, возвращайся, не стесняясь нисколько"». (1: 451)

Do you remember...
А помнишь, как мы читали Жака? О! если б для твоего счастья нужно было, чтоб я был Жаком, я был бы Жаком; я готов на всякую жертву. Но нет! что я говорю! Разве ты можешь любить другого? Разве ты можешь найти счастье с кем-нибудь, кроме Коли? Никогда, никогда!

The conversation...
разговор перешел к моим понятиям о супружеских отношениях. — «Неужели вы думаете, что я изменю вам?» — «Я этого не думаю, я этого не жду, но я обдумывал и этот случай». — «Что ж бы вы тогда сделали?» — Я рассказал ей «Жака» Жорж-Занда. «Что ж бы вы, тоже застрелились?» — «Не думаю», и я сказал, что постараюсь достать ей

Жорж-Занда (она не читала его или во всяком случае не помнит его идей). (1: 528-29)

I am the proponent...

Я проповедник идей, но у меня такой характер, что я ими не воспользуюсь; да если б в моем характере и была возможность пользоваться этою свободою, то по моим понятиям проповедник свободы не должен ею пользоваться, чтоб не показалось, что он проповедует ее для собственных выгод. (1: 444)

How she would...

как сиживала она здесь, окруженная молодежью [...] как многие мужчины ее любили [...] А вот Иван Федорович (Савицкий, польский эмигрант, Stella) ловко вел свои дела, никому и в голову не приходило, что он мой любовник... Канашечка то знал: мы с Иваном Федоровичем в алькове, а он пишет себе у окна.

I knew from Olga Sokratovna...

я слышала от Ольги Сократовны, что один из товарищей и хороших знакомых Николая Гавриловича в Петербурге просил ее с ним поселиться, и у них по этому поводу было совещание втроем, один убедительно просит, другой колеблется, а третий говорит: «Если желаешь — ступай, я в претензии не буду. В этих делах человек должен быть свободен». И вот, колеблющаяся сторона осталась по старому.

Wild amusements...

Удалое веселье было стихией Ольги Сократовны. Зимой катанье на тройках с бубенцами, песнями, гиканьем. Одни сани обгоняют другие. Отчаянная скачка. Догонят или не догонят? «Догоним и перегоним», — с восторгом кричит она, схватит вожжи сама, стоит и правит. Летом пикники... Лодка...

На жизнь Ольга Сократовна смотрела, как на вечный, словно для нее созданный праздник. Она любила быть окруженной, но только теми, кто ей нравился, кто ею восхищался и кто был ей послушен [...]

О.С. рассказывала мне, что любила, незаметно для гостей, выбежать в разгар танцев на улицу, чтобы полюбоваться на залитые светом окна своей квартиры, и говорить прохожим: «это веселяться у Чернышевских».

The house would be full...

Полон дом гостей, а Ник.Гавр. стоит в передней за конторкой и пишет.

In the fifth part...

В пятой части скандал Князя должен быть слишком крупен. Публич-

ное оскорбление (жена Ч[ернышевского]). Объяснение Князя, Флигель-
адъютанта, почти дуэль.

You think...
Вы думаете, что в Сибири мне жилось не хорошо? Я только там и
счастлив был.

But in essence...
Но в сущности она будет весьма верною женой, верною, как немногие.
(1: 513)

Transformations of Reality

My dear...
Я женился, мой милый, с совершенною уверенностью, что вообще
никакая жена не стала бы любить меня, а моя невеста — меньше
всякой другой девушки может любить меня. (13: 138-39)

Uneducated...
Я неученая, увидела это из первых разговоров, пустых, обо мне, о
пустяках, о моем счастье, — я увидела, какая разница между ним и
другими! — И ошиблась ли я? Вы знаете, как теперь начинают думать
о нем [...] Тогда все думали, что он пролежит весь свой век на диване
с книгою в руках, вялый, сонный. Но я поняла, какая у него голова,
какой характер! (13: 90)

Justification of Reality

I am in...
Здоровье мое хорошо, и надеюсь, очень долго останется хорошо. Я
не тратил его в молодости на обыкновенные дурачества юношей, ни
разу в жизни не изменял правилам нравственной и физической гигиены. Теперь видна польза от этого. (14: 502)

A firm conviction...
в нашем обществе сложилось твердое, общее всем сословиям и под-
держиваемое ложно наукой, убеждение о том, что половое общение
есть дело, необходимое для здоровья, и что так как женитьба есть
дело не всегда возможное, то и половое общение вне брака, не
обязывающее мужчину ни к чему, кроме денежной платы, есть дело
совершенно естественное и потому долженствующее быть поощря-
емым.

When a girl...
«Девушка сделав ошибку по незнанию жизни, теряет честное имя».

Для меня это кажется мыслью очень глупою... Юноша не теряет «честного имени», наделав и в тысячу раз худших ошибок — целыми десятками наделав их. (14: 215)

Remember, my dove...

Заботься, моя милая голубочка, о соблюдении правил гигиены. Будешь заботиться, то я буду совершенно счастлив. (14: 284)

Oh, how I...

«Уж как я завидовала вашим светлым локонам и васильковым глазам», — говорила Ольга Сократовна. «Да что вы, дорогая, — возражала Капочка, — но кого же можно было заметить рядом с вашим огненным взглядом, вашими черными, как смоль, чудными волосами...», и подруги принялись перебирать романы юных лет.

You cannot, my dear...

Как не можешь ты стать блондинкою, так не можешь ты, мой милый друг, стать робкою. (15: 293)

Fictitious Marriage: Reality-Literature-Reality

It was not the novel...

[...] не автор романа списал с него [П.И. Бокова] свой тип, а напротив, сам доктор вдохновился романом и разыграл его в жизни: порукой в том хронология.

I beg you...

Умоляю Вас поверить мне, что мы с моей дорогой, неоцененной Машей живем, как только подобает самым мирным супругам [...] Уверяю Вас, как честный человек, что мы живем с ней в самых лучших отношениях и если она по характеру сошлась более с удивительным из людей русских, дорогим сыном нашей бедной родины, Иваном Михайловичем, так это только усилило наше общее счастье [...] Вы можете представить, до какой степени наша жизнь счастливей, имея членом семьи Ивана Михайловича! [...] Теперь я пользуюсь случаем, чтобы умолять Вас повидать Ивана Михайловича, как родного своего детища, коим я считаю себя уже с давних пор сам, и умоляю не отказать мне в этом.

The Triple Union

Why all this...

Из-за каких пустяков какой тяжелый шум! Сколько расстройства для всех троих, особенно для вас, Вера Павловна! Между тем как очень спокойно могли бы вы все трое жить по-прежнему, как жили за год, или как-нибудь переместиться всем на одну квартиру, или иначе переместиться, или как бы там пришлось, только совершенно без всякого расстройства, и по-прежнему пить чай втроем, и по-прежнему ездить в оперу втроем. К чему эти мученья? К чему эти катастрофы?

The solution...

Исход ясен. Для других он невозможен, другим нельзя, а тебе можно, потому именно, что ты милая девушка. Ты женщина, но по чистоте и ясности чувства ты девушка. Согласись же на мой исход, хотя и будем помнить, что другим нельзя.

Each of them...

У обоих есть, конечно, свои особенности ума и характера, есть и недостатки; но все это природа распределила между ними так, что черты одного дополняют черты другого.

The Triple Union in a Romantic Key: Herzen

In my pure-hearted...

в моей чистой близости с твоей подругой был для меня новый залог нашего trio. [...] Быть ближе того, как я к N. — другу, брату нельзя, всю мою любовь к вам обоим я употреблю на сохранение всего. Нет в мире силы, страсти, которые бы отторгли меня от тебя. — Что N. сильно любит меня — это так и быть должно — но известный характер этой любви не приходится мне — но — Друг мой — его элиминировать можно только с чрезвычайной кротостью.

For some time...

я на некоторое время увлекся любовью к тебе и к ней, я поверил мечте соединения трех в одну любовь; да я и теперь верю в возможность этого.

The Triple Union in a Realistic Key: Shelgunov

The marriage...

брак, который связал нас, может и развязать, и Вы будете свободны [...] Вы можете выбрать себе нового мужа, можете наслаждаться с ним счастьем возможным на земле, а обо мне можете и не думать. Насчет обеспечения жизни вы не будете иметь хлопот, я буду заботиться о Вас и нужда не заглянет в дом, в котором Вы будете жить.

What should I do?

Что делать мне? [...] Не надобно быть пророком, чтобы угадать, что плоть восторжествует над духом.

Nikolai Vasil'evich...
Мы с Николаем Васильевичем остались прежними идеалистами; выходили из своих комнат вполне одетыми и продолжали говорить друг другу «вы».

My darling...
Действительно, голубчик, мы имеем на то [празднование нашей свадьбы] некоторое право, потому, если не в начале, то когда сами развились и созрели, сумели размежеваться в жизни и создали себе счастье, которое дается не многим, да еще долго не будет даваться, пока наши обыкновенные супруги будут пребывать в том остроумном турецком миросозерцании, в каком они обретаются.

The New Meaning of Adultery

In general they...
между ними было много сходства, так что если бы их встречать только порознь, то оба они казались бы людьми одного характера. А когда вы видели их вместе, то замечали, что хоть оба они люди очень солидные и очень открытые, но Лопухов несколько сдержаннее, его товарищ несколько экспансивнее.

He brought them...
Он сблизил их. Да, в самом деле сблизил.

I saw that I was to be free from coercion...
[...] я видел, что становлюсь совершенно свободным от принуждения.

Literary Parallels: Tolstoy and Dostoevsky

This novel...
Это [«Что делать?»] — удивительная комментария ко всему, что было в 60-67, и зачатки зла также тут.

Neither you...
Ни ты, ни Чернышевский в романе — вы ничего не разрешили в этом вопросе.

Constantly reading...
Читает все романы. Изучает вопрос. Все невозможно.

badly brought-up writers...
[...] дурно воспитанные писатели, музыканты, живописцы, которые не умели благодарить за чай, когда она им подавала его.

What is to be done?...
Что делать? Что делать? [...] Нельзя жить втроем.

A Russian at a Rendezvous: Collectivity in Love

Let us forget...
Бог с ними, с эротическими вопросами, — не до них читателю нашего времени, занятому вопросами об административных и судебных улучшениях, о финансовых преобразованиях, об освобождении крестьян. (5: 166)

3   The Embodiment of the Model: Texts

Dissertation: Ideal and Reality

Dreaming whips...
Желания раздражаются мечтательным образом до горячечного напряжения только при совершенном отсутствии здоровой, хотя бы и довольно простой пищи. Это факт, доказываемый всей историей человечества и испытанный на себе самом всяким, кто жил и наблюдал себя. (2: 36)

The sensation...
Ощущение, производимое в человеке прекрасным, — светлая радость, похожа на ту, какою наполняет нас присутствие милого для нас существа. Мы бескорыстно любим прекрасное, мы любуемся, радуемся на него, как радуемся на милого нам человека. (2: 9)

The image of Olga Sokratovna...
Образ Ольги Сократовны незримо присутствует на этих страницах как выражение основного тезиса «Прекрасное — есть жизнь».

There is only one...
наилучшая красавица, конечно, одна в целом свете, — и где же отыскать ее? (2: 40)

As a rule...
Обыкновенно, если лицо не изуродовано, то все части его бывают в такой гармонии между собою, что нарушать ее значило бы портить красоту лица. Этому учит нас сравнительная анатомия. Правда, очень часто случается слышать: «как хорошо было бы это лицо, если бы нос был несколько приподнят кверху, губы несколько потоньше» и т.п., — нисколько не сомневаясь в том, что иногда при красоте всех остальных частей лица одна часть его бывает некрасива, мы думаем, что обыкновенно, или, лучше сказать — почти всегда, подобное недовольство проистекает или от неспособности понимать гармонию,

или от прихотливости, которая граничит с отсутствием истинной, сильной способности и потребности наслаждаться прекрасным. (2: 56)

What, is a painted...
Как, неужели живое лицо не прекрасно, а изображенное на портрете или снятое в дагерротип прекрасно? (2: 45)

That a work...
Математически строго можно доказать, что произведение искусства не может сравниться с живым человеческим лицом по красоте очертаний: известно, что в искусстве исполнение всегда неизмеримо ниже того идеала, который существует в воображении художника. А самый этот идеал никак не может быть по красоте выше тех живых людей, которых имел случай видеть художник. (2: 56)

Reality presents...
Действительность представляется нашим глазам независимо от нашей воли, большею частью невовремя, некстати. Очень часто мы отправляемся в общество, на гулянье вовсе не за тем, чтобы любоваться человеческой красотою. (2: 74)

Life presents...
[...] для каждого отдельного человека жизнь представляет особенные явления, которых не видят другие, над которыми поэтому не произносит приговора целое общество, а произведения искусства оценены общим судом. Красота и величие действительной жизни редко являются нам патентованными, а про что не трубит молва, то немногие в состоянии заметить и оценить, явления действительности — золотой слиток без клейма. (2: 75)

Beauty is life...
[...] прекрасное есть жизнь, прекрасно то существо, в котором видим мы жизнь такою, какова должна быть она по нашим понятиям. (2: 10)

Real Life—Literature—Science

In order to stop...
Для прекращения мотовства конфисковать все имущества, превышающие известную меру, для прекращения хвастовства именами запретить употребление фамильных имен и приказать, чтобы подданные отличались друг от друга только нумерами, для улучшения характера воспитания брать всех детей по достижению пяти или шести лет из отцовского дома и отдавать в какие-нибудь казармы для малолетних. (5: 586)

innumerable number...
бесчисленного множества фактов, обстоятельств и документов, чуждых публичной известности и часто неизвестных даже тому лицу, к которому они относятся. (5: 617)

The question is...
Тут нет вопроса о том, действительно ли Иван Захаров есть Иван Захаров, а не какой-нибудь подкидыш или самозванец, действительно ли Иван Захаров — законный сын Захара Петрова, законен ли был брак Захара Петрова, не было ли других детей у Захара Петрова, не было ли завещания у Захара Петрова, не было ли долгов у Захара Петрова, и так далее, и так далее. До всего этого никому дела нет. Принадлежность участка Ивана Захарова так же ясна для всех и так же бесспорна, как принадлежность ему тех мозолистых рук, которыми он кормит свою семью. (5: 618)

Let everybody...
Пусть каждый рассудит, может ли это быть иначе. 2×2=4, это — штука, или нет, не «штука»: будем говорить ученым языком, это — формула известная, рассмотрим же эту формулу по-ученому. По-ученому 4 тут результат, производимый взаимодействием факторов 2×2. Положим теперь [...] (7: 555)

The natural sciences...
Естественные науки еще не дошли до того, чтобы подвести все эти законы под один общий закон, соединить все частные формулы в одну всеобъемлющую формулу. Что делать! Нам говорят, что и сама математика еще не успела довести некоторых своих частей до такого совершенства. (7: 294)

No one has done...
Со времени Аристотеля не было делано еще никем того, что я хочу сделать, и я буду добрым учителем людей в течении веков, как был Аристотель. (14: 456)

Scholar and Writer

I smiled...
Я улыбнулся. Теперь опять возобновятся предложения занять кафедру в университете. (14: 370)

I am a scholar...
Я — ученый. [...] Я один из тех мыслителей, которые неуклонно держатся научной точки зрения. Они, в самом строгом смысле слова, «люди науки». Таков я с моей ранней молодости. (15: 165)

My style...
Язык мой в них [повестях и романах] несколько неуклюж; как у
Гоголя, например. Но это недостаток маловажный. Все остальное,
что нужно для хорошего сказочника — вроде Диккенса или Фильдинга,
или, из наших, Пушкина и Лермонтова (в их прозе), у меня есть в
достаточно хорошем качестве и изобилии. Версификация не дана мне
природою. Но проза моя — хорошая поэзия. (15: 390)

Reconciling Opposites

I am an author...
У меня нет ни тени художественного таланта. Я даже и языком-то
владею плохо. (14)

As for the celebrated...
[Сравнительно] с прославленными сочинениями твоих знаменитых
писателей ты смело ставь наряду мой рассказ по достоинству испол-
нения, ставь даже выше их — не ошибешься! (14)

thought in man...
[...] ведь у мужчины мыслительная способность и от природы сильнее,
да и развита гораздо больше, чем у женщины [...] (12)

Now, women have...
Женщинам натолковано: «вы слабы» — вот они и чувствуют себя
слабыми, и действительно оказываются слабы. (259)

the feminine organism...
[...] женский организм крепче [...] крепче выдерживает разрушитель-
ные материальные впечатления [...] (258-59)

But in reality...
На деле мы видим слишком много примеров противного. [...] Это —
сила предубеждения [...] фальшивое ожидание [...] (259)

No, she is not a cold and insensitive girl...
Нет, она не холодная девушка без души. (53)

not human beings...
[...] не люди, а рыбы [...] меня смущает их холодное обращение между
собою. (325-26)

Colorless eyes...
бесцветные глаза, бесцветные жиденькие волосы, бессмысленное, бес-
цветное лицо. (23)

Russians are...
[Русские] смесь племен, от беловолосых, как финны [...] до черных,

гораздо чернее итальянцев [...] У нас блондинки, которых ты ненавидишь, только один из местных типов. (23)

Is she a brunette...
Она брюнетка или блондинка? [...] Это тайна. (55)

Her expression...
[...] и лицо, и походка, все меняется, беспрестанно меняется в ней, вот она англичанка, фрацуженка, вот она уж немка, полячка, вот стала и русская, опять англичанка, опять немка, опять русская [...] но только какая же она красавица! (81)

Totally naive...
Совершенно наивные девушки без намеренья действуют как опытные кокетки [...] (34)

true coquetry...
[настоящее] кокетство — это ум и такт в применении к делам женщины с мужчиною. (34)

It is thus that the Lord inspires children...
Господь умудряет младенцы. (38)

Marriage! The yoke! Prejudice!
Брак? Ярмо? Предрассудок? (25)

I have a passion...
науки — моя страсть, я родилась быть м-ме Сталь. (23-24)

We all talk...
Мы все говорим и ничего не делаем. А ты позже нас всех стала думать об этом — и раньше всех решилась приняться за дело. (117)

I am not...
Я не то, чем вам показалась. Я не жена ему, а у него на содержаньи. Я известна всему Петербургу как самая дурная женщина. Но я честная женщина. (31)

It is better...
Лучше умереть, чем дать поцелуй без любви. [...] Жюли Ле-Телье, погибшая женщина [...] она знает, что такое добродетель. (35)

was so shameless...
Была такая бесстыдная, хуже других. (158)

That was because...
Оттого, Настасья Борисовна, что, может быть, на самом-то деле были застенчивы, совестились. (158)

Is this the Julie...

Та ли это Жюли, которую знает вся аристократическая молодежь Петербурга? Та ли это Жюли, которая отпускает шутки, заставляющие краснеть иных повес? Нет, это княгиня, до ушей которой никогда не доносилось ни одно грубоватое слово. (29-30)

He is not such a barbarian...

Однако ж он вовсе не такой дикарь. Он вошел и поклонился легко, свободно. (51)

Monsieur Lopukhov...

— Мосье Лопухов, я никак не ожидала видеть вас танцующим [...]
— Почему же? Разве это так трудно, танцевать?
— Вообще — конечно нет, для вас — разумеется, да. (55)

If he had been...

Если б он был русский, Полозову было бы приятно, чтоб он был дворянин, но к иностранцам это не прилагается, особенно к французам. И к американцам еще меньше: у них в Америке человек — ныне работник у сапожника или пахарь, завтра генерал, послезавтра президент, а там опять конторщик или адвокат. (322)

Do not think of me...

Не думай обо мне. Только думая о себе, ты можешь не делать и мне напрасного горя. (196)

A in B's place...

А на месте B есть B, если бы на месте B не было B, то оно еще не было бы на месте B, ему еще недоставало бы чего-нибудь, чтобы быть на месте B [...] (188)

Oh perceptive reader...

О проницательный читатель, — говорю я ему, — ты прав, синий чулок подлинно глуп и скучен, и нет возможности выносить его. Ты отгадал это. Да не отгадал ты, *кто* синий чулок. Вот ты сейчас увидишь это, как в зеркале. [...] Видишь, чья это грубая образина или прилизанная фигура в зеркале? Твоя, приятель. (268)

Kirsanov was...

Кирсанов был сын писца уездного суда, то есть человека, часто не имеющего мяса во щах, — значит, наоборот, часто имеющего мясо во щах. (147)

Doubles

I see nothing...
Я ничего удивительного не нахожу в тебе, может быть, половина девушек, которых я знал и знаю, а может быть, и больше, чем половина, — я не считал, да и много их, что считать-то, — не хуже тебя, а иные и лучше, ты меня прости. (61)

Yes, it is herself...
Да, Вера Павловна видела: это она сама, это она сама, но богиня. Лицо богини — ее самой лицо, это ее живое лицо, черты которого так далеки от совершенства, прекраснее которого видит она каждый день не одно лицо, это ее лицо, озаренное сиянием любви, прекраснее всех идеалов, завещанных нам скульптурами древности и великими живописцами великого века живописи, да, это она сама, но озаренная сиянием любви, она, прекраснее которой есть сотни лиц в Петербурге, таком бедном красотою, она прекраснее Афродиты Луврской, прекраснее доселе известных красавиц. (281-82)

On a chair...
Сидит офицер. На столе перед офицером бутылка. На коленях у офицера она, Верочка. (127)

Now you are engaged...
теперь вы занимаетесь дурными делами, потому что так требует ваша обстановка, но дать вам другую обстановку, и вы с удовольствием станете безвредны, даже полезны, потому что без денежного расчета вы не хотите делать зла, и если вам выгодно, то можете делать что угодно — стало быть, даже и действовать честно и благородно, если так будет нужно. (114)

Double Count

He should nevertheless...
[...] он все-таки должен был на всякий случай приготовить вас к чему-нибудь подобному, просто как к делу случайности, которой нельзя желать, которой не за чем ждать, но которая все-таки может представиться: ведь за будущее никак нельзя ручаться, какие случайности может привести оно. (225)

Upon this word...
На этом «просто дурак» сошлись все, даже и те, которые отвергали, что он застрелился. Действительно, пьяный ли, промотавшийся ли

застрелился, или озорник, вовсе не застрелился, а только выкинул штуку, — все равно, глупая, дурацкая штука. (8)

Now the mystification...
Теперь уже ничего нельзя было разобрать — и дурак, и умно. (9)

What form...
В какую форму должно было развиться это недовольство? Если бы вы и он, оба, или хоть один из вас, были люди не развитые, не деликатные или дурные, оно развилось бы в обыкновенную свою форму — вражда между мужем и женой, вы бы грызлись между собою, если бы оба были дурны, или один из вас грыз бы другого, а другой был бы сгрызаем. (223)

If you have...
Если вы имеете возразить что-нибудь, я жду [...] если предлагаемое мною пособие покажется вам достаточно, я выскажу условия, на которых согласна оказать его [...] Вы можете принять или не принять их, вы принимаете их — я отправляю письмо, вы отвергаете их — я жгу письмо, и т.д., все в этой же бесконечной манере. (32-33)

Either he...
[...] либо наш, либо наша приходятся либо братом, либо сестрой, либо генералу, либо генеральше. (121)

Both dresses...
[...] оба платья обошлись 174 рубля; по крайней мере так сказала Мария Алексеевна мужу, а Верочка знала, что всех денег вышло на них меньше 100 рублей [...] (18)

I make...
Это я дарю вашей жене. Оно стоит 150 руб. (85 руб.). Я его только два раза (гораздо более 20) надевала [...] (42)

Illusion and Reality

This house is...
Теперь этот дом отмечен каким ему следует нумером, а в 1852 году, когда еще не было таких нумеров, на нем была надпись: «Дом действительного статского советника Ивана Захаровича Сторешникова». Так говорила надпись, но Иван Захарыч Сторешников умер еще в 1837 году, и с той поры хозяин дома был сын его, Михаил Иванович, — так говорили документы. Но жильцы дома знали, что Михаил Иванович — хозяйкин сын, а хозяйка дому — Анна Петровна. (15)

They both...
они оба твердо помнили, что ведь по-настоящему-то хозяйка-то не
хозяйка, а хозяинова мать, не больше, что хозяйкин сын не хозяйкин
сын, а хозяин. (40)

How Petrovna...
Каким образом Петровна видела звезды на Серже, который еще и не
имел их, да если б и имел, то, вероятно, не носил бы при поездках на
службе Жюли, — это вещь изумительная, но что действительно она
видела их, что не ошиблась и не хвастала, это не она свидетельствует,
это я за нее также ручаюсь: она видела их. Это мы знаем, что на нем
их не было, но у него был такой вид, что с точки зрения Петровны
нельзя было не увидеть на нем двух звезд, — она и увидела их, не
шутя я вам говорю: увидела. (120)

This one, in French...
«[...] французскую-то я сама почти разобрала: «Гостиная» — значит,
самоучитель светского обращения [...]». «Нет, Марья Алексеевна, это
не «Гостиная», это Destiné — судьба». «Какая же это судьба? роман,
что ли, так называется, или оракул, толкование снов?» «А вот сейчас
увидим, Марья Алексеевна, из самой книги [...] Тут о сериях больше
говорится, Марья Алексеевна, — ученая книга». «О сериях? Это
хорошо, значит, как денежные обороты вести». (66)

The New Gospel: The Background

Treatises of this sort...
[...] такие трактаты должны были совершить окончательный пере-
ворот в философских исканиях русской интеллигенции, и сделали это
дело вполне.

The Catechism of Russian Atheism

It is difficult...
В бессмертие личное снова трудно сказать, верю ли, — скорее нет, а
скорее, как Гегель, верю в слияние моего «я» с абсолютною субстан-
циею, из которой оно вышло [...] смотря по достоинству моего «я».
(1:279)

The immortality...
Бессмертие души есть вредная мечта, удерживающая человека от
прямого пути главнейшей цели жизни — улучшение собственного
быта на земле.

Under certain circumstances...

[...] при известных обстоятельствах человек становится добр, при других — зол. (7: 264)

Sacrifice is...

[...] это фальшивое понятие: жертва — сапоги всмятку. Как приятнее, так и поступаешь. (98)

Science says...

Наука же говорит: возлюби, прежде всех, одного себя [...]

Man is...

Человек произошел от обезьяны, а потому положим душу за други своя.

if it were mathematically...

[...] если бы математически доказали вам, что истина вне Христа, то вы бы согласились лучше остаться с Христом, нежели с истиной [...]

Atheism became...

Атеизм превратился в религию своего рода, и ревнители этой новой веры разбрелись подобно проповедникам по всем путям и дорогам, разыскивая везде душу живу, чтобы спасти ее от христианския скверны. [...] каждый из нас охотно пошел бы на эшафот и сложил свою голову за Молешотта и Дарвина.

Russians do not...

Наши не просто становятся атеистами, а непременно уверуют в атеизм, как бы в новую веру, никак и не замечая, что уверовали в нуль.

on three stands...

[...] разложил на подставках, в виде трех налоев, сочинения Фохта, Молешотта и Бюхнера, и перед каждым налоем зажигал восковые церковные свечки.

It may be that...

Атеизм самый полный ближе всех, может быть, к вере стоит.

He has not...

> Его еще покамест не распяли,
> Но час придет — он будет на кресте,
> Его послал Бог гнева и печали
> Царям земли напомнить о Христе.

The Theology of What Is to Be Done?

Strange...
«Странное дело — в этой книге ни разу не упоминается о Боге» — о какой книге говорил он — неизвестно.

As for you...
ты теперь будешь здорова, вот только я коснусь твоей руки, — видишь, ты уже и здорова, вставай же [...]. Верочка встала. (81)

It is Easter...
[...] нынче Пасха, Саша, говори же Катеньке: воистину воскресе. (332)

Far away...
На далеком северо-востоке две реки, которые сливаются вместе прямо на востоке от того места, с которого смотрит Вера Павловна; дальше к югу, все в том же юго-восточном направлении длинный и широкий залив, на юге далеко идет земля, расширяясь все больше к югу между этим заливом и длинным узким заливом, составляющим ее западную границу. Между западным узким заливом и морем, которое очень далеко на северо-западе, узкий перешеек. (286)

Vera Pavlovna's Fourth Dream: the Kingdom of Heaven

Half of them...
Шумно веселиться в громадном зале половина их, а где же другая половина? «Где другие? — говорит светлая царица, — они везде [...] но больше, больше всего — это моя тайна. Ты видела в зале, как горят щеки, как блистают глаза, ты видела, они уходили — это я увлекала их, здесь комната каждого и каждой — мой приют, в них мои тайны ненарушимы, занавесы дверей, роскошные ковры, поглощающие звук, там тишина, там тайна [...] (289-90)

Chernyshevsky ends...
Он оканчивает фаланстером, борделью. Смело.

Sept. 10...
10 сент[ября 1873 г.], середа. Сегодня во сне мне пришел на ум вопрос: каким образом может устроиться коммуна? Какая разница между понятием коммуны и равенства? Каким средством уравнять владение почвой и всяким иным имуществом? Каким средством сплотить силы труда отдельных лиц в общинный труд? Можно ли дело кончать ровным разделом посемейно или поголовно, или разделить только труд, т.е. доход?
    Вопрос не так легок, как кажется.

Christian Mysteries in a Positive Key

Although you revealed...
[...] ты являлась мне, я видела тебя, но ты окружена сиянием, я не могла видеть тебя. (281)

For your sake...
[...] для тебя на эту минуту я уменьшаю сиянье моего ореола [...] на минуту я для тебя перестаю быть царицею. (281)

Yes, it is herself...
Да, Вера Павловна видела: это она сама, это она сама, но богиня. Лицо богини — ее самой лицо, это ее живое лицо, черты которого так далеки от совершенства [...] она прекраснее [...] доселе известных красавиц. (281-82)

There is nothing...
[...] нет ничего выше человека, нет ничего выше женщины. (281)

Let the disposition...
[...] пусть немного переменится расположение атомов и выйдет что-нибудь другое. (123)

Notes

Introduction

[27][The young people] will be...
[...] молодежь проникнется глубочайшим уважением и пламенной любовью к распластанной лягушке [...] Тут-то именно, в самой лягушке-то и заключается спасение и обновление русского народа.

Part One

[6]Read Rousseau's...
[...] прочтите «Confessions» Руссо, там рассказывается многое из моей жизни, но далеко не все. (15: 360)

I feel so close...
Многие страницы его [Руссо] так близки мне, что мне кажется я их написал сам.

[23]In a trembling...
Я ему дрожащим голосом рассказывал «Двойника», и он сначала думал, что это я писал. (1: 365)

[28]Looking at them...
Я и тут, глядя на них, думал о тех ясных и целомудренных семьях первых протестантов, которые безбоязненно пели гонимые псалмы, готовые рука в руку спокойно и твердо идти перед инквизитора. Они мне казались братом и сестрой [...]

[71]Once I attempted...
Раз я хотел похвастаться перед ними своими знаниями в литературе, в особенности французской, и завел разговор на эту тему. К удивлению моему оказалось, что, хотя они выговаривали иностранные заглавия по-русски, они читали гораздо больше меня [...] Пушкин и Жуковский были для них литература (а не так, как для меня, книжки в желтом переплете, которые я читал и учил ребенком) [...] В знании музыки я тоже не имел перед ними никакого преимущества [...] Одним словом, все, чем я хотел похвастаться перед ними, исключая выговора французского и немецкого языков, они знали лучше меня и нисколько не гордились этим.

And I think...
«Думаю себе: я не умею обходиться в гостиных, не умею болтать по-французски, как другие, и завидно мне бывало салонным господам. Ну, да думаю, зато я образован, как никто [...] да я и не знаю никого с этим всесторонним и глубоким образованием. Есть ли наука, в которой я не чувствовал бы в себе силы сделать открытия — филология, история, а естественные науки? Все мне знакомо [...]

Part Two

[11]For the honest...
За честных богатых и знатных людей, представители которых составляют большинство находящегося здесь общества! [...] За тех из слушавших мой рассказ небогатых людей, которые не порицали меня за сочувствие честным богатым и знатным! (13: 851)

[12]Even before...
[...] уж и прежде, не зная Дуни, [Лужин] положил взять девушку честную, но без приданого, и непременно такую, которая уже испытала бедственное положение; потому, как объяснил он, что муж ничем не должен быть обязан своей жене, а гораздо лучше, если жена считает мужа за своего благодетеля.

I decided...
[...] я решился вас взять, так сказать, после городской молвы, разнесшейся по всему околотку насчет репутации вашей. Пренебрегая для

вас общественным мнением и восстанавливая репутацию вашу, уж, конечно, мог бы я, весьма и весьма, понадеяться на возмездие и даже потребовать благодарности вашей [...]

[62]Panaev is dead...

Умер [...] Панаев. Что же делать? Обрядили покойника, положили в передний угол на стол. Знакомые и жена умершего собрались в гостиной и стали рассуждать, как теперь устроить жизнь Некрасова с Панаевой, находившихся в связи друг с другом. Вдруг дверь из зала открывается и в гостиную входит Панаев, шагов которого никто не слыхал, так как он был приготовлен на тот свет в мягких туфлях. Панический страх, изумление были так велики, что не скоро все оправились. Оказалось, что Панаев не умирал, а находился в летаргическом сне.

Notes

For full authors' names, titles, and publication data on works cited in short form in the Notes, see the Works Cited section, pp. 289–97. Unless otherwise identified, Dostoevsky citations by volume number are to the 30-volume collection, *Polnoe sobranie sochinenii v tridtsati tomakh*; Herzen citations by volume number are to the 30-volume collection, *Sobranie sochinenii v tridtsati tomakh*; and Tolstoy citations by volume number are to the 90-volume collection, *Polnoe sobranie sochinenii v devianosta tomakh*. Chernyshevsky's 16-volume collection, *Polnoe sobranie sochinenii*, is cited as *PSS*; and Lidia Ginzburg's work *O psikhologicheskoi proze* (2d ed., 1977) is cited as Ginzburg, *PP*.

BOOK EPIGRAPH: Alexander Herzen, "Bazarov Once Again" ("Eshche raz Bazarov"; 1868). English translation from Brown, "Pisarev," pp. 163–64.

Introduction

1. Ginzburg, *PP*, pp. 6–33. See also Gasparov, p. 15.
2. See the following works: "Vvedenie" and chap. 1, "Chelovecheskii dokument i postroenie kharaktera," in Ginzburg, *PP*; chap. 1, "Literaturnaia rol' i sotsial'naia rol'," in Ginzburg, *O literaturnom geroe*; and Iu. Lotman, "Teatr i teatral'nost'," "Stsena i zhivopis'," "Dekabrist," "O Khlestakove," and "Poetika." Many of these works have been translated into English, as indicated in the Works Cited section. The translations are cited in the Notes. See Gasparov, "Introduction," for a detailed treatment of the history and significance of this field.

3. Iu. Lotman, "Decembrist," p. 98.

4. Mukařovský, p. 169.

5. See Gasparov, pp. 25–26; and Iu. Lotman, "Concerning Khlestakov," pp. 186–87.

6. N. Annenskii, cited in Bogdanovich, p. 6.

7. On the intelligentsia, see Malia, "What Is the Intelligentsia?"; Berlin; and Nahirny. On the general characteristics of the historical development and ideology of the 1860s, see Gleason; Emmons; Lampert; and Venturi. For a different view, see Brower.

8. Shtakenshneider, p. 161.

9. Wellek, p. 241.

10. See Ginzburg, *Literatura*, p. 11; and Gasparov, p. 25.

11. See Iu. Lotman, "Concerning Khlestakov," p. 186; Wellek, pp. 242–45; and Ginzburg, *O literaturnom geroe*, pp. 5–56.

12. Dostoevsky, *The Idiot*, p. 439 (Dostoevsky, 8: 383). See Ginzburg, *O literaturnom geroe*, p. 52.

13. Berlin, pp. 127–31. For an outline of views on the relations between literature and life in modern Russian literature, see McLean.

14. Saltykov-Shchedrin, 7: 455.

15. Shelgunov, p. 98.

16. Cited in Piksanov and Tsekhnovitser, p. 175.

17. See, for example, Pisarev, 4: 316; and Dobroliubov, *Polnoe sobranie*, 2: 208.

18. For information on the polemic, see Reifman.

19. Antonovich and Eliseev, p. 563.

20. Pisarev, 3: 51. On this issue, see Brown, "Pisarev," p. 162.

21. Herzen, 20: 335.

22. Ginzburg, *O literaturnom geroe*, pp. 52–54.

23. Reifman, p. 90, points out that "younger generation" was not a matter of age, but a purely symbolic term; in 1862 Chernyshevsky was 34 years old.

24. N. G. Chernyshevsky, *Chto delat'*, pp. 148–49.

25. Brown, "Pisarev," pp. 163–64 (Herzen, 20: 337).

26. Stepniak-Kravchinsky, 1: 371.

27. In his article "Motivy russkoi dramy," Pisarev wrote: "[The young people] will be inspired with deep respect and ardent love for the spread frog [*rasplastannoi liagushke*]. . . . It is here, in this same frog, that the salvation and renewal of the Russian people lies" (Pisarev, 2: 392). A curious illustration of the special symbolic aura that surrounded science in the popular consciousness is the reception of Ivan Sechenov's *Refleksy golovnogo mozga* (*The Reflexes of the Brain*; 1863). A treatise in

physiology, materialist in outlook, it was originally intended for publication in the *Contemporary* (because of difficulties with the censorship, it appeared instead in a scholarly medical journal, *Meditsinskii vestnik*). In his autobiography, Sechenov wrote (p. 115) that after the appearance of his book, public opinion, to his astonishment, "promoted [him] to a philosopher of nihilism." Holquist offers an ingenious explanation for this phenomenon in suggesting that the public perceived Sechenov in terms of Turgenev's Bazarov. "What we get is a reverse of the process by which a living figure becomes the basis of a fictional character." Holquist also suggests that "the connection between the two appears even more ineluctable to anyone who has seen the famous photo of Sechenov, taken in 1861, the year Turgenev completed *Fathers and Sons*: we see a fierce-eyed, hirsute young man sitting at his work table in the Medico-Surgical academy, complete with Bunsen burner, electrical charging mechanism and a laboratory clamp from which are suspended—of course—three frogs. It is less the portrait of an individual man than it is the icon of an era" (Holquist, "Bazarov and Sechenov," pp. 363, 373). It seems that "the frogs" in Pisarev's article and in the photo of Sechenov were intended to suggest an association with a representation of crucifixion.

28. Skabichevsky, p. 249. On patterns of behavior, see Brower.

29. Ibid., p. 250.

30. *Vest'*, 46 (1864); cited in Moser, p. 44.

31. Debogory-Mokrievich, p. 4.   32. Leffler, p. 11.

33. Kropotkin, *Memoirs*, p. 300.   34. Shelgunov, p. 256.

35. Kropotkin, *Memoirs*, p. 297.   36. Kotliarevsky, p. 257.

37. Panteleev, p. 578.

38. See Shelgunov et al., 1: 165.

39. See Steklov, 2: 324. For two participants' accounts of this episode, see Dostoevsky, 21: 25–26; and *PSS*, 1: 777.

40. See Shelgunov et al., 1: 157.

41. Malyshenko, pp. 102–3.

42. Chernyshevskaia-Bystrova, *Delo Chernyshevskogo*, pp. 146–47.

43. *Literaturnoe nasledstvo*, 67 (1959): 130.

44. For a review of the controversy, see Pereira, pp. 112–19; and Woehrlin, chap. 9. New arguments on the proclamation are made in Perper.

45. For a detailed outline and penetrating analysis of Chernyshevsky's views, see Pereira.

46. For concrete evidence, see Chernyshevskaia-Bystrova, *Delo Chernyshevskogo*, p. 119; Steklov, 2: 212–15; and Pereira, p. 13.

47. Nikoladze, p. 29, cited in Pereira, p. 13.

48. Cited in Steklov, 2: 221. 49. Ibid., p. 212.

50. Ibid., 1: 153. 51. Oksman, 1: 373–74.

52. For a review of this curious episode, see Reiser, pp. 783–87.

53. Published in *Katorga i ssylka*, 44 (1928): 50.

54. Fet, 1: 429.

55. See *N. G. Chernyshevsky: Stat'i*.

56. Skabichevsky, pp. 248–49.

57. Antonovich and Eliseev, p. 300.

58. Piksanov and Tsekhnovitser, p. 418.

59. Kropotkin, *Ideals*, p. 281.

60. Plekhanov, *Literatura*, 2: 175.

61. Plekhanov, *Chernyshevsky*, p. 71, cited in Pereira, p. 85.

62. Tsitovich, pp. iv–v.

63. For information about the circulation of the novel, see Reiser, pp. 788–91, and for reminiscences, E. M. Chernyshevskaia, p. 143, and Vodovozova, 2: 199. For interesting characterizations of the readership in the 1860s, see Barenbaum's articles "'Kruzhkovoe' chtenie," "Iz istorii chteniia," and "Raznochinno-demokraticheskii chitatel'"; and Brodskii.

64. Skabichevsky, pp. 249–50.

65. See Chukovsky, pp. 232–66. On communes, see Stites, pp. 108–11, 118–21. For reminiscences, see Zhukovskaia, pp. 154–224; Panaeva, pp. 327–35; Skabichevsky, p. 226; and Vodovozova, 2: 199–207.

66. Vodovozova, 2: 206–7. 67. Stites, p. 110.

68. Dostoevsky, 8: 349. 69. Cited in Steklov, 2: 217.

70. Ibid. 71. Ibid., p. 219.

72. Ibid., p. 132.

73. See Valentinov, pp. 76, 101–8.

74. N. Rusanov made this comment; see *Russkoe bogatstvo*, 11 (1909).

75. *Sobranie materialov*, p. 182; cited in *PSS*, 11: 706.

76. See Knizhnik-Vetrov, p. 153; cited in Stites, p. 106.

77. On fictitious marriages, see Stites, pp. 106–7; and Brower, pp. 25–26. For reminiscences, see Vodovozova, 2: 223–24; Shelgunov et al., 1: 139–40; and Zhukovskaia, p. 106.

78. Sinegub, no. 9: 95, 109.

79. See Stites, p. 107.

80. *Mayakovsky*, p. 354. See also documentary evidence and an outline of this episode in Jangfeldt, pp. 21, 31–32, 40–41.

81. Koblitz, describing the marriage of Sofia and Vladimir in its early stages, comments (p. 82): "It is possible that Sofia and Vladimir consciously modeled their behavior on that of the characters of *What Is to Be*

Done? On the other hand, they might have taken their cues from the couple whose marriage was probably Chernyshevsky's model: Maria and Petr Bokov." In fact, the Kovalevskys had many friends among the people of the sixties; among their closest ones were the Bokovs, the Shelgunovs, the Pypins, and the Chernyshevskys (see Koblitz, pp. 70–139 passim). I discuss the relationship between literary texts and real-life examples in the section "Fictitious Marriage: Reality–Literature–Reality" in the second part of this work.

82. Kovalevskaia, p. 223.

83. Ibid., p. 182; Leffler, p. 31.

84. Leffler, p. 40.

85. This is the interpretation of Stites, p. 106, and Koblitz, p. 131. For a different one, see Kochina, p. 65.

86. Kovalevskaia, p. 384.

87. Leffler, p. 119. For more information on these enterprises, see Leffler, p. 41; Kochina, p. 89; and Koblitz, pp. 132–33. Koblitz, p. 133, following the Soviet historian S. Ia. Shtraikh, sees these enterprises as inspired by "the industrializing fever."

88. Leffler, p. 119. See also Leffler, pp. 112–19, and Kovalevskaia, pp. 431, 438, for more information on the drama.

89. See Moser for a detailed review of this literature.

90. See Bakhtin, pp. 90–91; and Struve. For a view of Chernyshevsky's artistic achievements, see Tamarchenko, pp. 370–71, 381.

91. Pereira, p. 39.

92. Mathewson, p. 63.

93. This interpretation of Chernyshevsky's role is modeled after Iurii Lotman's interpretation of the role of the Decembrists in the development of Russian culture. For Lotman, the Decembrists' social and political ideas and their creative and critical writings were less important than their success in creating a particular type or model of behavior (Lotman, "Decembrist," p. 99).

94. *PSS*, 14: 456. On this issue, see Ginzburg, *O literaturnom geroe*, pp. 50–51.

1. Exposition

1. On the clergy and clerical education in Russia, see Freeze, *Russian Levites*; and *Freeze, Parish Clergy*.

2. See *PSS*, 1: 632. On his early reading, see also Oksman, 1: 76.

3. See Oksman, 1: 20, 75.

4. Shelgunov, p. 29.

5. The diaries were written in a personal code. Concerned that a fu-

ture biographer would not be able to read them, Chernyshevsky provided a key to the code by rewriting Lermontov's *Kniazhna Meri* in it (*PSS*, 1: 216). A part of the diary was seized during Chernyshevsky's arrest in 1862, and sections of it were decoded by the investigators. This part of the diary was published by Chernyshevsky's son Mikhail in 1906 in vol. 10 of *Polnoe sobranie sochinenii N. G. Chernyshevskogo*. The whole diary was published in 1928 in vol. 1 of *Literaturnoe nasledie*. A second, revised edition appeared in 1931 (*Izdatel'stvo Politkatorzhan*), and a third in 1939 (vol. 1 of *PSS*).

6. For a detailed review of Chernyshevsky's connection to Rousseau, see Scanlan. Scanlan, p. 105, comments on Chernyshevsky's identification with Rousseau and on his "urge to transfer the image of the French philosopher to a Russian setting." During the period of the diaries, Chernyshevsky did not refer to Rousseau's *Confessions* (they are mentioned for the first time in 1856; his first mention of Rousseau, in 1850, was in connection with *Emile*), but in retrospect he apparently linked his own confessional writings to Rousseau's. *Confessions* was one of the books Chernyshevsky asked for in prison, and Rousseau was one of the few authors whose works he took to penal servitude. While in the Peter-and-Paul Fortress, Chernyshevsky worked on a translation of the *Confessions* and on a biography of Rousseau. During his exile, he tried—in both writing and oral improvisations—to adapt the *Confessions* to Russian conditions, making Rousseau a Russian and a contemporary (Oksman, 2: 175). (His translation of the *Confessions* is published in Chernyshevsky, *Neopublikovannye proizvedeniia*.) The following statement, made in a letter to Dobroliubov, shows that he read Rousseau's *Confessions* as though they were his own: "Read Rousseau's *Confessions*, it tells many things about my life, though far from everything" (*PSS*, 15: 360). It is interesting that Tolstoy made a similar confession in his diary: "I feel so close to many of his [Rousseau's] pages that it seems to me I wrote them myself" (Biriukov, 1, 279).

7. Herzen, *My Past*, 2: 400 (Herzen, 9: 20).

8. See Ginzburg, "*Byloe i dumy*," pp. 82–84.

9. Annenkov, p. 327.

10. See Belinsky, 11: 170–72.

11. Ibid., p. 195. See the discussion of these issues in Ginzburg, *PP*, pp. 80–83.

12. Wellek, pp. 241, 253.

13. On Tolstoy's diaries, see Eikhenbaum, *Molodoi Tolstoy*, pp. 46–47. On similarities in the method of psychological analysis in the diaries of Tolstoy and Chernyshevsky, see Morozenko.

14. For a psychological analysis of this phenomenon, see Shapiro, pp. 49–51.

15. For a detailed list of the works written during this period and calculations of their volume, see Shchegolev, pp. 75–76. By the unit he uses, *pechatnyi list*, which contains 40,000 letters, he puts the oeuvre of this period at 68 units of belletristic works; 12 units of scholarly writings; 10 units of autobiographical materials; 4 units of evidence related to his trial; 11 units of compiled materials; and 100 units of translations. Taking into account 50 units of drafts, Shchegolev estimates that Chernyshevsky had to write 11.5 typographical units (or 212.75 pages) a month.

16. See *PSS*, 14: 660–61; and Skaftymov, "Sibirskaia belletristika N. G. Chernyshevskogo," in *Stat'i*, p. 236. On memory, see *PSS*, 15: 407.

17. See Oksman, 2: 126.

18. Chernyshevskaia-Bystrova, *Letopis'*, pp. 608–9. For a transcription of the delirium, see M. N. Chernyshevsky.

19. See *PSS*, 13: 916.   20. Oksman, 2: 165.

21. Cohn, p. 215.   22. See Struve.

23. These techniques apparently had a Western source: Dostoevsky in *A Gentle Creature* (*Krotkaia*) referred to Victor Hugo's *Le Dernier Jour d'un condamné*. The matter is treated in Cohn, pp. 208–16. See also Friedman, pp. 59, 67, pointing out similar experiments by Stendhal (who also used the image of the stenographer). On *The Double*'s impact on Chernyshevsky, consider the following entry in the diary of 1849: "In a trembling voice I was recounting *The Double* to him [Lobodovsky], and at first he thought that it was my work" (*PSS*, 1: 365).

24. For information on the intellectual life of the 1830s–40s, see Malia, "Schiller"; Malia, *Alexander Herzen*; Ginzburg, *PP*, pp. 37–130; Gershenzon, *Istoriia*; Gershenzon, "Liubov' Ogareva"; Miliukov, "Liubov' u idealistov tridtsatykh godov," in *Iz istorii*; Carr, *Romantic Exiles*; Carr, *Michael Bakunin*; Brown, *Stankevich*; Kornilov, *Molodye gody Bakunina*; Kelly; and Chizhevsky.

25. Bakunin, 1: 396–97.

26. On this issue, see Manuel and Manuel; Manuel, *Prophets*; and Riasanovsky.

27. Quoted in Gershenzon, "Liubov' Ogareva," p. 341. See also Ginzburg, *PP*, p. 51.

28. See Malia, *Alexander Herzen*, pp. 137, 178. In *My Past and Thoughts* Herzen made the following comment about Granovsky and his young wife: "Looking at them, I used to think of the serene, chaste families of the early Protestants, who fearlessly sang forbidden psalms, ready

to go hand in hand, calmly and firmly, to face the Inquisition. They seemed to me like brother and sister." Herzen, *My Past*, 2: 502 (Herzen, 9: 125).

29. For a discussion of George Sand's influence, see Stites, pp. 19–20.

30. By Vasily Botkin, according to Natalie Herzen in her diary (published in *Russkie propilei*, vol. 1, Moscow, 1915, p. 238).

31. N. Ia. Danilevsky, expounding the system of Fourier (*Delo Petrashevtsev*, 2: 293).

32. See Eikhenbaum, *Tolstoy. 70-e gody*, pp. 245–49.

33. Malia, *Alexander Hertzen*, p. 266.

34. See Ginzburg, *PP*, p. 72.

35. On Hegel's influence, see Chizhevsky.

36. Stankevich, p. 650.

37. Belinsky, 11: 386–87.

38. Ibid., 6: 268.

39. Ibid., 12: 41.

40. Ibid., p. 38.

41. Herzen, *My Past*, 2: 400 (Herzen, 9: 20).

42. Belinsky, 12: 69. See also Ginzburg, *PP*, p. 103.

43. Kotliarevsky, p. 296. Kotliarevsky dedicates a chapter to the influence of the materialist philosophy: pp. 288–322.

44. Cited in Lange, 2: 252.

45. See Lange, 2: 249; and Feuerbach, p. 49.

46. Pereira, p. 35.

47. See de Rougemont, p. 166.

48. Feuerbach, p. 48.

49. For the argument on the primacy of the physical and mental in metaphor, see de Rougemont, pp. 164–66.

50. Pereira, p. 102.

51. Herzen, *My Past*, 2: 758 (Herzen, 10: 134).

52. See Korman, pp. 63–64.

53. Shelgunov et al., 1: 143. On education, see Brower.

54. Herzen, 18: 348.

55. Herzen to Ogarev, July 29, 1867, in Herzen, 29, part 1: 157.

56. Cited in Steklov, 2: 65–66.

57. Ibid., p. 27.

58. Ibid., pp. 19–20; Chukovsky, p. 7.

59. Panaeva, p. 252.

60. Fet, 1: 132.

61. Belinsky to V. P. Botkin, April 1840, in Belinsky, 12: 512.

62. Ibid.

63. Belinsky to Bakunin, Nov. 1, 1837, in ibid., 11: 196–97. See Ginzburg, *PP*, pp. 108–9.

64. Herzen, *My Past*, 2: 410–11 (Herzen, 9: 30–31; first published in *Poliarnaia zvezda* in 1855). The story is also related in the memoirs of Ivan Panaev, published in *Sovremennik* in 1861. For a modern edition, see Panaev, pp. 296–300.

65. For the connections between the image of Myshkin and the new men (including direct references to *What Is to Be Done?*), see Lidia Lotman, pp. 244–55, 320–32. See also Dostoevsky, 9: 366.

66. Dobroliubov to I. I. Bordiugov, Dec. 17, 1858, in Dobroliubov, *Polnoe sobranie*, 9: 340.

67. The grim story of Belinsky's loves includes his infatuation with a "woman of easy virtue," described in his letters of 1838 (see Belinsky, 11: 232, 329); his hopeless passion for a sister of Bakunin's, conceived in the "harmony" of Bakunin's estate, Premukhino, where Belinsky spent three months as a guest (see Korman, p. 80); and his unhappy marriage to a woman of the petite bourgeoisie. Dobroliubov made an attempt at "saving" a prostitute: he persuaded her to leave the brothel and planned to marry her. He soon became deeply disappointed in her, though, and with the intervention of Chernyshevsky, the marriage was called off.

68. Cited in Korman, p. 81. Korman gives a remarkable analysis of the theme of shyness. See also Ginzburg, *PP*, pp. 108–9.

69. Published in *Russkaia starina* in 1904–5.

70. Dobroliubov, *Polnoe sobranie*, 9: 307–8.

71. Tolstoy, *Childhood, Boyhood and Youth*, pp. 338–39 (Tolstoy, 3: 172–73). In chap. 43 of *Iunost'* Tolstoy described the confrontation between his protagonist (a student of noble origin at Moscow University) and a group of non-gentry students whom, judging by such signs as bad French and German accents and dirty, closely bitten nails, he thought to be inferior in every way. "Once I attempted to brag before them of my knowledge of literature, and particularly of French literature, and I led the conversation to that topic. It turned out, to my amazement, that although they pronounced titles of foreign books in Russian, they had read much more than I. . . . Pushkin and Zhukovsky were literature to them (and not, as to me, those books in yellow bindings which I had read and studied as a child). . . . Neither had I any advantage over them in music. . . . In a word, with the exception of the French and German accents, they knew everything that I attempted to brag about before them, much better than I did, and were not in the least proud of it" Tolstoy, *Childhood, Boyhood and Youth*, p. 397 (Tolstoy, 3: 218).

And yet in his play *The Infected Family* (*Zarazhennoe semeistvo*; 1863–

64), written as a reproof to *What Is to Be Done?*, Tolstoy gave a penetrating and cruel parody of the situation of an educated *raznochinets* endeavoring to enter polite society by marrying a young girl from a gentry family; this young *raznochinets* is tormented by his sense of social inadequacy despite his awareness of his superiority in education and intelligence. "And I think to myself: I don't know how to act in living rooms, I don't know how to chatter in French like the others, and I've sometimes envied the salon crowd. Well, but then I think, even so, none of them is as educated as I . . . and, well, I don't know anyone with such a broad and deep education. Is there any field in which I don't feel I have the ability to make discoveries—philology, history, or the sciences? I know them all" (Tolstoy, 7: 212). What is being parodied here is also Chernyshevsky's characteristic personal style.

72. Oksman, 1: 140–41.
73. For a discussion of this episode, see Shklovsky, pp. 154–56.
74. N. A. Dobroliubov, 1: 272.   75. Kropotkin, *Memoirs*, p. 299.
76. Dostoevsky, 8: 476.   77. Skabichevsky, p. 250.

2. Recapitulation: Marriage

1. Tanner, p. 15.
2. See Ginzburg, *PP*, p. 104.
3. Belinsky, 12: 30.
4. On the social institution of the salon, see Lougee; Tinker; Todd.
5. Todd, p. 43.
6. For a Russian variant of the teacher scheme, see Herzen's novel *Who Is to Blame?* (*Kto vinovat?*; 1847). The initial situation can be viewed as a recasting into contemporary Russian life of the situation in Rousseau's *La Nouvelle Héloïse*: an educated young *raznochinets*, a tutor in a wealthy gentry family, falls in love with and marries the gentleman's daughter. However, the girl's origin (she is the illegitimate daughter of a landowner and a peasant mother) makes her social position intermediate; this marriage does not involve a move up the social ladder (Herzen's novel is discussed in more detail below).
7. On the role of the aristocrat in the European love myth, see de Rougemont; and Girard. Both authors point out the nobility's seminal role in mediating emotion.
8. Skabichevsky, pp. 124–25.
9. Shelgunov et al., 1: 200.
10. Tinker, pp. 16, 21.
11. A curious psychological phenomenon is Chernyshevsky's feeling of awe, in the years of exile, for the wealthy and the noble. In his Si-

berian letters and belletristic writings, he was preoccupied with the theme. In his letters to Alexander Pypin, he fantasized about the possibility of becoming a financial adviser to Rothschild, who (he supposed) could have benefited from the advice of a political economist of his rank. His novels are full of noble and wealthy ladies (their exact income is usually specified), who are traveling on a yacht or residing in a villa in exotic parts of the world (always in a warm climate—a touching detail in view of Chernyshevsky's confinement to the severe climate of eastern Siberia) in the company of their poor and non-noble but highly valued friends. The motif of the wealthy and the noble culminated in the 1888 novel *Evenings at Princess Starobelskaia's* (*Vechera u kniagini Starobel'skoi*). An autobiographic character, Viazovsky (the name of the immediate superior of Chernyshevsky's father, whose position he eventually received), a world-famous scholar of modest means and common origins, is unexpectedly taken to the palace of an aristocratic lady, to whom he was recommended by an Italian princess. Viazovsky's guess that the princess wants to make him her children's tutor turns out to be a comical misunderstanding of the situation. The wealthy and the noble need Viazovsky as a valuable interlocutor, adviser, and confidant. A brilliant society gathers to listen to his improvisation, which is being recorded by a team of stenographers. Addressing his illustrious listeners, Viazovsky proposes the following toast: "For the honest among the rich and noble people whose representatives are in the majority in the present gathering! . . . For those not so rich, who listened to my story and did not blame me for my sympathy for the rich and noble!" (*PSS*, 13: 851). Another detail is worth mentioning: Princess Starobel'skaia's name is Lidia Vasil'evna—a name given to Volgina, a character in *The Prologue* who bears an unmistakable likeness to Olga Sokratovna Chernyshevskaia.

12. A parody of such reasoning appears in Dostoevsky's *Crime and Punishment*. Luzhin, who is mockingly characterized as "a man of the persuasion of our new generation" and a "rational man," is expounding to his fiancée a "theory of the advantages of wives taken from poverty": "Even before he knew Dunia he had intended to take as his wife an honest girl without a dowry, who must have known poverty, because, as he explained, a husband ought not to be under any sort of obligation to his wife, and it was much better if she looked upon him as her benefactor" (Dostoevsky, 6: 32). In Dunia (as he explains to her), Luzhin found an alternative candidate for such marriage design: "I decided to take you, so to say, when the gossip of the town about your reputation had spread all over the district. Scorning public opinion for

your sake and vindicating your reputation, I was certainly completely and absolutely entitled to count on being recompensed and even to demand your gratitude" (ibid., p. 234). This parody is aimed at demonstrating that the utilitarian calculus in human relations advocated by the new men is dangerously close to vulgar practicality and petty self-interest. The degree of insight into the psychology of the new men is indeed remarkable (Dostoevsky could not have known of Chernyshevsky's diary). And yet, as we know from the diary, Chernyshevsky's motivations in choosing a bride with a blemish were entirely noble.

13. See Siegel; and Matich.

14. For a review of these references, see Dostoevsky, 5: 379–80. See Holquist, *Dostoevsky*, pp. 64–71, for a discussion of the "literariness" of the underground man's behavior.

15. Pypina, p. 12.   16. Belinsky, 11: 286.

17. Ibid., 12: 32.   18. Shapiro, p. 46.

19. For a detailed review of Chernyshevsky's ethical system, see Pereira, pp. 36–39.

20. See, for example, Tolstoy to V. Arsen'eva, Nov. 12–13, 1856, in Tolstoy, 60: 108–9. For a discussion of this episode, see Eikhenbaum, *Tolstoy. 50-e gody*, p. 346.

21. Dostoevsky, 6: 50. Among the new men, the calculated marriage seems to have been accepted as normal. There is an extreme example of it—almost an inadvertent parody—in an episode in the life of Dmitry Pisarev. It occurred between 1862 and 1866, during the time of his mental illness. While incarcerated in the Peter-and-Paul Fortress, Pisarev sent several letters to Lidia Osipovna, a young lady he had never met, asking her hand in marriage. His motivation for marrying was that he needed a stimulus to activity. And as a rational man, free of romantic notions about love, he regarded it as inconceivable that she could prefer someone else. "Lidia Osipovna," he wrote, "don't ruin your life! You absolutely have to marry a new man!" Their marriage would be happy. This notion was supported by a chain of carefully calculated arguments: (1) they would subscribe to all Russian journals and read many articles together; (2) they would subscribe to several foreign newspapers and journals; (3) many books would always be at their disposal; (4) they would be acquainted with peaceful, simple, hard-working, and totally unceremonious people; (5) Lidia Osipovna would always be able to ask her learned husband to explain difficult questions; (6) she would be able, with his help, to master German or English; and (7) their life would be devoid of luxury, while the "Ministry of Finance" would be entirely in his wife's hands. Lidia Osipovna declined. See Volynsky,

pp. 498–500. The letters were published in the January and February 1893 issues of *Russkoe obozrenie*.

22. Oksman, 1: 96.   23. Cited in ibid., p. 99.
24. Demchenko, p. 93.   25. Iudin, p. 884.
26. Demchenko, p. 97.

27. For a review of the theme of Hamlet, which appears in the works of Belinsky and Turgenev, see Turgenev, 8: 555–65.

28. Belinsky, 7: 313.

29. Kathryn Feuer, Introduction to N. G. Chernyshevsky, *What Is to Be Done?*, tr. Dole and Skidelsky, p. xiii.

30. Cited in Gershenzon, "Liubov' Ogareva," p. 356.

31. Herzen, My Past, 2: 630–38 (Herzen, 9: 255–62: "Epizod iz 1843 goda").

32. Pypina, p. 36.   33. *Zven'ia*, 8 (1950): 576.
34. Pypina, p. 105.   35. Ibid.

36. Chernyshevskaia-Bystrova, *Letopis'*, pp. 257–60; *PSS*, 14: 833.

37. Dostoevsky, 9: 389. See Nazirov for a discussion of this issue.

38. Pypina, p. 33.

39. See *N. G. Chernyshevsky. Estetika.*

40. Oksman, 2: 370 (13n).   41. Ibid., p. 65–66.
42. Ibid., p. 68.   43. Ibid., pp. 127–28.
44. Ibid., pp. 171–73.

45. See Manuel and Manuel, p. 537.

46. Stites, p. 21 (Belinsky, 3: 398).

47. Tolstoy, "Kreutzer Sonata," p. 155 (Tolstoy, 27: 79).

48. See Reiser, p. 827. Stites, p. 91, gives a different date.

49. Reiser, p. 820. For a review of the controversy over the question of a real-life prototype and documentation of the case, see ibid., pp. 819–33.

50. Zhukovskaia, p. 216. See also Reiser, p. 823.

51. Reiser, p. 828.   52. *Zven'ia*, 3–4 (1934): 887.
53. See Leffler, pp. 10–11.   54. Ibid., p. 17.

55. Kovalevskaia, p. 380.

56. The question was first discussed in Skaftymov, pp. 203–27.

57. N. G. Chernyshevsky, *Chto delat'?*, p. 241.

58. Ibid., p. 227.   59. Oksman, 2: 171.
60. Ibid., p. 86.   61. Ibid., p. 304.

62. Ibid. The theme of the ménage à trois is also found in a bizarre anecdote Chernyshevsky told to amuse a visitor (D. I. Miliukov, who saw him in Viliuisk, where Chernyshevsky was otherwise totally isolated): "Panaev is dead. So what is to be done? The body was dressed

and placed on the table. His friends and his wife sat in the parlor discussing the plans of Mrs. Panaev's future life with Nekrasov, who had been her lover. Suddenly the door opens and Panaev walks in—no one heard him because they put soft slippers on his feet. Panic and pandemonium. It was some time before they got over their surprise. As it turned out, Panaev was not dead. He was in a state of lethargy" (cited in ibid., p. 250). This macabre story can be interpreted as an allegory of Chernyshevsky's own situation. Confined in Siberia, he was (for his wife), in a manner of speaking, suspended in "lethargy" and had every reason to believe that she was involved in similar arrangements. It is notable that the prolonged absence of one of the participants in the menage is a constant element of the scheme.

63. N. G. Chernyshevsky, *Chto delat'?*, p. 197.

64. Rousseau, p. 194.

65. See Tanner, pp. 145–51.

66. For more information on Chernyshevsky and Rousseau, see note 6 to Part One.

67. See Malia, *Alexander Herzen*, p. 270.

68. For a detailed treatment of this episode, see Carr, *Romantic Exiles*. The documents pertaining to the story were published in *Literaturnoe nasledstvo*, 64 (1958). Natalie Herzen's letters to Herwegh were written in French.

69. *Literaturnoe nasledstvo*, 64 (1958): 82, 189, 269–70, 292.

70. Ibid., p. 285.   71. Ibid., p. 106.

72. Ibid., p. 292   73. Ibid., p. 272.

74. Ibid., p. 292.   75. Ibid., p. 298.

76. Herzen, *My Past*, chap. 46.   77. Herzen, 24: 308.

78. Carr, *Romantic Exiles*, p. 120.

79. Herzen, 24: 295–99.

80. Carr, *Romantic Exiles*, p. 120.

81. *Literaturnoe nasledstvo*, 64 (1958): 312; Herzen, *My Past*, chap. 47.

82. Herzen, 24: 326.

83. Ibid., 26: 62–63. See also Carr, *Romantic Exiles*, p. 195.

84. *Russkie propilei*, 4 (1917): 211.

85. See Carr, *Romantic Exiles*, chaps. 8, 12, 16. For the documents, see Gershenzon, *Arkhiv N.A. i N.P. Ogarevykh*.

86. The Shelgunov affair is related in Bogdanovich, pp. 35–50. See pp. 264–420 for documents.

87. Ibid., p. 272.   88. Ibid., p. 282.

89. Ibid., p. 288.   90. Ibid., p. 339.

91. See Stites, pp. 40–44.   92. Bogdanovich, p. 341.

93. P. Zasodimsky, cited in Bogdanovich, p. 409.

94. Bogdanovich, p. 398.

95. Manuel, pp. 241–42.

96. Manuel and Manuel, p. 535.

97. N. G. Chernyshevsky, *Chto delat'?*, p. 49.

98. Ibid., p. 179.   99. Ibid., pp. 240–41.

100. Herzen, 29, part 1: 185.   101. Ibid., p. 170.

102. See Eikhenbaum, *Lev Tolstoy. 70-e gody*, pp. 124–38.

103. Tolstoy, 20: 3–4.   104. Ibid., p. 43.

105. Ibid., p. 44.   106. Ibid., p. 334.

107. Herzen, 29, part 1: 326.

108. See Mochulsky, pp. 159–64, 183–84, 237–38. See also Girard, pp. 45–52.

109. Mochulsky, pp. 207–8.   110. Armstrong, p. 93.

111. Ibid., p. 82.   112. Tanner, p. 13.

113. Shelgunov, in his article "Russian Ideals, Heroes, and Types" ("Russkie idealy, geroi i tipy"; 1868), remarked that the new man was "a collective man."

114. On the problem of mediated emotion, see Girard.

3. The Embodiment of the Model: Texts

1. Chernyshevsky's dissertation is discussed in Pereira, pp. 40–42; Terras, pp. 235–43; and Usakina, pp. 228–49.

2. The passages from the dissertation are from the English translation in N. G. Chernyshevsky, *Selected Philosophical Essays*. The first set of numbers in the citations refers to the Russian text in *PSS*; the italic number is the page in the English translation.

3. See Usakina, p. 233.

4. N. M. Chernyshevskaia, p. 124.

5. In his book *Lessing, His Time, His Life and Work* (*Lessing, ego vremia, ego zhizn' i deiatel'nost'*, 1856–57), Chernyshevsky intended to demonstrate that Lessing's Germany was a society similar to Russia's in the 1860s (see *PSS*, 4: 890). The most important point of this parallel was the idea that in Lessing's time (and because of his efforts) literature was the driving force in the social and intellectual development of the German nation (see Heier, p. 59). Iu. Steklov, Chernyshevsky's first biographer, noted: "Almost everything that he says about the character of Lessing's literary activity is applicable to Chernyshevsky himself, and in this respect his judgments of Lessing are to a certain degree autobiographical in nature" (Heier, p. 61 [Steklov, 1: 162]). It is remarkable that Chernyshevsky sees in Lessing not only a fellow enlightener of his na-

tion (and a creator of "realistic" aesthetics), but also a fellow *raznochi-nets* who rose to cultural prominence. In this respect, Lessing is for him a figure similar to Rousseau. He dwells on such details of Lessing's youth as his upbringing as the son of a pastor and his seminary educa-tion; his intellectual brilliance; and his initial shyness, clumsiness, and reticence. He also dwells on young Lessing's association with a more active, sociable, and outgoing friend (a fellow student at Leipzig Uni-versity). However, having established Lessing as his double, Cherny-shevsky then endows him with desirable (but unattained) qualities: in the final analysis, Lessing was more outgoing—bolder and even row-dier than his friend, a great drinker and womanizer. He mastered danc-ing, fencing, and riding, and gained entrée to polite society (*PSS*, 4: 88–89, 96).

6. For a review of this polemic, see Dostoevsky, 5: 379 and 17: 306–7.

7. Yet Chernyshevsky did write poetry. He even attempted to write English poetry, hoping that it would be easier to publish:

> We all who sing this song of Love,
> We are all of the same, great, Nation.
> Our blood is one, our Language one,
> The same our feelings' inclination.

8. See Morson, pp. 99–102.

9. All subsequent references to *What Is to Be Done?* are given in the text. Except as explained below, the quotations are drawn from the En-glish translation of Benjamin R. Tucker. The first number in the cita-tions is the page in the original (N. G. Chernyshevsky, *Chto delat'?*); the second, italic number is the page in the Tucker translation. This transla-tion is not complete, however; an "n.p." in italic indicates that the pas-sage is not present in Tucker, and that the translation is Slava Paperno's. The complete text of the novel is published in the Ornatskaia and Reiser scholarly edition. An English translation based on this edition was pub-lished in Moscow in 1983 (tr. Laura Beraha), but it is stylistically flawed. A translation of the full text of the first edition of the novel (less com-plete than the Ornatskaia and Reiser edition) was published in 1986 (tr. Dole and Skidelsky, with an introduction by Kathryn Feuer). At this writing, a scholarly, annotated English translation is being prepared by Michael Katz and William Wagner for Cornell University Press.

10. See the notes to N. G. Chernyshevsky, *Chto delat'?*, p. 836.

11. On the poetics of dreams in Russian literature, see Katz.

12. See Abrams, pp. 61–63.

13. Dostoevsky, 21: 130.

14. Annenkov, p. 210. For a review of the influence of these Western ideas in Russia, see Komarovich. See also Frank, *Dostoevsky: Seeds of Revolt*, pp. 183–98.

15. See Malia, *Alexander Herzen*, pp. 119–28, 226.

16. Oksman, 1: 158.

17. For a detailed review and analysis of Chernyshevsky's system, see Pereira, pp. 35–40.

18. The problem is discussed in Ginzburg, "Belinsky v bor'be."

19. Connections between Ivan Karamazov and Herzen are discussed in Perlina, pp. 121–35. On the Belinsky connection (Belinsky's private letter of 1841 served as a source and inspiration of Ivan's famous monologue on "returning his entrance ticket"), see Kirpotin, pp. 228–48; and Ginzburg, *PP*, pp. 128–29.

20. Frank shows that Dostoevsky used a similar technique (carrying the opponent's initial premises to their ultimate conclusion) in his polemics with Chernyshevsky in *Notes from Underground* (*Dostoevsky: Stir of Liberation*, pp. 312–19).

21. Dostoevsky, 10: 198. A similar statement appeared in Dostoevsky's letter to N. D. Fonvizina of Feb. 1854 (see 12: 297).

22. Dostoevsky, 15: 81, 73.

23. See Dostoevsky, *Pis'ma*, 4: 59.

24. Dostoevsky to A. N. Maikov, Dec. 11, 1868, in ibid., 2: 150. See also Wellek, p. 232.

25. Feuerbach, p. 32.

26. See Berdyaev, p. 45; Shils, p. 17; and Pereira, p. 103.

27. Stepniak-Kravchinsky, 1: 368–69.

28. V. Zaitsev, a critic of *Russkoe slovo*, cited in ibid., p. 369.

29. Ibid., p. 369.

30. Dostoevsky, *The Idiot*, p. 520 (Dostoevsky, 8: 452).

31. Dostoevsky, 10: 269.

32. Ibid., 11: 10, 268.

33. Cited in Steklov, 2: 216.

34. Oksman, 1: 158. According to a contemporary, Chernyshevsky's teachings had a following in some theological seminaries. There was a circle of "Chernyshevtsy" in the Vologda seminary, and one of the high-ranking members of the administration (he belonged to the black clergy, i.e., the monastic clergy) considered himself a proselyte of both Chernyshevsky and Feuerbach (Sazhin, p. 27).

35. See Odoevsky, p. 179.

36. For reminiscences of the ceremony, see Oksman, 2: 19–54.

37. Herzen, 13: 222.

38. M. N. Chernyshevsky, pp. 143, 146.

39. Ibid., p. 134.

40. For a review of the possible literary sources of the title, see Reiser, p. 833.

41. Frank sees in Rakhmetov "the fateful fusion between the hagiographic pattern of Russian religious kenoticism and the coldly dispassionate calculations of English Utilitarianism" ("N. G. Chernyshevsky," pp. 83–84).

42. See Clark, pp. 48–51.

43. Herzen, 29, part 1: 167.

44. Kathryn Feuer comments on the prominence of the theme of gaiety in the novel; see her Introduction to Chernyshevsky, *What Is to Be Done?*, tr. Dole and Skidelsky, p. xix.

45. See *Literaturnoe nasledstvo*, 39–40 (1941): 354.

46. Feuerbach, p. 131.

47. On Liebig's influence in Russia, see the notes to Chernyshevsky, *Chto delat'?*, p. 844.

48. Feuerbach, p. 131.

Works Cited

Abrams, W. H. *Natural Supernaturalism: Tradition and Revolution in Romantic Literature.* New York, 1971.

Annenkov, P. V. *Vospominaniia i kriticheskie ocherki.* St. Petersburg, 1881.

Antonovich, M. A., and G. Z. Eliseev. *Shestidesiatye gody. Vospominaniia.* Moscow-Leningrad, 1933.

Armstrong, Judith. *The Novel of Adultery.* New York, 1976.

Bakhtin, M. M. *Problemy poetiki Dostoevskogo.* Moscow, 1963.

Bakunin, M. *Sobranie sochinenii i pisem.* 2 vols. Moscow, 1934.

Barenbaum, I. E. "Iz istorii chteniia raznochinno-demokraticheskoi molodezhi vtoroi poloviny 50-kh—nachala 60-kh godov XIX veka." In *Istoriia russkogo chitatelia,* vol. 2. Leningrad, 1976, pp. 29–44.

———. "'Kruzhkovoe' chtenie raznochinnoi molodezhi vtoroi poloviny 50-kh—nachala shestidesiatykh godov XIX veka." In *Istoriia russkogo chitatelia,* vol. 1. Leningrad, 1973, pp. 77–92.

———. "Raznochinno-demokraticheskii chitatel' v gody demokraticheskogo pod'ema (vtoraiia polovina 50-kh—nachalo 60-kh godov XIX veka)." In *Istoriia russkogo chitatelia,* vol. 3. Leningrad, 1979, pp. 23–62.

Belinsky, V. G. *Polnoe sobranie sochinenii.* 13 vols. Moscow, 1953–59.

Berdyaev, Nicolas. *The Origin of Russian Communism.* London, 1948.

Berlin, Isaiah. *Russian Thinkers.* New York, 1978.

Biriukov, P. *Lev Nikolaevich Tolstoy: Biografiia po neizdannym materialam.* 2 vols. Moscow, 1911.

Bogdanovich, T. A. *Liubov' liudei shestidesiatykh godov.* Leningrad, 1929.

Brodskii, N. L. "N. G. Chernyshevsky i chitateli 60-kh godov." In N. L. Brodskii, *Izbrannye trudy.* Moscow, 1964, pp. 9–26.

Brower, Daniel R. *Training the Nihilists: Education and Radicalism in Tsarist Russia.* Ithaca, N.Y., 1975.

Brown, E. J. "Pisarev and the Transformation of Two Novels." In W. M. Todd III, ed., *Literature and Society in Imperial Russia.* Stanford, Calif., 1978, pp. 151–72.

———. *Stankevich and His Moscow Circle, 1830–1840.* Stanford, Calif., 1966.

Carr, E. H. *Michael Bakunin.* London, 1937.

———. *The Romantic Exiles.* Cambridge, Mass., 1981.

Cassirer, Ernst. *The Philosophy of Symbolic Form.* Tr. Ralph Manheim. 3 vols. New Haven, Conn., 1955.

Chernyshevskaia, E. M. "Vospominania E. M. Chernyshevskoi," *Russkaia literatura,* no. 2, 1978.

Chernyshevskaia, N. M. "Ozarena toboiu zhizn' moia . . . (N. G. i O. S. Chernyshevskie)," *Russkaia literatura,* no. 11, 1978.

Chernyshevskaia-Bystrova, N. M., ed. *Delo Chernyshevskogo.* Saratov, 1968.

———. *Letopis' zhizni i deiatel'nosti N. G. Chernyshevskogo.* Moscow-Leningrad, 1953.

Chernyshevsky, M. N. "Poslednie dni zhizni Chernyshevskogo," *Byloe,* no. 8, 1907, 128–50.

Chernyshevsky, N. G. *Chto delat'? Iz rasskazov o novykh liudiakh.* Ed. T. I. Ornadskaia and S. A. Reiser. Leningrad, 1975.

———. *Literaturnoe nasledie.* Ed. N. A. Alekseev et al. 3 vols. Moscow, 1928–30.

———. *Neopublikovannye proizvedeniia.* Saratov, 1935.

———. *Polnoe sobranie sochinenii.* 16 vols. Moscow, 1939–53.

———. *Selected Philosophical Essays.* Moscow, 1953.

———. *What Is to Be Done?* Tr. N. Dole and S. S. Skidelsky, with an introduction by K. Feuer. Ann Arbor, Mich., 1986.

———. *What Is to Be Done? Tales About New People.* Tr. Benjamin R. Tucker, expanded by Cathy Porter, with an introduction by E. H. Carr. London, 1982.

Chizhevsky, D. I. *Gegel' v Rossii.* Paris, 1939.

Chukovsky, Kornei. *Liudi i knigi shestidesiatykh godov.* Leningrad, 1934.

Clark, Katerina. *The Soviet Novel: History as Ritual.* Chicago, 1981.

Cohn, Dorrit. *Transparent Minds: Narrative Modes for Presenting Consciousness in Fiction.* Princeton, N.J., 1978.

Debogory-Mokrievich, V. K. *Vospominaniia.* Paris, 1894.

Delo Petrashevtsev. Pub. Akademiia nauk SSSR. Institut istorii. 3 vols. Moscow, 1937–51.

Demchenko, A. A. *N. G. Chernyshevsky: Nauchnaia biografiia*, vol. 1. Saratov, 1978.

———, ed. *N. G. Chernyshevsky v vospominaniiakh sovremennikov.* 2d ed. Leningrad, 1982.

Dobroliubov, N. A. *Dnevniki, 1851–1859.* Moscow, 1932.

———. *Polnoe sobranie sochinenii v deviati tomakh.* 9 vols. Moscow-Leningrad, 1961–64.

Dostoevsky, F. M. *The Idiot.* Tr. Constance Garnett. New York, 1935.

———. *Pis'ma.* Ed. S. A. Dolinin. 4 vols. Moscow-Leningrad, 1930.

———. *Polnoe sobranie sochinenii v tridtsati tomakh.* 30 vols. Leningrad, 1972–.

Eikhenbaum, B. M. *Lev Tolstoi. 50-e gody.* Leningrad, 1928.

———. *Lev Tolstoi. 60-e gody.* Leningrad-Moscow, 1931.

———. *Lev Tolstoi. 70-e gody.* 2d ed. Leningrad, 1974.

———. *Molodoi Tolstoi.* Petrograd-Berlin, 1928.

Emmons, Terence. *The Russian Landed Gentry and the Peasant Emancipation of 1861.* Cambridge, Mass., 1967.

Fet, A. *Moi vospominaniia: 1848–1889.* 2 vols. Moscow, 1890.

Feuerbach, Ludwig. *The Essence of Christianity.* New York, 1957.

Frank, Joseph. *Dostoevsky: The Seeds of Revolt, 1821–1849.* Princeton, N.J., 1976.

———. *Dostoevsky: The Stir of Liberation, 1860–1865.* Princeton, N.J., 1986.

———. *Dostoevsky: The Years of Ordeal, 1850–1859.* Princeton, N.J., 1983.

———. "N. G. Chernyshevsky: A Russian Utopia," *The Southern Review,* no. 1, 1967, 68–84.

———. "Nihilism and *Notes from the Underground,*" *Sewanee Review,* 69 (1961), 1–33.

Freeze, G. L. *The Parish Clergy in Nineteenth-Century Russia: Crisis, Reform, Counter-Reform.* Princeton, N.J., 1983.

———. *The Russian Levites: Parish Clergy in the Eighteenth Century.* Cambridge, Mass., 1977.

Friedman, Melvin. *Stream of Consciousness: A Study in Literary Method.* New Haven, Conn., 1965.

Gasparov, Boris. "Introduction." In A. D. Nakhimovsky and A. Stone Nakhimovsky, eds., *The Semiotics of Russian Cultural History.* Ithaca, N.Y., 1985, pp. 13–29.

Gershenzon, M. *Istoriia molodoi Rossii.* Moscow, 1908.

———. "Liubov' P. Ogareva." In M. Gershenzon, *Obrazy proshlogo.* Moscow, 1912.

———, ed. *Arkhiv N. A. i N. P. Ogarevykh.* Moscow-Leningrad, 1930.

Ginzburg, Lidia. "Belinsky v bor'be a zapozdalym romantizmom." In L. Ginzburg, *O starom i novom*. Leningrad, 1982, pp. 229–44.

——. *"Byloe i dumy" Gertsena*. Leningrad, 1957.

——. *Literatura v poiskakh real'nosti*. Leningrad, 1987.

——. *O literaturnom geroe*. Leningrad, 1979.

——. *O psikhologicheskoi proze*. 2d ed. Leningrad, 1977. Chapter 1 translated into English as "The 'Human Document' and the Formation of Character," in A. D. Nakhimovsky and A. Stone Nakhimovsky, eds., *The Semiotics of Russian Cultural History*. Ithaca, N.Y., 1985, pp. 188–224.

Girard, René. *Deceit, Desire, and the Novel*. Baltimore, 1965.

Gleason, Abbot. *Young Russia: The Genesis of Russian Radicalism in the 1860s*. New York, 1980.

Heier, E. "Chernyshevskii's Lessing." In S. D. Cioran, W. Smyrniw, and G. Thomas, eds., *Studies in Honor of Louis Shein*. Hamilton, Canada, 1983, pp. 55–64.

Herzen, A. I. *My Past and Thoughts*. Tr. Constance Garnett. 4 vols. New York, 1968.

——. *Sobranie sochinenii v tridtsati tomakh*. 30 vols. Moscow, 1954–65.

Holquist, Michael. "Bazarov and Sechenov: The Role of Scientific Metaphor in *Fathers and Sons*," *Russian Literature*, 16.4 (Nov. 1984), 359–74.

——. *Dostoevsky and the Novel*. Princeton, N.J., 1977.

Iudin, P. L. "N. G. Chernyshevsky v Saratove," *Istoricheskii vestnik*, no. 12, 1905.

Jangfeldt, Bengt, ed. *Vladimir Maiakovsky and Lilia Brik: Correspondence 1915–1930*. Stockholm, 1982.

Katz, Michael. *Dreams and the Unconscious in Nineteenth-Century Russian Fiction*. Hanover, N.H., 1984.

Kelly, A. *M. Bakunin: A Study in the Psychology and Politics of Utopism*. Oxford, 1982.

Kirpotin, V. Ia. *Dostoevsky i Belinsky*. Moscow, 1960.

Knizhnik-Vetrov, I. S. *Russkie deiatel'nitsy Pervogo Internatsionala i Parizhskoi kommuny*. Moscow, 1964.

Koblitz, Anna Hibner. *A Convergence of Lives. Sofia Kovalevskaia: Scientist, Writer, Revolutionary*. Boston, 1983.

Kochina, P. Ia. *Sof'ia Vasil'evna Kovalevskaia*. Moscow, 1981.

Komarovich, V. L. "Iunost' Dostoevskogo," *Byloe*, no. 28, 1924, 3–43.

Korman, B. O. *Lirika Nekrasova*. 2d ed. Izhevsk, 1978.

Kornilov, A. A. *Molodye gody Mikhaila Bakunina. Iz istorii russkogo romantizma*. Moscow, 1915.

Kotliarevsky, Nestor. *Kanun osvobozhdeniia*. Petrograd, 1916.

Kovalevskaia, S. V. *Vospominaniia i pis'ma*. Moscow, 1961.

Kropotkin, P. A. *Ideals and Realities in Russian Literature*. New York, 1916.

———. *Memoirs of a Revolutionary*. Boston, 1899.

Lampert, Eugene. *Sons Against Fathers*. Oxford, 1965.

Lange, F. A. *History of Materialism*. 2 vols. Boston, 1880.

Lebedev, A. A. "N. G. Chernyshevsky (Nabroski po neizdannym materialam)," *Russkaia starina*, no. 3, 1912.

Leffler, A. C. *Sonia Kovalevsky: Biography and Autobiography*. New York, 1895.

L. N. Tolstoi i russkaia literaturno-obshchestvennaia mysl'. Leningrad, 1979.

Lotman, Iurii. "Dekabrist v povsednevnoi zhizni." In V. G. Bazanov and V. G. Vatsuro, eds., *Literaturnoe nasledie dekabristov*. Leningrad, 1975, pp. 25–74. Translated into English as "The Decembrist in Daily Life," in A. D. Nakhimovsky and A. Stone Nakhimovsky, eds., *The Semiotics of Russian Cultural History*. Ithaca, N.Y., 1985, pp. 95–149.

———. "O Khlestakove," *Trudy po russkoi i slavianskoi filologii* (Tartu), no. 26, 1975, 19–53. Translated into English as "Concerning Khlestakov," in A. D. Nakhimovsky and A. Stone Nakhimovsky, eds., *The Semiotics of Russian Cultural History*. Ithaca, N.Y., 1985, pp. 150–87.

———. "Poetika bytovogo povedeniia v russkoi kul'ture XVIII veka," *Trudy po znakovym sistemam* (Tartu), no. 8, 1977, 65–89. Translated into English as "The Poetics of Everyday Behavior in Eighteenth-Century Russian Culture," in A. D. Nakhimovsky and A. Stone Nakhimovsky, eds., *The Semiotics of Russian Cultural History*. Ithaca, N.Y., 1985, pp. 67–94.

———. "Stsena i zhivopis' kak kodiruiushchie ustroistva kul'turnogo povedeniia cheloveka nachala XIX stoletiia." In Iu. Lotman, *Stat'i po tipologii kul'tury*. Tartu, 1973, pp. 74–89. Translated into English as "The Stage and Painting as Code Mechanisms for Cultural Behavior in the Early Nineteenth Century," in Ju. M. Lotman and B. A. Uspenskij, *The Semiotics of Russian Culture*. Ed. A. Shukman. Ann Arbor, Mich., 1984, pp. 165–76.

———. "Teatr i teatral'nost' v stroe kul'tury nachala XIX veka." In Iu. Lotman, *Stat'i po tipologii kul'tury*. Tartu, 1973, pp. 42–73. Translated into English as "The Theater and Theatricality as Components of Early Nineteenth-Century Culture," in Ju. M. Lotman and B. A. Uspenskij, *The Semiotics of Russian Culture*. Ed. A. Shukman. Ann Arbor, Mich., 1984, pp. 141–64.

Lotman, Lidia. *Realizm russkoi literatury 60-kh godov*. Leningrad, 1974.

Lougee, Carolyn C. *La Paradis des Femmes: Women, Salons, and Social Stratification in Seventeenth-Century France*. Princeton, N.J., 1976.

Mayakovsky v vospominaniiakh sovremennikov. Comp. N. V. Reformatsky. Moscow, 1963.

Malia, Martin E. *Alexander Herzen and the Birth of Russian Socialism, 1812–1855.* Cambridge, Mass., 1961.

———. "Schiller and the Early Russian Left." *Harvard Slavic Studies,* no. 4, 1957, 169–200.

———. "What Is the Intelligentsia?," *Daedalus,* Summer 1960, 441–58.

Malyshenko, G. "Nikolai Gavrilovich Chernyshevsky," *Russkaia mysl',* no. 3, 1906, 73–121.

Mantzaridis, Georgios I. *The Deification of Man.* Crestwood, N.Y., 1984.

Manuel, F. E. *The Prophets of Paris.* Cambridge, Mass., 1962.

Manuel, F. F. and F. P. Manuel. *Utopian Thought in the Western World.* Cambridge, Mass., 1979.

Mathewson, Rufus W. *The Positive Hero in Russian Literature.* 2d ed. Stanford, Calif., 1975.

Matich, Olga. "A Typology of Fallen Women in Nineteenth-Century Russian Literature." In *American Contributions to the Ninth International Congress of Slavists, Kiev, September 1983,* vol. 2. Columbus, Ohio, 1983, pp. 325–43.

McLean, Hugh. "The Development of Modern Russian Literature," *Slavic Review,* Sept. 1962, 389–410.

Miliukov, P. *Iz istorii russkoi intelligentsii.* St. Petersburg, 1903.

Mochulsky, K. *Dostoevsky: His Life and Work.* Princeton, N.J., 1978.

Morozenko, L. N. "U istokov novogo etapa v razvitii psikhologizma (Rannie dnevniki Tolstogo i Chernyshevsky)." In *L. N. Tolstoy i russkaia literaturno-obshchestvennaia mysl'.* Leningrad, 1979, pp. 112–32.

Morson, Gary Saul. *The Boundaries of Genre: Dostoevsky's Diary of a Writer and the Tradition of Literary Utopia.* Austin, Tex., 1981.

Moser, Charles. *Anti-nihilism in the Russian Novel of the 1860's.* The Hague, 1964.

Mukařovský, Jan. "The Individual and Literary Development." In *The Word and Verbal Art. Essays by Jan Mukařovský.* Tr. J. Burbanck, ed. P. Steiner. New Haven, Conn., 1977, pp. 161–79.

Nabokov, Vladimir. *Dar.* Ann Arbor, Mich., 1975. Translated into English as *The Gift* by M. Scammel, with the collaboration of the author. New York, 1979.

N. A. Dobroliubov v vospominaniiakh sovremennikov. Comp. S. A. Reiser, Moscow, 1961.

Nahirny, Vladimir. *The Russian Intelligentsia.* New Brunswick, N. J., 1983.

Nazirov, R. G. "Geroi romana 'Idiot' i ikh prototipy," *Russkaia literatura,* no. 2, 1970, 114–23.

Nekrasov, N. A. *Polnoe sobranie sochinenii i pisem.* 12 vols. Moscow, 1948–53.

N. G. Chernyshevsky. *Estetika. Literatura. Kritika.* Leningrad, 1979.

N. G. Chernyshevsky: Stat'i, issledovaniia i materialy, vol. 2. Saratov, 1962.

Nikitenko, A. V. *Dnevnik v trekh tomakh.* 3 vols. Moscow, 1955–56.

Nikoladze, N. "Vospominaniia o shestidesiatykh godakh," *Katorga i ssylka,* no. 5, 1929.

Odoevsky, V. F. 'Dnevnik,' *Literaturnoe nasledstvo,* 22–24 (1935).

Oksman, Iu. G., ed. *N. G. Chernyshevskii v vospominaniiakh sovremennikov.* 2 vols. Saratov, 1959.

Ovsianiko-Kulikovsky, D. N. *Istoriia russkoi literatury XIX veka,* vol. 3. Moscow, 1911.

Panaev, I. I. *Literaturnye vospominaniia.* Moscow-Leningrad, 1950.

Panaeva, Avdot'ia. *Vospominaniia.* Moscow, 1972.

Panteleev, L. F. *Iz vospominanii proshlogo.* Moscow-Leningrad, 1934.

Pelikan, Jaroslav. *The Spirit of Eastern Christendom (600–1700).* Chicago, 1974.

Pereira, N. G. O. *The Thought and Teachings of N. G. Chernyshevsky.* The Hague, 1975.

Perlina, Nina. *Varieties of Poetic Discourse: Quotations in the Brothers Karamazov.* Lanham, N.Y., 1983.

Perper, M. I. "Proklamatsiia 'Barskim krest'ianam ot ikh dobrozhelatelei poklon,'" *Russkaia literatura,* no. 1, 1975, 138–54.

Piksanov, N. K., and O. G. Tsekhnovitser, eds. *Shestidesiatye gody.* Moscow-Leningrad, 1940.

Pisarev, D. I. *Sochineniia v 4 tomakh.* 4 vols. Moscow, 1955–56.

Plekhanov, G. V. *Literatura i estetika.* 2 vols. Moscow, 1958.

———. *N. G. Chernyshevsky.* St. Petersburg, 1910.

Pypin, A. N. *Moi zametki.* Moscow, 1910.

Pypina, V. A. *Liubov' v zhizni Chernyshevskogo.* Petrograd, 1923.

Randall, Francis B. *N. G. Chernyshevskii.* New York, 1967.

Reifman, P. S. "Bor'ba v 1860-kh godakh vokrug romana I. S. Turgeneva 'Ottsy i deti,'" *Trudy po russkoi i slavianskoi filologii* (Tartu), no. 6, 1963, 82–94.

Reiser, S. A. "Nekotorye problemy izucheniia romana." In N. G. Chernyshevsky, *Chto delat'? Iz rasskazov o novykh liudiakh.* Ed. T. O. Ornadskaiia and S. A. Reiser. Leningrad, 1975, pp. 782–833.

Riasanovsky, Nicholas V. *The Teaching of Charles Fourier.* Berkeley, Calif., 1969.

de Rougemont, Denis. *Love in the Western World.* Tr. Montgomery Belgion. Princeton, N.J., 1983.

Rousseau, Jean-Jacques. *The Confessions.* Tr. J. M. Cohen. London, 1953.

Rusanov, N. "Ucheniki Marksa o Chernyshevskom," *Russkoe bogatstvo,* no. 11, 1909.

Saltykov-Shchedrin, M. E. *Polnoe sobranie sochinenii v dvadtsati tomakh.* 20 vols. Moscow, 1933–41.

Sazhin, A. M. *Vospominaniia.* Moscow, 1925.

Scanlan, James P. "Chernyshevsky and Rousseau." In A. Mlikotin, ed., *Western Philosophical Systems in Russian Literature: A Collection of Critical Studies.* Los Angeles, Calif., 1978, pp. 103–20.

Sechenov, I. M. *Avtobiograficheskie zapiski.* Moscow, 1907.

Shapiro, David. *Neurotic Styles.* New York, 1965.

Shchegolev, P. "Chernyshevsky v raveline," *Zvezda,* no. 3, 1924, 71–77.

Shelgunov, N. V. *Vospominaniia.* Moscow-Petrograd, 1923.

Shelgunov, N. V., L. P. Shelgunova, and M. L. Mikhailov. *Vospominaniia.* 2 vols. Moscow, 1967.

Shils, E. "The Intellectuals and the Power: Some Perspectives in Comparative Analysis," *Comparative Studies in Society and History,* 1.1 (1958), 5–22.

Shklovsky, V. *Za i protiv: zametki o Dostoevskom.* Moscow, 1957.

Shtakenshneider, E. A. *Dnevnik i zapiski.* Moscow-Leningrad, 1934.

Siegel, George. "The Fallen Women in Nineteenth-Century Russian Literature," *Harvard Slavic Studies,* no. 5, 1970.

Sinegub, S. S. "Vospominaniia chaikovtsa," *Byloe* (3 parts), nos. 8–10, 1906.

Skabichevsky, A. M. *Literaturnye vospominaniia.* Moscow-Leningrad, 1928.

Skaftymov, A. *Stat'i o russkoi literature.* Saratov, 1958.

Sobranie materialov o napravlenii razlichnykh otraslei russkoi slovesnosti. St. Petersburg, 1865.

Stankevich, N. V. *Perepiska N. V. Stankevicha 1830–1840.* Moscow, 1914.

Steklov, Iu. M. *N. G. Chernyshevskii: Ego zhizn' i deiatel'nost', 1828–1889.* 2d ed. 2 vols. Moscow-Leningrad, 1928.

Stepniak-Kravchinsky, S. *Sochineniia.* 2 vols. Moscow, 1958.

Stites, Richard. *The Women's Liberation Movement in Russia.* Princeton, N.J., 1978.

Struve, Gleb. "Monologue Interieur: The Origin of the Formula and the First Statement of its Possibilities," *PMLA,* 69 (1954), 1101–1111.

Tamarchenko, G. E. *Chernyshevsky-romanist.* Leningrad, 1976.

Tanner, Tony. *Adultery in the Novel: Contract and Transgression.* Baltimore, 1979.

Terras, Victor. *Belinsky and Russian Literary Criticism: The Heritage of Organic Aesthetics.* Madison, Wis., 1974.

Tinker, C. B. *The Salon and English Letters*. New York, 1915.

Todd, W. M. III. *Fiction and Society in the Age of Pushkin: Ideology, Institutions, and Narrative*. Cambridge, Mass., 1986.

Tolstoy, L. N. *Childhood, Boyhood and Youth*. Tr. Louise and Aylmer Maude. London, 1930.

———. "The Kreutzer Sonata." In *The Novels and Other Works of Lyof N. Tolstoï*, vol. 16. New York, 1913.

———. *Polnoe sobranie sochinenii v devianosta tomakh*. 90 vols. Moscow, 1928–58.

Tsitovich, P. P. *Chto delali v romane "Chto delat'?"* Odessa, 1879.

Turgenev, I. S. *Polnoe sobranie sochinenii i pisem*. 28 vols. Moscow-Leningrad, 1961–68.

Usakina, T. *Istoriia. Filosofiia. Literatura*. Saratov, 1968.

Uspenskaia, A. "Vospominaniia shestidesiatnitsy Aleksandry Uspenskoi," *Byloe*, no. 18, 1922.

Valentinov, N. [Vol'sky]. *Vstrechi s Leninym*. New York, 1953.

Venturi, Franco. *Roots of Revolution: A History of the Populist and Socialist Movements in Nineteenth-Century Russia*. Tr. Francis Haskell. London, 1960.

Vodovozova, E. N. *Na zare zhizni i drugie vospominaniia*. 2 vols. 3d ed. Moscow, 1964.

Volynsky, A. L. *Russkie kritiki*. St. Petersburg, 1890.

Wellek, René. "The Concept of Realism in Literary Scholarship." In R. Wellek, *Concepts of Criticism*. New Haven, Conn., 1963.

Woehrlin, William. *Chernyshevsky: The Man and the Journalist*. Cambridge, Mass., 1971.

Zhukovskaia, E. *Zapiski*. Leningrad, 1930.

Index

In this Index, an "f" after a number indicates a separate reference on the next page and an "ff" indicates separate references on the next two pages; "*passim*" is used for clusters of references in close but not consecutive sequence. Literary works are listed under the authors' names, not separately by title, except for *What Is to Be Done?*, entered under the W's.

Library of Congress Cataloging-in-Publication Data

Paperno, Irina.
  Chernyshevsky and the age of realism.

  Bibliography: p.
  Includes index.
  1. Chernyshevsky, Nikolay Gavrilovich, 1828–1889.
2. Authors, Russian—19th century—Biography.
3. Critics—Soviet Union—Biography. I. Title.
PG2947.C3P3   1988   891.73'3   88-2311
ISBN 0-8047-1453-3 (alk. paper)